the favorite child

ellen weber libby, phd

the favorite child

preface by
howard m. halpern, phd
author of the bestselling
How to Break Your Addiction to a Person

PB Prometheus Books
59 John Glenn Drive
Amherst, New York 14228–2119

Published 2010 by Prometheus Books

Inquiries should be addressed to
Prometheus Books
59 John Glenn Drive
Amherst, New York 14228–2119
VOICE: 716–691–0133
FAX: 716–691–0137
WWW.PROMETHEUSBOOKS.COM

14 13 12 11 10 5 4 3 2 1

Library of Congress Cataloging-in-Publication Data

Libby, Ellen Weber, 1946–
The favorite child / Ellen Weber Libby.
p. cm.
Includes bibliographical references and index.
ISBN 978–1–59102–762–1 (pbk.)
1. Entitlement attitudes. 2. Child development. 3. Child rearing.
I. Title.

RC569.5.E48L53 2010
649'.64—dc22

2009039242

Printed in the United States of America on acid-free paper

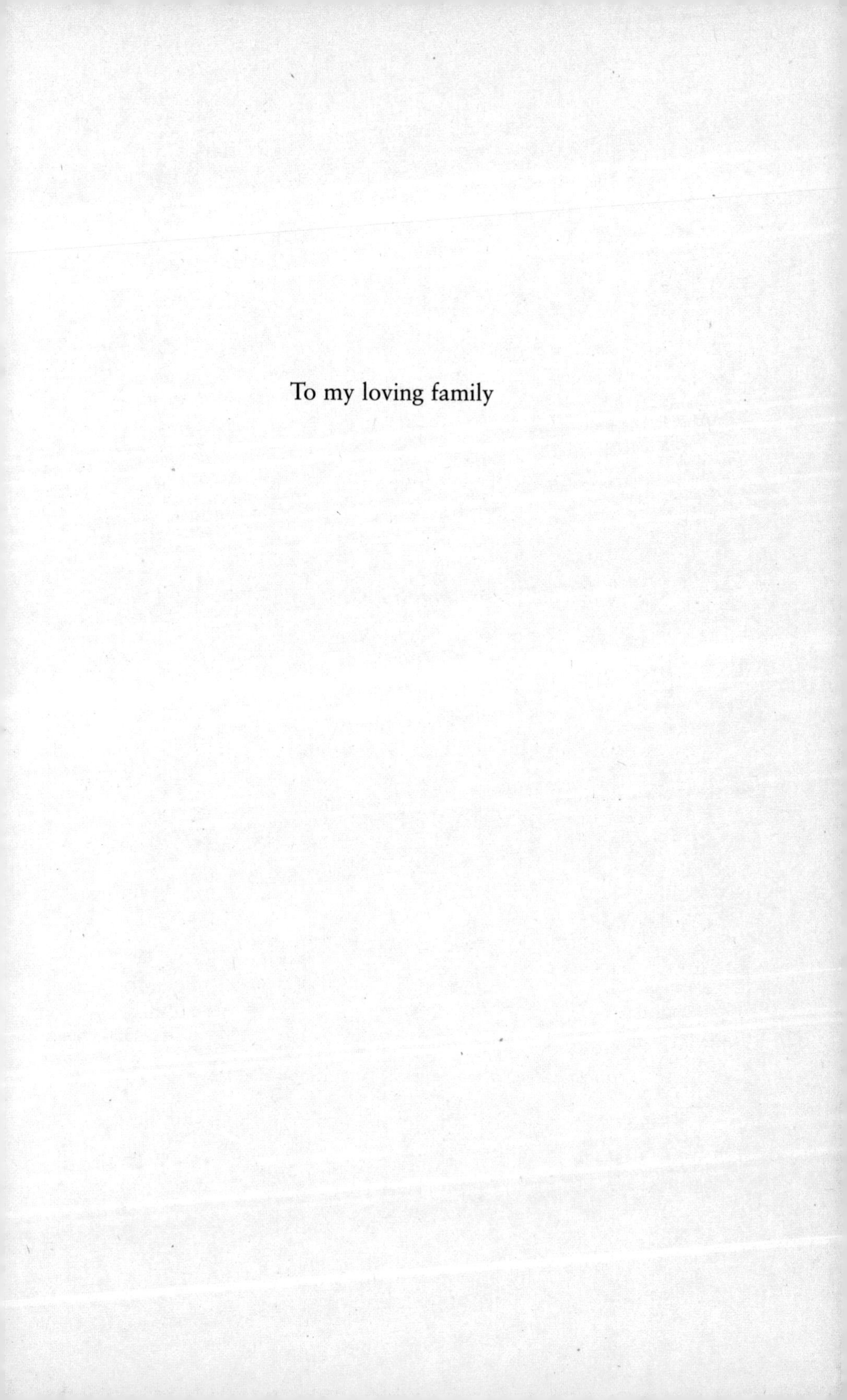

To my loving family

CONTENTS

SECTION THREE: CHILDREN'S STORIES

PREFACE

Most people are aware that the conflict they experienced as children revolved around their powerful need to have the love and approval of their parents. Not only is the love of both parents desired and prized, but it must be greater than the love going from the parents to any or all of the competing siblings. To accomplish this ongoing mission, each child longs to be the favorite.

Few parents admit to having a favorite child. "I love all my children equally" is a familiar refrain. This is rarely, if ever, true. Children differ in so many ways and often evoke dissimilar reactions from the parents. For example, brash and aggressive behavior that might be a turnoff to one parent may make that same child the other parent's favorite.

We will see that being the favorite child in a family, while having many pluses, is not an unmitigated joy, advantage, and blessing. Some who are in the role of the favorite child benefit greatly from that position. Their feelings of self-worth, competence, and general well-being are promoted by knowing they are favored. Others feel that the pressures to retain their favored status make them uneasy and shape their personalities in ways that are full of strain and anxiety. They feel pressure to do whatever is necessary to maintain their special position. Such strivings often have an impact on the relationships between siblings. They appear in the developmental journey from the classroom to the playground, from the dining room to the workplace, and perhaps to the boardroom and to the halls of government.

When the Smothers Brothers appeared on television, the whole nation seemed to enjoy their hilarious altercations. The format was always the same—they would get to some point in a frustrating disagreement, and Tommy would sputter helplessly in his efforts to put together arguments in the face of the much swifter, more verbal, more aggressive Dickie. When Tommy seemed helpless and hardly able to speak, he would stammer, "Mom always loved you best." The audience would laugh in delighted recognition of these words. What was it about these words, the seeming non sequitur in Tommy's reply, that struck such a chord in this large TV audience?

Tommy, the adult, still retained wishes from his childhood to be recognized by his mother as worthy, valued, and loved. If she loved him, particularly in comparison to her special feelings toward Dickie, there was still no doubt in Tommy's mind that "Mom always loved [Dickie] best." In this family, being the favorite child was the key to being loved.

Dr. Libby's professional expertise in the area of the favorite child—struggles growing up, adolescent conflicts, and adult choices—and her experience with patients give her a powerful professional and personal viewpoint on resolving a difficult problem.

Readers who are aware that either they or people they know have been bedeviled by the conflict involved in achieving and maintaining the position of being the favored child will find this book a great source of insight and understanding with regard to this often hidden influence in their lives.

Howard M. Halpern, PhD
New York City

ACKNOWLEDGMENTS

This book was written in my head several times over many years. But, after long days of sitting in my office and exploring with clients their apprehensions and ambitions, I craved physical activity or idle conversation during weekends and evenings. I resisted time alone at the computer, transferring to paper those thoughts on favoritism that occupied my mind. It took the enthusiasm of my loving family and supportive friends to impel me to undertake this project. I was motivated by their confidence in my ability to conceptualize the dynamics of favoritism and to write about it.

The most encouraging person was my husband, Hank. First, he gave me the courage to learn about favoritism firsthand as we parented our children. He respectfully challenged my favored treatment of one child over the other. And, when one child challenged me about my favored treatment of the other, Hank helped me to appreciate the truth, and often the humor, of the point of view of the child who challenged me. Second, as I was writing this book, Hank motivated me with his pride and offered endless counsel in helping to ensure that my thoughts translated into language that was easily grasped.

Two colleagues have actively nurtured my curiosity for all that is psychological, personal, and professional: Dr. Ellen Schiff and Dr. Steve Shere. Ellen, my friend from graduate school, and I have had dinner together every other week for about thirty-five years. Additionally, for the past twelve years, we have spoken on the phone every Tuesday morning from 6:15 to 6:55 a.m., during my commute to work. During these times, Ellen has challenged my thinking on favoritism, always guiding me to a more thoughtful and articulate position. When writing this book seemed too daunting, she listened to me patiently and then, with the wisdom only a trusted friend can provide, reminded me of all the times when an undertaking that loomed large brought me pleasure and fulfillment.

Steve, my co-therapist of thirty years, and I have had lunch every Thursday over these years. In this time together, we flush out thoughts regarding our work. We explore interventions that we have made during group sessions, curious as to whether they were primarily driven by our unique histories or those of the clients. We contrast our own life experiences, his as the son of an adoring mother and mine as the daughter of an adoring father. From our honest, respectful, and trusting discussions, much of my initial thinking regarding favoritism emerged.

A third colleague, Dr. Howard Halpern, instilled in me a desire to write. Over the years, I was stirred by his recounting of the satisfaction he gleaned from writing. It reminded me of my father's appreciation for the written word. When I decided to take on this project, Howie offered wise counsel and endless encouragement.

The formal version of this book was born during my participation in the Harvard Writers' Workshop. My colleague, Dr. Eileen Dunn, spoke with fervor about her experiences there the previous year. Tired of hearing me say, "The next time you go, I really want to go with you," she took me from dinner to my office and watched me register online for the course. From there, this book sprang to life. At the seminar, four middle-aged aspiring female writers, Nancy Rozen, Billie Pivnick, Eileen, and I, banded together to form a support group that we named "The Harvard Hussies." It was our purpose to infuse in one another the "can-do-it" attitude. Thank you Hussies!

It was at Harvard that I met Regina Brooks, my agent, and Lisa

Tener, my writing coach. These extraordinary women, individually and collectively, were my mentors and guides. Without Regina, this project would not have morphed from my thoughts and dreams to the world. Without Lisa, I would not experience the pride of knowing what I can accomplish.

Once I had completed the manuscript, it was the team at Prometheus Books, first orchestrated by Linda Greenspan Regan, executive editor, and then by Ann O'Hear, my copyeditor, who worked thoughtfully with me to help ensure that the book would read smoothly. With every edit, the book was improved.

To each of you, my heartfelt thanks for helping me to undertake and complete this significant project.

INTRODUCTION
FAVORITE CHILD—THE ROAD TO POWER

Every family has favorites. During my thirty-year practice as a clinical psychologist, I have seen just about every conceivable variation on this theme. All family members live with the profound effects, good and bad, of favoritism. The importance of this subject, favorite children—their power and possible moral corruption—motivated me to write this book.

DYNAMICS OF FAVORITISM

Elected and appointed public officials are among the clients I see in my large psychotherapy practice in Washington, DC. I have observed that a disproportionate number of these powerful people had been favorite children when growing up. My conclusion is that growing up as the favorite child teaches children necessary skills to take on difficult challenges, but accompanying this potential benefit are possible burdens. The behaviors learned as favorite children profoundly influence the molding of their personalities and, as adults, their continued behaviors and reactions in relationships. Throughout my career, I have thought about and discussed how the complexities of favoritism—good and bad—affect all members of a family. From my own life experiences, both personal and professional, my theory of the favorite child complex emerged.

The favorite child complex involves conscious and unconscious behaviors, enacted by all family members, in reaction to a favored relationship between one parent and one child. This favored relationship may be fluid, lasting for hours, days, or months, and rotating among all children in the family. This type of fluidity fosters health within the family. Alternatively, the favored relationship may be fixed, between one parent and one child. This rigidity can often undermine the health of the designated child as well as that of other family members.

The favorite child complex is generated by those interactions within a family that result from preferential treatment given by one parent to one child. The effect of this treatment reverberates throughout the family, influencing all relationships between adults, between each adult and each child, and among the children themselves.

All family members are players in the drama of favoritism. There are five predictable themes that play out. The first recounts a story of parents, with one perceived as powerful and the other absent, and children, with one locked into the role of favorite while others feel overlooked. The second portrays the less visible parent as moderating the more visible parent's involvement with the favorite child. The third shows one parent favoring different children at different times. The fourth features both adults shifting their focus of favorite child among all the children in the family: both parents favor all the children at different times. The fifth theme conveys the dynamics of favoritism in single-parent households.

The scripts enacting these themes are infinite, every family has its own, and each member possesses a personal version reflecting his own bias. *The Favorite Child* illustrates the impact of the favorite child complex on different family members as they live their lives influenced by their unique role in their family's enactment of favoritism. The experiences are recounted of those children who are favored, not favored, or overlooked. Each parent also has his or her own story. Each script illuminates diverse factors that influence the individual's behavior and relationships within the family, factors such as sex, age, temperament, intelligence, religion, sexual orientation, creativity, physical skills, and appearance.

The story of each person is told from his or her unique perspective, often alongside the stories of other family members. These stories, considered together, foster an understanding of how a family operates. I heard hundreds of families and thousands of people recount their stories and saw favoritism emerge as a powerful, universal, and predictable force driving family dynamics.

Favoritism may be an expression of honest feelings, reflecting sincere preferences deeply rooted within a parent. When selecting children for the exalted role of favorite, parents may not expect anything from the favorite children in return for their selection. Alternatively, the designation of favorite children may be a manipulation designed by parents, consciously or unconsciously, to elicit from these children desired behaviors. In these cases, parents do expect something in return.

The advantages of favoritism are profound. It provides a laboratory to develop those psychological and interpersonal skills required for personal power. Confidence, a by-product of such power, evolves and prepares favorite children to tackle challenges that would be daunting for most. Favorite children often develop into adults who are focused—determined to achieve whatever they set out to do. They expect success, seldom contemplating the alternative. Favorite children master the art of achieving challenging goals.

Among the disadvantages of favoritism is that it can potentially mar favorite children's moral fiber. When growing up favored, children may come to believe that they can get away with behaviors that other children cannot. To get what they want, they learn to spin the truth and manipulate their relationship with the powerful person in their family. Boundaries defining acceptable behaviors are usually fluid for them, so these children may not learn necessary lessons about the consequences of their behaviors. Favorite children tend to be oblivious to the impact of their actions on others.

In public officials, we often see people with numerous traits that are characteristic of favored children. These people take on with focus, determination, and confidence the difficult challenges of our society, such as public safety, war and peace, and the economy. To be elected or appointed, they present themselves successfully to the electorate or other powerful politicians by using the same charm they mastered as children, once again, to appeal to powerful adults. Once they have achieved their goals, public officials are vulnerable to exploiting the power of their positions, as they exploited the position of favorite child. We see many public officials freely spinning truth to obtain their desired ends. These are behaviors that they perfected when growing up as favorite children.

The confidence and determination to achieve desired ambitions have steered many favorite children to public service and have offered to our country men and women committed to solving difficult and perplexing dilemmas. In many of these people, however, we have witnessed the tragic repercussions of favoritism—lies, deceit, and corruption that lead to their downfall. As a nation, we are robbed of further contributions from these people, while our general distrust of politicians grows.

Despite developing this theory over many years, I never, in my wildest dreams, imagined that my knowledge would be so relevant to my own family. In 2007, my brother-in-law, I. Lewis "Scooter" Libby, chief of staff to the vice president of the United States, was found guilty of obstructing justice, lying to the FBI, and perjury. Here, in the experiences of my brother-in-law, was an example of the potential dangers of growing up as the favorite child. My theory of favoritism was further solidified as I struggled to make sense of his criminal conviction in the context of the person I knew, and as I worked to square his behaviors with accusations of deceptiveness and lying by other public officials, such as Richard Nixon or Bill Clinton.

My career permitted me to understand why my brother-in-law's career ended sadly with shame and notoriety. It helped me identify those dynamics that seemed to fuel the tragedy. My in-laws did not appear to have the willingness to confront personal truths about themselves that might have helped to mitigate the possible negative ramifications of favoritism in Scooter's life. Open communication among all family members, as well as a respectful relationship between parents—whether married, divorced, remarried, or otherwise single—helps to minimize the potential risks of favoritism. My mother-in-law defended herself against hearing truths that would potentially make her uncomfortable, such as her inappropriate, favored treatment of Scooter. Her husband seemed to observe in silence her unhealthy, preferential relationship with Scooter, seldom intervening.

Favoritism in families follows patterns. Generally, sons growing up as the unquestioned favorite of one parent are likely to achieve great professional success. This, too, is characteristic of daughters who were their father's favorite. As adults, these children are more likely to struggle with issues of intimacy, as evidenced by unfulfilling marriages, alienation from siblings, or issues of addiction. Many daughters growing up as the unquestioned favorite of their mother are likely to live their lives as caretakers of others, compromising their freedom in adulthood.

Family dynamics are reenacted from one generation to the next. Parents reflect how they were parented, either in their wholesale acceptance of childhood experiences or in their rejection of these experiences. Left undefined, the reenactment of favoritism within a family results in greater and greater consequences: while children's feelings of power and confidence may increase from one generation to the next, so do the potential negative consequences that emanate from their feelings of entitlement.

TRUTHS OF FAVORITISM

Six underlying truths are essential to appreciating the dynamics of the favorite child complex.

First, favoritism is normal, a fact of life. People are more comfortable identifying a favorite color, activity, or food than a favorite person. Children of all ages have favorite outfits they insist on wearing day after day. We ask friends familiar with a city we plan to visit for names of their favorite restaurants or parks. We are disappointed if the baker is out of our favorite cookies or the grocer is out of our favorite brand of strawberry ice cream. Our preferences reflect associations, strong and subtle, with past experiences that gave us pleasure.

Second, while it is clear who is selected as favorite, those doing the selecting generally obfuscate the truth of their preference. Parents are likely to deny they have favorites, insisting all their children are treated the same. In truth, no two children are identical and no two children can be treated exactly the same. Children know who their parents prefer and generally understand the reasons for it. Children know what a given child does to invite favored status. Just ask them! Parents may delude themselves, but children are not fooled.

Third, favoritism just is. It is not inherently good or bad. The family dynamics around favoritism create the atmosphere that renders favoritism either "good" or "bad." When children grouse about the unfairness of a sibling receiving extra privileges, the tension created by the defensiveness of parents unwilling to hear and accept the potential truth of this perspective generates stress within the family. As this pattern is repeated over time, families acclimate to living with increased stress. Alternatively, if parents are receptive to hearing the truths of children who feel overlooked, a culture is built within the family to resolve unhappy feelings, which benefits all family members.

Fourth, every family has idiosyncratic dynamics, which dictate how favoritism is expressed in that family. The dynamics can be spontaneous responses to what is transpiring in the moment or unconscious enactments rooted in family history, genetics, or early childhood experiences. Rewarding a child for achieving a goal is an example of a spontaneous response generated in the moment. Rewarding a child for not having snowball fights or rewarding the child for not dressing in a particular style because it makes the mother uneasy are examples of a response connected to the parent's unconscious life.

When families permit and encourage their members to react truthfully to the expression of favoritism, then the potential hazards of unhealthy family relationships are diluted. Through awareness and honesty, families more successfully cope with the complexities of feelings and alliances generated by favoritism. The emotional health of all family members is supported.

Fifth, the relationship between parents sets the tone for the family. At one level, there are no secrets in families. Children sense the tone of their parents' relationship from how they relate to each other: whether their communication is open and receptive, or closed and defended. Children surmise whether parents respect each other and work as a team or whether they are at odds, competing with each other and resentfully surrendering. The relative openness and respectfulness of communication between the parents establishes the framework for family functioning.

How parents relate to each other around issues of favoritism is critical in determining the potential consequences of favoritism within the family. For example, since favoritism within a family is inevitable but may sometimes be inappropriate, parents working as a team in monitoring each other are crucial to containing the potential risks of favoritism for both the favored child and the entire family. If the observing parent is silent, that parent colludes in perpetuating the unhealthy alliance between his spouse and the child. If the observing parent is attacking, then the attacked parent will probably become defensive, entrenching herself in the potentially destructive behavior of increased favoritism. If the parent demonstrating inappropriate preferential treatment defends herself against her partner's respectful observations, then all family members come to fear the potential destructiveness of the powerful parent. Any of these possible scenarios cultivates unhealthy alliances within the family.

Conversely, if the observing parent respectfully conveys concerns to the involved parent, and that parent trusts her partner, then the dynamics between the involved parent and the child of focus can be modified. In this sequence, the interests of all family members are met.

Sixth, the dynamics of favoritism exist in families with one child or multiple children, as well as in traditional two-parent families, nontraditional two-parent families, one-parent families, and families where parents are divorced. In the less common family structures, the dynamics of favoritism may be insidious and the dynamics more difficult to ferret out, requiring a trusted outside observer.

THE FAVORITE CHILD COMPLEX

Being favored offers children important life advantages, such as confidence and power. But, without healthy family dynamics, these children may be scarred by feelings of entitlement or their lives may be encumbered by their relationships with their parents. Mothers and fathers want to nurture their children to be effective adults—desiring that every child in the family should experience the advantages taught by favoritism without being saddled with its risks. To foster this objective, *The Favorite Child* seeks to provide an understanding of the dynamics surrounding issues of favoritism in the family, and to help families to be open and honest about favoritism. No family is without its uncomfortable issues. In making families conscious of the favorite child complex, we can make them become more aware of its dynamics in their home. This knowledge can be used to help mitigate the potential destructiveness of favoritism.

The first section of *The Favorite Child*, "Favoritism: It's All around Us," illustrates the fact that the issues generated by favoritism profoundly affect all families and all their members. Feelings stemming from the dynamics of favoritism may remain unconscious; yet they profoundly influence the behaviors and personal development of all family members. To help foster an appreciation of the power of favoritism, this section examines the dynamics of infant-mother bonding and how nonverbal communication can have an impact on babies

The second section of the book, "The Favorite Child Complex," explores the complex in its many guises and manifestations. This section examines families in which favoritism rests in the relationship between one parent and one child. Here you will learn the factors that influence the selection. The section also examines families in which favoritism is fluid, flowing from both parents to different children, creating a healthier dynamic. Finally, this section examines in great detail the blessings and curses of favorite child status, rich with stories of those whose experiences fall into one or another of the categories mentioned above. It brings into formulation the theory of the favorite child complex.

The third section of the book, "Children's Stories," relates detailed stories of several patients. These chapters convey multifaceted family histories, exploring their impact on family dynamics. It appreciates the impact of dynamics passed down from prior generations to the present. You will learn how these histories and dynamics impacted my clients by creating both successes and serious problems. And you will learn how these clients went about healing the ills stemming from favoritism and turned their lives around. You will read about the different permutations of favoritism: father's favorite son, father's favorite daughter, mother's favorite son, and mother's favorite daughter. We will also examine the story of overlooked children and nonfavorites. While each chapter in this section tells one story in great detail, I highlight the commonalities of each story with those of other men and women.

CONFIDENTIALITY

Interspersed throughout this book are examples of public figures who are not my clients. My knowledge of these people, except for Scooter Libby, is generally acquired through research. My knowledge of Scooter comes from having married into the Libby family. The purpose of including content on public people is to demonstrate the possible repercussions of favoritism.

In this book, I do not use the actual names of clients. I also alter details surrounding their lives, including their government positions. Each case study and vignette presented is a composite of multiple clients struggling with similar issues. To maintain the power and ethics of psychotherapy, confidence is an absolute requirement. In writing this book, my respecting the anonymity of the many men and women with whom I have worked, as well as those who have approached me in the writing of this book, has been an objective equal to that of elucidating the favorite child complex. As a result, I have gone to great lengths to conceal the identities of my clients, clinical supervisees, and others who have confided in me. I have worked to protect the identities of the members of their families. It is important to note that my clients have been my instructors, teaching me the profound lessons necessary for articulating the favorite child complex. It is my expectation that they will find throughout the book aspects of the complex that resonate with pieces of their own stories.

All my sources have been courageous in traveling into the depths of their "Shadow," those parts of their characters unknown to them but profoundly influencing their personality, behavior, and relationships. I hope that the theory, vignettes, and anecdotes stimulate your own thoughts on this rich and complicated, yet common, family experience.

SECTION ONE

FAVORITISM

It's All around Us

CHAPTER ONE
EVERY FAMILY HAS ITS STORY

When I was forty-four, my brother picked me up from work on a rainy evening. The driver of another car lost control and hit us head on. The doctors and my wife later told me that as I drifted in and out of consciousness, I repeatedly asked, "My brother, is he okay?" My younger brother walked away with a small cut on his nose covered with a little Band-Aid. I, on the other hand, broke two hips and an arm, had glass embedded in my eyelids, and suffered a concussion. I always believed that, if one of us had to be injured, it should be me. I wanted his life to be unencumbered, so he could do whatever he wanted.

—Hank's reflections

The wisdom I gleaned from spending thousands of hours with individual patients, couples, and families prepared me for an ultimate challenge: witnessing the public trial of my brother-in-law, Scooter Libby, and coping with my disappointment in learning that a jury had found him guilty of lying. Scooter's story graphically illustrates the familiar dynamics of favoritism that I have witnessed in the therapies of influential people with whom I have worked. Scooter's story offers a vivid illustration of the widespread benefits and liabilities that favoritism confers on the individual, family, and society.

MY FAVORITE BROTHER-IN-LAW

Hank, my husband, is seven years older than his brother, Scooter. Since Hank and I started dating as young college students, I have known Scooter since he was thirteen years old. After Hank and I married, I thought of Scooter more as a younger brother than as a brother-in-law. From my twenties through my fifties, I spent more time and shared more intimacies with Scooter than I did with my own brother, Richard. Scooter lived in closer proximity to Hank and me, and because he did not get married until his forties, he found refuge from the loneliness of bachelorhood in our home and family. He shared in the excitement of our growing family.

I remember first meeting Scooter. He talked about his upcoming graduation from Eaglebrook, a boarding school in Massachusetts, and his anticipation of enrolling in Andover, a prep school. We talked as the Kingston Trio played on the record player, and waited for Hank to finish dressing for our evening out. During those early years, Hank and I would take our brothers, Scooter and Richard, to cheer the New York Mets to victory, or to Mystic, Connecticut, to lose ourselves in maritime history, or just to Compo Beach in Westport to throw a Frisbee and eat hot dogs at the Big Top.

During Scooter's years at Yale, our small apartment provided shelter for his classmates journeying to Washington to participate in peace marches. Long after they returned to New Haven, the smell of tear gas that permeated their clothes lingered. When Hank and I moved into our first house, the guest room became Scooter's room, where he camped out during summers and other school breaks, and our attic became a refuge for his precious memorabilia.

Scooter and I fought for dominance over the shower—whether or not the spigot would direct water to the bathtub or the shower. Those mornings he showered first, as I turned on the water, my hair got wet. In total fury I would scream, "SCOOTER! You did it again!"

He calmly replied, "El, thought you'd learn by now." He won again, not only the battle of water, but also the battle of shame. I retreated, feeling stupid, wondering why I had not learned to check the spigot and forgetting my anger that my brother-in-law, a welcomed guest in my home, refused to comply with one of my few demands—turning the spigot to the tub after showering.

Scooter was the favorite uncle to our young children. Vividly, I remember him driving up our driveway in his green Saab, which he affectionately called "Patrick," and our daughter, Corinne, bolting to the door, shouting, "Scoots, Scoots!" He picked her up and spun her around, both of them laughing and screeching with delight. This loving greeting between them remained predictable until Corinne grew too big to be twirled in the air.

When our son, Mark, played soccer or football, Scooter joined my husband and me on the muddy sidelines of many athletic fields, cheering on Mark and his teams. Scooter, bundled up in black ski clothes, sipped hot coffee, enjoying his nephew's skills.

After Scooter's son was born, it was at our home that he had his early birthday parties. In our home, Scooter's young family spent several holidays, his daughter, as a toddler, running away from Misty, our playful black Labrador, and toward her admired, older cousin Corinne. Mark and his cousins would throw a football or kick soccer balls, coming to the holiday table caked in mud.

From college to law school to his first professional job, our home remained Scooter's refuge. Eventually, Scooter received an appointment at the State Department and moved to Washington. Yet he kept the key to our home, freely coming and going, and he often shared whatever leftovers filled our refrigerator. Over the years, Scooter built his own life, marriage, and family. Though he stayed in Washington, as we did, our lives steered us in different directions. Hank and I continued to harbor the sentimental feelings that reflected our rich history with his brother.

Day of Reckoning

Sitting alone in my office and reclining in my slightly worn and very comfortable black leather chair, I enjoyed a moment of respite. Stimulated by my morning's work, I relaxed, breathing deeply, and contemplated "Moon Rise over Sedona," my favorite photograph. Taken by Hank, this picture captures the majesty of nature, a full moon in broad daylight.

Forcing myself out of my reverie, I checked my phone messages. There were several, which was unusual for this time of day. The first, from Hank, startled me. Generally, we did not talk or exchange phone messages during the day: days were devoted to work and evenings to each other. For Hank to call now, the message had to be particularly important.

"Elly," he said with urgency in his voice, "the jury returned. Scooter was found guilty on four of the five charges. Call me. I'm in the office."

The grand jury testimony, the indictment, the months and days leading up to the trial, the trial, and the long jury deliberations were all over. Trying to grasp a truth I had long sensed, I sat, my body trembling from shock. My heart raced as it does after I push myself on the treadmill. During Scooter's years in government service, Hank and I witnessed Scooter evolve from a person we trusted entirely to a person who seemed to be driven by a growing arrogance and sense of entitlement. This metamorphosis evolved gradually as he pursued his developing dream of being an esteemed public servant.

As a young litigator at Schnader, Harrison, in Philadelphia, Scooter worked hard, pursuing excellence. After moving to Washington, he continued to work hard, but we noted that his desire to cultivate relationships with senior partners slowly began to overshadow other commitments. Routinely, he would be late for dinners that had been arranged for set times. Everyone, including Hank and me, would pretend that was okay. The family smiled, enjoying Scooter's trappings of Washington success, where running late because of "unavoidable demands" often determines a person's importance. We laughed, having learned to expect this treatment, and we chose to eat cold turkey rather than eat without Scooter. The family never confronted Scooter, although, between ourselves, Hank and I began to question the choices Scooter seemed to be making.

Decisions driven by Scooter's apparent hunger to please his mentors became more apparent during his years of government service, first under the tutelage of Paul Wolfowitz at the State Department and then at the Department of Defense, and later under the tutelage of Dick Cheney, first at the Department of Defense and then at the White House. During these years, the richness and ease of our conversations with Scooter diminished. While our time with him was always pleasant, the impoverishment of our conversations with him increased and the sense of closeness among trusted loved ones gradually melted. Scooter's speech patterns, always noncommittal, became more so.

Our family, and Scooter's, often joined by the seniors, continued to celebrate birthdays and holidays together but, over the years, the ritual grew shallower. History could no longer secure these gatherings. Increasingly, we were bothered by Scooter's lack of communication with us. We sensed and accepted his growing feelings of entitlement and his seeming inclination to spin stories to further his interests. He seemed to care less than before about being truthful with us. We were unable to discuss with him our awareness of this dwindling relationship. Thus, estrangement between Scooter and us was inevitable; we became uncomfortable around Scooter and, most likely, Scooter around us.

Despite this recent history, the day's sadness rested heavily on me. The career of this brilliant, creative, hardworking man—sullied because the jury found that he had lied—potentially robbed our nation of his future contributions. With this verdict, his years of government service and aspirations had probably come to a grinding halt. His trajectory toward honor had become laden with shame. Having witnessed, here in my office, the fall of some of Washington's best and brightest public servants, I understood the fall of my brother-in-law.

His is the story of a person driven by the burdens of the role of family favorite. Scooter's adult life was affected adversely by behaviors that potentially harm favorite children and those around them. Scooter, mastering the skills of being his mother's favorite son, longed to know that he was his father's favorite as well. In his relationships with Paul Wolfowitz and Dick Cheney, he had the opportunity to be the favorite of powerful men.

Mother's Favorite Son

Janis, my mother-in-law, who was born to an upper-middle-class Southern family, never learned the simple details of living on one's own—cooking, doing laundry, handling routine household chores, or shopping for food. When Hank was born, my in-laws lived in Connecticut, where my father-in-law, Irve, struggled with his young clothing store business. Years later, Janis reported that she panicked throughout her pregnancy, fearing herself inadequate to care for a child without the help of Frances, her childhood caretaker, and her indulgent mother, grandmother, grandfather, and great-uncle. After Hank was born, she laughed when telling the story of taking him as a newborn by train to her family home in Louisiana.

"We were on the train," she'd say, "and I couldn't get Henry to stop crying. It was during World War II and the train was packed with GIs. They picked him up, held him, and sang to him. Henry smiled. I don't know how I would have survived the trip without them."

In the telling, the story is all about Janis as a victim: "I don't know *how I would have survived* the trip without them." The story ignores the tension absorbed by the innocent baby: how would *he* have survived the trip without the doting GIs? Hank responded to her tension, crying as babies do, and Janis became more anxious. Her baby became fussier and she became more anxious and frustrated, feeling more inadequate. As Hank grew up, he became the symbol of her inadequacy and lived with the tension she imposed on their relationship. He was affirmed by his loving grandmother.

Scooter was born after his father achieved financial security. This permitted Janis the luxuries of childcare and household help, which helped to assuage her insecurities. With this assistance, she could hold her infant son until he became fussy and then hand him off to someone more adept at calming him. She enjoyed this baby, feeling affirmed in her role as mother and not having to confront personal anxieties or shortcomings.

When Scooter was young, my father-in-law's absence from the family was felt. A successful investor, he traveled to oversee his businesses. When he was in town, he and my mother-in-law had a full social schedule. When at home, he spent time holed up in his office, working. The tension between Janis and Irve was always present, felt by Hank and remembered vividly by friends of my in-laws.

Scooter grew up as the family favorite, providing this contentious family a focus for agreement. Hank commented, "Scooter was always the favorite son—he was even *my* favorite. I would do anything in the world for him." Hank continued: "Scooter didn't argue with Mom and Dad. He smartly agreed to what they asked and then proceeded to ignore the whole matter. No one, including me, ever confronted Scooter with his deception."

Quiet, bright, articulate, Scooter held the position of favorite, and no one challenged him. Outwardly, he could do no wrong. Seven years older than Scooter, Hank seldom said "no" to his brother. When Scooter was about twelve years old and boarding at Eaglebrook, unexpectedly, he could not come home for a holiday. Hank changed his plans so he could be with Scooter, no questions asked. To Hank, his own plans were irrelevant if he could do something for Scooter.

Two days before Hank and I married, when we were eager to be at home and to prepare for the festivities, we spent the night and wee hours of the morning at Newark Airport instead, waiting for Scooter to arrive from Yakima, Washington. Hank would not consider having Scooter take public transportation if he could pick him up himself.

My in-laws also seldom held Scooter accountable. When Hank worked a summer job at a boatyard, one of Scooter's few responsibilities at home was to move the sprinkler around the lawn during the day. Hank recalled one night arriving home at the same time as his father, Irve. As they walked together to the house while his father chomped on his pipe, they passed by patches of scorched grass. Irve took the pipe from his mouth, put it into his left hand, yellowed from pipe handling, bit down on his lower lip, and turned to Hank with a scowl: "Hank, why wasn't the sprinkler moved?" Hank swallowed hard, nodded his head, and accepted the reproach.

Family culture required Hank to take the blame for his brother's mistakes. Because of this, Scooter did not seem to take responsibility for his behaviors within the family that might be unacceptable. The family pretended that Scooter never stirred the pot. Even when his behavior caused wrath, that wrath was projected onto Hank. Everyone believed the spin: "Scooter is a good boy." He, as well as his parents and brother, believed he never caused any fights or generated family tension. He mastered the art of operating beneath the radar screen whenever tension surfaced in the family.

After Scooter completed a year at Columbia Law School, he considered a leave of absence to go to Breckenridge, Colorado, to work on his novel. Hank remembers Scooter asking for his counsel, recalling the conversation between them: "Hank, what do you think?" he asked.

"Why now? Why not finish law school first?"

"I'm more interested in the book than law school. I need to finish it and get it published, and a friend from Andover and Yale has a house in Breckenridge. I can stay there for free."

"To be a good lawyer, you have to have your heart in it. You have to want it," Hank counseled.

"I know, replied Scooter. "I'm pretty sure I do want to finish law school. I just need a break."

Moving to the harder subject of telling my father-in-law, Scooter requested Hank's help.

"Will you talk to Dad with me?" Hank remembers Scooter asking.

"Sure," said Hank, which, in the shorthand of brothers, was Hank's agreement to the familiar role of taking the heat, as he had done concerning the sprinklers so many years earlier. Contemplating a leave from law school would undoubtedly provoke Irve to fury. Hank, again, accepted the role of depository of Dad's anger.

Scooter began his life as his mother's favorite. As Janis told me, from the time he was born, he made her feel good. In exchange, it was apparent to me that this insecure woman made few other demands on Scooter and indulged him. She put little apparent pressure on him to meet family obligations that were appropriate to children his age, such as finding his own summer jobs or doing regular chores around the house. While she expected Irve, Hank, and me to pay homage to her mother in Louisiana, she never thought it important enough to pressure Scooter to make arrangements to travel there.

When Scooter was in college and Irve required heart bypass surgery, Janis hesitated over telling Scooter, fearing it would interfere with his ski plans during spring break. She expected Hank at her side. Hank and I conspired with Janis, encouraging Scooter to enjoy his break skiing and hanging out with friends. We all assumed that Hank and I would easily juggle the pressures of our burgeoning professional careers to be in Florida so we could assist Janis and Irve.

Ultimately, Scooter opted for a quick visit. I remember it vividly. The previous day, Hank and I had worked long hours, pressured to complete assignments, in anticipation of our absence for the remainder of the week. We flew to Florida and arrived late in the afternoon, feeling exhausted. We met my mother-in-law at the hospital and waited with her for Irve to come out of surgery. The next morning we left the house at 6:30 a.m. at Janis's insistence. She did not want to miss the doctors when they made rounds, even though they assured her they would not see Irve before 10:00 a.m. because they had early procedures scheduled for other patients. Hank and I complied readily with Janis, and got up at the crack of dawn, appreciating how my mother-in-law's chronic anxiety was aggravated by this family crisis.

Throughout the morning we coped with Janis's anxious state, as well as our own complicated emotions, in reaction to experiencing Irve as an angry patient recovering from bypass surgery. He growled and yelled, not appreciating our presence but scowling if we left his bedside. When Scooter arrived, Irve calmed down. The next day, Scooter left to join friends for a skiing vacation in Colorado. After taking Scooter to the Fort Lauderdale Airport, Hank returned to the hospital to visit his father.

As he entered the room, Irve turned to Hank, saying, "I want my son."

Hank responded, "I'm here, Dad."

"No, the other one!" said Irve.

When Scooter had been there for his brief visit, he made everyone feel good, including me. When he entered the hospital room, he charmed me with the sweetness of his greeting. He appreciated my helping to "hold down the fort," which contrasted with what I sometimes felt was my own family's indifference to my generosity and availability. Any resentment I may have had of his role in the family, or envy of his ski trip, dissipated. Because he made everyone in the family feel good, Scooter was able to do what he wanted. He was not challenged but encouraged!

That week, the family script was perfectly enacted without a glitch: Janis was anxious and all the family members appeased her; Irve was demanding and all the family members jumped through hoops, hoping to contain his potential fury; Hank absorbed the family tension while trying to lessen his own by working hard at being a perfect son and brother; Scooter, the favorite son, was celebrated for his brief visit. Janis, Irve, and Hank skillfully colluded in furthering Scooter's role as the favored child, encouraging him to live a life filled with shallow praise and with minimal responsibility as a family member. As for me, I did not challenge the family charade. I was taken in by the smoothness of the enactment.

With skills reinforced by his mother when he was a child, and perfected over years of practice, Scooter mastered the art of making people like him and feel good about themselves. He calmed people, defusing their anxiety. Never one to draw attention to himself, my brother-in-law sensed what he needed to do and did it. He was smart and a quick study, and he worked hard at the office while utilizing his keen intellect. He cultivated a circle of male friends, generally making the time to play a game of Sunday morning softball or flag football with them. Scooter's professional and social skills enabled him to get him what he wanted and ensured favored treatment for him where he deemed it mattered.

The roles of mother's favorite son and favorite person in the family seemed to be insufficient for Scooter. He did not appear secure, even though he was the son his father favored. As close as he wanted to be to his father, Scooter did not fully expose his name, formally giving his name as "I. Lewis Libby" and not "Irve L. Libby, Jr." Did this reflect unease on Scooter's part or my father-in-law's? It was my father-in-law who nicknamed his son Scooter, a name explained by one of the few anecdotes about his childhood that my brother-in-law seemed to enjoy. Scooter's secretiveness surrounding his true name, maybe encouraged by his father, suggests the confusion of this relationship.

Scooter longed for Irve's approval. Despite the fact that his father gave him preferential treatment, his father was not as affirming as Scooter seemed to crave. My father-in-law, who was an obstinate man, lectured and demanded, criticized and demeaned. He loved the activity of engaging his sons in endless discussions about business, but Irve seldom followed their advice or carried out their suggestions. While both Hank and Scooter were frustrated by this dance and both came to dread these "family meetings," their styles of responding were different: Hank tried to talk out his frustration with his father while Scooter said little.

After the fact, it appeared to Hank that Scooter was more disturbed than Hank was by their father's disregard for their counsel, a symbol of their father's disrespect. It seemed that, for Scooter, having his father's trust was of utmost importance. Hank sensed that Scooter, not having achieved this, tried to obtain it from others. He sought it from professional mentors. He seemed to find it in professors, senior partners, Paul Wolfowitz, and later Dick Cheney.

THE SHADOW

Hank and Scooter enjoyed the interchange, "Who knows what evil lurks in the hearts of men? Only the Shadow knows."[1] Mimicking Lamont Cranston at the opening of the radio show, *The Shadow*, this banter foreshadowed the tragedy of Scooter's being found guilty in a court of law on one count of obstructing justice, one count of lying in the FBI investigation, and two counts of perjury. The jury rejected Scooter's version of the truth. In defining his actions as "lies," the jury found Scooter guilty of a federal offense and held him accountable for his behavior. He could no longer avoid responsibility for his actions.

All humans possess a hidden side. Freud termed this unknown the unconscious, and Jung called it the Shadow. James Hollis, in his thoughtful book, *Why Good People Do Bad Things*, writes that the human psyche is not a single, unified whole but is often divided. Our unconscious intentions are frequently in conflict with each other. In his interpretation of Jung, Hollis posits that the Shadow is more extensive than just the unconscious. It includes those feelings that "haunt" us or make us uncomfortable with ourselves.[2]

Hiding from feelings, either conscious or unconscious, can create tension that, in turn, generates psychological disequilibrium. Commonly, we are unaware of our defensiveness. We are blind to the tension generated by our unconscious need to "not know" and unaware of the psychic energy required to keep hidden these forbidden truths. It is at the cost of our emotional or physical well-being, and often that of those we love, that we resist expanding our consciousness. Fighting to maintain rigid defenses protects our unconscious, and it prevents us from facing our dark side.

Like many clients I see in my practice, Scooter probably believes himself to be an honorable person. Experiencing himself differently would threaten the world as he knows it, pushing him beyond tolerable levels of discomfort. Electing to maintain his current boundaries between consciousness and unconsciousness, Scooter may well protect himself from viewing as lies his statements before the grand jury and permit the perpetuation of the spin that he was a victim of Special Counsel Patrick Fitzgerald's pursuit.

Acceptance of the truth—that we have a Shadow—is the prerequisite to containing its potential danger. "[T]hose who do not consider the implications of a divided human soul remain unconscious and therefore dangerous to self and other," Hollis writes.[3] Increased self-awareness permits us greater psychic harmony and is the antidote to the destructive potential of the unconscious. As our psyches become more united and we become more conscious of who we are in the world, the split between our conscious and unconscious lessens. As our decisions become more conscious, we can more reliably evaluate the rewards and risks of given behaviors and decisions.

Hollis reminds us that the Shadow is not necessarily evil, "although it may do things that we or others later judge evil."[4] He points out that even when questionable actions are rooted in the unconscious, "in the end we are wholly accountable for the actions and consequences of the Shadow."[5]

As I see it, for the following three reasons, Scooter's Shadow prevented him from knowing what he needed to do to better protect himself during Patrick Fitzgerald's investigation and the grand jury testimony. First, his Shadow interfered with the possibility that he would take seriously Fitzgerald's warning, a warning that, as a successful attorney, Scooter knew well: on March 5, 2004, at the beginning of his testimony to the grand jury, Fitzgerald reminded Scooter of his "constitutional right to refuse to answer any question if a truthful answer would tend to incriminate [him]."[6]

Fitzgerald further reminded Scooter that at any time he could stop the proceedings to consult with his attorney. Fitzgerald explicitly stated that "any testimony that you give is under oath" and that "if you make any deliberate false statement about a material or important fact, you could be prosecuted for perjury. . . . And if, if someone does commit a false statement or commit perjury, they could be prosecuted [*sic*] by up to five years in jail for each such false statement."[7] In the grand jury transcripts, Scooter stated clearly that he understood all of the above.

Second, after his guilty verdict, political analysts debated why Libby was indicted and not Karl Rove. The consensus seemed to be that Rove was better counseled for his testimony before the grand jury. Emma Schwartz wrote in the *Legal Times* that "many lawyers who followed the trial say the biggest handicap lay in Libby's early legal strategy—to speak to the grand jury multiple times."[8] If Scooter had accepted the truth of his situation, its seriousness, it seems likely that he would have been counseled by a lawyer who regularly dealt with high-profile criminal investigations in Washington, DC. Having grown up as a favorite child, Scooter may have been ill prepared to accept that he *was* in danger, despite the fact that he himself was a lawyer.

Schwartz reported that in Scooter's eight-hour, tape-recorded testimony before the grand jury, he "came across as kind and gracious, his voice soothing and calm, even under repetitious questioning."[9] Even under pressure, Scooter conveyed the confidence and certainty that is characteristic of favorite children.

Third, the jury sitting during the criminal trial found Scooter guilty of not telling the truth during the federal investigation of the Valerie Plame leak and during Scooter's grand jury testimony. Throughout his life, this behavior, coupled with his charm, had absolved him of responsibility for his actions. Indeed, just as the Libby family had let him off the hook for much of his life, members of the criminal trial jury wanted to do so as well. Denis Collins, a jury member speaking to the press, commented that the jury liked Scooter and wanted to acquit him, feeling dismay that the evidence precluded this option.[10]

With hindsight, we could say that Scooter's role in his family, starting with the role of his mother's favorite son and morphing into the role of family favorite, with his father's unhealthy participation, harmed him. He grew up seemingly believing that he could do anything he chose. He appeared to develop the skills necessary to navigate life without adequate accountability or clarity about right and wrong. He learned to be slick.

ONE POWERFUL PARENT AND ONE ABSENT PARENT

Scooter Libby's story invites interest because of his public position as well as the widespread interest in the functioning of former vice president Cheney's office. But all favorite children have their stories to tell. Commonly, one child at a time occupies that role in the family. This position may be held exclusively by one child or rotated among many. When occupying the role of favorite, children learn traits—positive and negative—that impact the rest of their lives. Favored children grow up against the backdrop of complicated, often subtle, family dynamics that influence their growth and development.

Libby's story illustrates the theme of favoritism in the type of family in which the other parent does not challenge the spouse's indulging of the favorite child. In this story, Libby's father colluded silently with Janis, observing her indulging of Scooter, maybe as a reward for Scooter's calming her and not aggravating her anxiety. Generally, Irve did not intervene and often participated in the charade.

Favored children, who grow up feeling entitled to do or have what they want, are vulnerable to living out the consequences of favoritism's dark underbelly. The power these people are likely to realize in their lives is significant, and so the impact of their downfall can be profound. Their injuries can have an impact on their families and colleagues, and sometimes on the nation and the world.

In order to reduce the likelihood of tarnished successes, favorite children must courageously confront their Shadows and expand the boundaries of their self-awareness. Later we will read stories of favorite children who have taken on this challenge. Each child grew up in a family with one adult who was more dominant and the other who was more absent. Each tells a detailed story of favoritism within a family from differing vantage points: mother's favorite son and mother's favorite daughter, and father's favorite son and father's favorite daughter.

DIFFERENT CHILDREN FILLING THE ROLE OF FAVORITE

The family in which I grew up illuminates different dynamics, those in which different children experienced favorite status. In my family of two children, my brother, Richard, and I each believed ourselves to be our father's favorite. When talking about our cherished relationship with our father, we agreed that I was probably his favorite until I left for college, when Richard, five years younger, replaced me. As our father's favorite, Rich and I developed confidence in ourselves. In my case this was necessary in order for me to overcome my frustrating relationship with my mother; in his case, it was necessary in order for him to take significant risks in establishing himself in the career he desired.

In exchange for my father's special treatment of me, I comforted him with my warmth and affection, responses that he craved but that were not forthcoming from my mother. I sensed what my dad wanted and gave it to him, which laid the groundwork for my career in psychology. My brother offered Dad laughter and relaxation, interplay that Dad sought in response to my mother's sternness. In my brother's case, his ability to laugh and relax helped to invite people into his life. His home, reflecting this personality, has a professional pool table in a central place in his living room and a state-of-the-art audio/visual room occupying adjacent space.

Until our mother's death, Richard was always her favorite. He was more like Mother—physically resembling the people on her side of the family, quieter, and more self-reliant than me. She preferred him because of his sex, as she wanted male engagement but felt uncomfortable with the demands of adult intimacy. Issues from her own childhood, buried deep in her Shadow, remained unresolved and were destructive to my development.

Being my father's favorite was insufficient for me. Like Scooter, I was driven by the desire for recognition as favorite of the less-affirming parent. For me, this was my mother and, for Scooter, his father. Pleasing my father evolved into rote behaviors, as Scooter's did in his response to his mother. For me, those skills, honed by years of anticipating my father's need for loving attention, were ineffectual in achieving what I wanted from my mother.

Not dissuaded by my brother's special status as mother's favorite, even as an adult, I continued to long for my mother's recognition. I falsely believed that if I worked hard enough or figured out the trick, I might get it. After my dad died, I put my life on hold to tend to my mother's health needs. I flew from Washington to Illinois, and later to Florida, at a moment's notice, putting a strain on others who had to carry my load. When I was at my mother's side, she sought my absent brother, as Irve sought Scooter.

Finally, when I was forty-three, only three months before my mother's unexpected death, I accepted the obvious: she did not want me in her life, so, of course, I would never feel special to her. Denying this truth, and struggling to recreate the reality I wanted, was costly and emotionally painful. While my father and I both sensed the truth throughout my mother's life, Dad and I wanted it to be different. Dad longed to have his wife's loving support and to witness my mother's love for me. Instead, he struggled with loneliness. His normal feelings of affection for me were made more complicated by the emotional absence of his adult female partner.

I knew that I could not ignore my mother if I wanted to maintain favored child status in my relationship to my dad. It was important to him that I should have a relationship with her. My skills, my knowledge of how to please him, faltered in my relationship with her. Ultimately, she wanted to be alone and she wanted me to be self-contained, which was not how I was wired. Obviously, I could not change my sex, and my mother never modified her contempt for women. During my visits with my mother before her unexpected death, I opened myself to the feared truth: I would never be the person she wanted, and she would never be the mother I wanted.

The family legacy passed from my parents to me made being female difficult, given my mother's conveying disdain for women and my father's valuing women as people to soothe men. Having pushed the boundaries of my own Shadow and explored my own truths, I have modified behaviors, learned as a child, aimed at trying to win my parents' favor. I have grown to treasure my identity as a woman and to appreciate the riches in my relationships with men. The family script I pass on to my children regarding their roles as female and male is different from the one passed to me. Their images of themselves are not tainted by my distorted requirements for a daughter or a son. My daughter is comfortable with being female, and my son with being male. Each claims the role, unconditionally, as my favorite.

DIFFERENT CONSTELLATIONS RESULT IN DIFFERENT OUTCOMES

The two families, my husband's and mine, enacted two vastly different dramas that are relevant to understanding the dynamics of the favorite child. In my husband's family, one child, Scooter, filled his mother's inappropriate needs and his father, a bystander, colluded. Rewarded for his role in soothing his mother, Scooter was the anointed favorite child. He grew up feeling confident and entitled, feelings that the whole family reinforced. Yet Scooter seemed still to long for more from his father.

In my family, both my brother and I enjoyed favorite child status. My brother was first rewarded by our mother and later by our father; I was rewarded by my father and, through much of my life, longed for this reward from my mother. Richard and I, having both reaped the rewards of special treatment, matured with confidence, which enabled our successes in life. Because my brother and I each experienced being a favorite child, neither one of us was burdened by holding that position exclusively, as was my brother-in-law.

The ensuing chapters explore the nuances of differing family dynamics that evolve from the designation of a child as the favorite. This process goes on in all families, in some with subtlety and in others more blatantly. But first, let us explore the frequency of favoritism within our society.

CHAPTER TWO
FAVORITISM
Known to All

Favoritism is a word that elicits a spontaneous response. Everyone has a story of or an association with it.

The word is *simple*, referring to the state or fact of being chosen, or showing partiality.

The word is *evocative*, provoking feelings of wanting to be desired or of jealousy toward the person chosen.

The word is *value laden*, triggering definitive reactions, positive or negative.

Whether I am giving a workshop or conversing with friends, people react passionately to the phrase *favorite children*:

"We treat all our children the same."

"I was the favorite!"

"Ugh! Who'd want to be the favorite? Just ask my sister. She has no life. She was mother's favorite and, at fifty, she's still glued to mother's side, still taking care of her."

"My brother. He was the favorite. Aren't all oldest sons in Irish families the favorite?"

The topic of favoritism has long intrigued me. Understanding the dynamics of favoritism is central to my work as a psychotherapist in Washington, DC. As I noted earlier, the city is a magnet for people who use the power of relationships to get things done, whether to save the environment or to build military hardware. It is a city for people who are experts in using power. It is not a city for amateurs; the culture magnifies the shortcomings of favoritism, which include a sense of entitlement and spinning the truth.

Growing up in a family as the favorite child provides a fertile training ground for perfecting the skills that are necessary for power. Just as a great basketball star does not begin shooting hoops at the age of twenty-five, a powerful person does not begin developing her power skills during adulthood.

The roots of favoritism go deep within a family. The implications are profound for the favorite child, as well as for all other family members. How a child assimilates the characteristics of favoritism affects his interactions beyond just those of the family. Whatever career he chooses, the implications are great, particularly in politics, where his sense of power and "can-do-it" attitude drive important legislation. However, a favorite child's feelings of entitlement, and her refusal to be held accountable, can undermine the moral structure of our society.

It is crucial to understand the dynamics of favoritism, and their implications, because they permeate many aspects of our own lives and society:

- When we elect people to represent us, understanding the dynamics that contribute to their attractiveness—their confidence in taking on difficult challenges—may confer a better appreciation of the risk that they possibly have a damaged character.
- The well-being of our children and the success of our nation depend upon our ability to raise children who have the confidence to take on challenges and yet are willing to play by the rules. Parenting such children demands an appreciation of the dynamics surrounding favoritism in a family.
- All people experience the effects of favoritism in their childhood: either they were favored or they were not. Either way, their personalities are impacted by their status in the family. The experience of having been the favorite ensures childhood pleasure and maybe opportunities, though sometimes in adult-

> hood that success is accompanied by tragedy. *Not* being the favorite may be painful to the child but may assure health and success in adulthood by insulating the person against tragedy. Understanding the dynamics of favoritism permits adults to enrich their lives as they use that knowledge to maximize the benefits of their role in the family and minimize its negative impact on them. A more satisfying life will likely follow.

At a conference where I spoke about favoritism, a thirty-five-year-old woman came up to me in an ecstatic state. "That's it! I've been divorced five years, still obsessing about my husband's 'not getting it.' Now I realize why he never will. I'm finally free to move on with my life and leave him behind."

She quickly explained that she had married her college sweetheart, the big man on campus. He had excelled in every endeavor and was adored by all. A few years into the marriage she learned of his affairs; he spun stories to try to convince her that he was not having affairs and pledged his love. The dance continued for five years, the wife confronting him with evidence of his infidelity and the husband spinning the story, still trying to convince her of his truth.

"Deep down, I knew I was being sold a bag of goods," she lamented. "I kept trying to believe him but I couldn't. I became depressed, crying all the time. I even had to take a leave of absence from my MBA program at Harvard." Ultimately, the couple divorced.

Five years after the divorce, she continued to ruminate about her inability to get her former husband to acknowledge the truth. Though she had completed graduate school and launched her career, she found that social relationships with men frightened her. Hearing me speak on the favorite child complex, she felt exhilarated when she realized a profound truth: her ex-husband was Mama's favorite. "He grew up believing he could have what he wanted without any consequences for his behavior. As a kid, his 'boring' younger brother ached with jealousy, but as an adult, his life is more fulfilling and is lived with more integrity."

Understanding the favorite child complex freed this woman from her painful marriage and divorce: her husband's mother's unwavering and irrational preference for him cultivated his feelings of power and entitlement to whatever he wished. In his adult relationship, he acted as if his partner would treat him as his mother had: in exchange for making her feel good, she would not hold him accountable for his behaviors. In contrast, this woman's former brother-in-law, who was overlooked as a child by his mother, grew up less encumbered by his relationship with his mother and became a more responsible person.

FAVORITISM—A COMMON DYNAMIC

As I work on developing concepts concerning favoritism or teasing out its dynamics, I have found that my attention to the topic can be all-consuming, and my day-to-day environment contributes to my thinking. Illustrations unexpectedly emerge in a restaurant, on the radio, and in a store, each one exposing different aspects of the phenomenon of favoritism.

My first experience occurred when observing my friend Beth interact with Carlos, a maître d' at a local restaurant where she was a regular. Since the weather was beautiful, the Logan Café bristled with impatient customers clamoring for tables outside on the patio.

"Carlos, my friend," Beth said in her soft and sensual voice, "how long a wait?"

"At least ninety minutes. I wished you'd called ahead," he replied.

"But you always take such good care of me," she added calmly and earnestly.

In response, Carlos's expression changed from a grimace to a smile. Within minutes, Beth and I were comfortably seated on the patio, sipping wine and ignoring the glares of the customers who were still waiting.

The scene reminded me of the last client I had treated that day, a working mother. This political appointee, hard working and brilliant, was internationally revered, but at home felt overlooked, disrespected, and inconsequential. My client described her bitterness in going directly from an intense work environment to the demands of three children, each needing help with homework and demanding special attention while she worked at preparing dinner. Her husband seemed oblivious to the unyielding pressure she felt. She experienced her family as expecting a lot from her but offering little.

Watching Beth express her appreciation of Carlos amidst a sea of complaining customers, I imagined that if one of my client's children expressed appreciation of her with a spontaneous kiss or hug, she might feel as valued as Carlos. As Beth was a favorite customer for treating Carlos as special when he most needed the affirmation, my client's affectionate child would be similarly favored for sensing this tired mother's need to be appreciated and loved.

As I was driving home, a country and western music station played Blake Shelton's "The Baby," written by Chip Taylor. This song expressed truths regarding favoritism with clear resonance:

> My brother said that I
> Was rotten to the core.
> I was the youngest child,
> So I got by with more.
> I guess that she [Mom] was tired by
> the time I came along.
> She'd laugh until she cried,
> I could do no wrong.
> She would always save me,
> Because I was her baby.[1]

"The Baby," in its exquisite simplicity, is replete with meaning. Because of the mother's needs, she anointed the baby as the favorite. The selection had little to do with who he was, only that he was the youngest. The ramifications of the selection on the child's developing personality were profound.

That "she was tired by the time [he] came along" and that he "was her baby" are both accidents of birth. For this mother, this child held the coveted status of "her baby," and throughout his life, he continued to be treated as "the baby." Not being held accountable for age-inappropriate behaviors, maybe because his mother was tired or maybe because she needed to have a baby child, this child grew up feeling entitled, believing that he "could do no wrong."

The fact that his brother found him "rotten to the core" challenges the belief that being favored is all positive. The listener to "The Baby" is left with the distinct impression of a child having grown up feeling entitled but inadequate in meeting adult responsibilities. Maybe occasionally the siblings who were *not* the favorites have more fulfilling lives as adults? Still, assuming this song has autobiographical elements, as do many of the songs that Taylor writes and Shelton sings, these men, who may have been irresponsible as children, forged careers as respected and prolific musicians.

My next brush with favoritism occurred at Barnes and Noble when I met my husband for a cup of cappuccino at the end of a long day. While I waited for him to arrive, two mothers with infants came to my attention. Both children fussed, maybe wanting a diaper change, or their mother's exclusive attention, or to sleep in their cribs at this late hour. The responses of the mothers differed dramatically.

One mother took her baby from the stroller. Holding the baby close to her, she rocked him and spoke softly to him. The mother's eyes sparkled and her loving smile conveyed affirmation. The baby became quiet, was put back in the stroller, and Mom continued her shopping.

The second mother, in contrast, communicated impatience and disapproval to her baby. "Stop it! Stop it! Stop crying," she shrieked at the baby, who was secured in a Snugli baby carrier across her chest. The baby, responding to his mother's agitation and her voice, and feeling her heart racing, cried more and more loudly, flailing his arms and legs with tremendous energy. The more irritating the mother's voice became, and probably the faster her heart beat, the more distressed the baby's cry became.

In the first example, both mother and baby enjoyed the success of their relatedness. The mother responded affirmatively to her baby's communication. The baby calmed down and the mother experienced herself as a competent caretaker. This interplay reinforced good feelings and the symbiotic nature of this relationship for both mother and child.

And so the roots of favoritism could take hold. When the mother responded positively to the child, the child responded positively to the mother. Each made the other feel better about herself. The behaviors reinforced each other while their attraction to one another grew stronger. Baby learned an important lesson in power: *mother heard you and responded to your needs*. Baby got what baby wanted. The challenge ahead for the mother is to affirm her child's power while still teaching her child right and wrong.

The second example demonstrated mother and child tension that probably left both feeling bad about themselves. Baby experienced disapproval of his expression, and he expressed his anguish at having been criticized by crying more. Mother experienced herself as an inadequate caretaker: the harder she tried to silence her child, the louder and unhappier the child became. To this child, the mother became a symbol of frustration. To this mother, the child may become a symbol of her incompetence.

Mother-Infant Attachment

John Bowlby, a British psychiatrist, wrote about the impact of maternal deprivation in the 1950s: Having worked with children scarred by World War II, he observed the negative impact on the development of those young children separated from their mothers during the war.[2] As his thinking matured, his writings, lectures, and supervision profoundly impacted the focus of researchers and the thoughts of clinicians. All grew to appreciate that children's functioning *is* rooted in their early attachment to their mothers.

Bowlby observed the impact of a mother's behavior on her infant.[3] Of equal importance, as pointed out by Nadia Bruschweiter Stern, is the impact of the infant's behavior on the mother.[4] Mothers successful in comforting their children are more likely to feel better about themselves than mothers who are frustrated in this endeavor. And, like all people, mothers are more likely to seek out experiences or people that make them feel good and reject those that make them feel bad—even when the person being rejected is their own infant.

Mothers may instinctively be more responsive to one child than another or may be genetically predisposed to preferring one child over another. This predilection, a mother's irrational attachment to one child, may last a lifetime. It may undermine the child's healthy development.

As this mother and child assumed a negative association for one another, they laid the groundwork for a lifetime of potential pain. Children, physically connected to their mothers from the moment of conception, spend a lifetime separating from their mothers while concurrently fearing their mothers' rejection. The infant I observed at Barnes and Noble experienced an infant's worst fear, maternal disapproval or rejection. As this baby grows from childhood into adulthood, many of his actions will probably be driven by his unconscious ambivalence: hunger for maternal approval and rage at her negativity.

Preoccupied by my thoughts on favoritism, I browsed the shelves in Barnes and Noble for books on the subject. I already owned the book most intriguing to me, *First Mothers: The Women Who Shaped the Presidents*, by Bonnie Angelos.[5] This book focuses on the relationships between the men who became presidents of the United States, from 1932 to 2008, and their mothers. Angelos describes these relationships as special and these men as favored children. Writing about Franklin Delano Roosevelt's relationship with his mother, Angelos quotes Sigmund Freud: "A man who has been the indisputable favorite of his mother keeps for life the feeling of a conqueror, the confidence of success that often induces real success."[6] This succinct statement captures the spirit of the favorite child growing up to believe that he can take on any challenge. He will not be easily deterred.

INFANTS KNOW THE TRUTH

First Mothers highlights the impact of the mother/child relationship, underscoring the power and confidence gleaned from the position of mother's favorite son. Like the Blake Shelton song, Angelos's book shows that the conferral of special status often reflects the mother's needs. Some communication may even predate the birth of the child, while other communication originates at birth. The complexity of factors influencing children's personality development has been studied in neuroscience.

Research physicians understand that childhood experiences have an impact on human growth and development, and adverse experiences can have profoundly negative results. These findings are the outcome of substantial research, spanning more than twenty years, in the Adverse Childhood Experiences (ACE) Study, carried out under the auspices of the United States Centers for Disease Control and Prevention (CDC) and Kaiser Health Plan's Department of Preventive Medicine in San Diego, California. The results of this study are consistent with those of neurobiologists who have found childhood stress to have a significant impact on the children's developing central nervous systems.[7]

Robert Anda, MD, senior research fellow at the CDC and co-principal investigator for the ACE study, said at a meeting that a logical extension of the research supports the hypothesis that a child's proclivity to adverse childhood experiences takes root at the moment of conception. He believes that a pleasurable sexual experience for the parents at the moment of conception influences the child's health in a positive fashion, while a negative experience increases the likelihood of illness. Anda's conjecture is consistent with the findings of neuroscientists who believe that the growing fetus develops personality traits that both reflect and react to those of the mother.[8]

The right side of a fetus's brain develops more fully than the left. The right side governs the development of affect. Raw experiences, not moderated by language, are absorbed into babies' psyches. It is not until infants are approximately two years old that the left side of their brains, controlling language, develops more fully. As language skills develop, so do children's capacities to temper the intensity of primitive emotion.

Louis Cozolino, PhD, clinical psychologist at Pepperdine University, has written on brain circuitry, having scrutinized volumes of existing literature and critically evaluated diverse brain-related research. He believes that human behavior is affected by the uniqueness of the individual brain. However, he contends that each person's brain reflects the evolution of the species, the genetic history of the given family, and the impact of given chemical signals on the brain cells of a given person.[9]

We can learn so much more about the growing brain, since

Infant Awareness

Louis Cozolino writes about the importance of infant/mother communication:

> Bonding in the first few weeks occurs at a very primitive level, with smell and touch playing primary roles. Although specific words are meaningless, the tone and prosody of the voice hold center stage. A mother instinctually embraces her baby after birth, maximizing [the] contact area of the skin and helping the infant's hypothalamus to establish a set point for temperature regulation. The infant and mother gaze into each other's eyes, linking hearts and brains.... Endorphin levels in both mother and child rise and fall as they touch, separate, and touch again, providing them with alternating rushes of well-being and distress.
>
> Orienting of the head to the sound of the mother's voice increases the possibility of eye contact.... Prolonged, shared, and emotionally stimulating gazes stimulate the growth of networks of attachment and the entire brain. In recent years, the image of the infant as a passive recipient of stimulation has been replaced with a view of the infant as a competent participant in getting its needs met by reacting to and impacting on specific aspects of the social environment.[10]

Cozolino continues by citing research completed by Tiffany Field. He summarizes her research in this way:

> Within 36 hours of birth, neonates are able to discriminate among happy, sad, and surprised facial expressions at a rate that exceeds chance. Looking at happy faces causes newborns to widen their lips, whereas sad faces elicit pouting.... Infants, it seems, look primarily at the mouth for happy and sad faces, whereas they alternate between the eyes and mouth in response to expressions of surprise. This suggests that they're capable of selecting different visual targets based on the information presented to them.[11]

studies of the brain, enhanced by technological advances in brain imaging, show the brain as a fluid organ, continually changing. The infant brain functions instinctively, communicating nonverbally to the world surrounding the infant. With no language to mitigate the newborn's reactions, the newborn expresses pleasure and pain by smiles or tears.

The child, as a fetus and infant, senses his mother's predisposition to him. This unhindered communication, conveyed through the mother's body chemistry and nonverbal communication, may forever have an impact on the mother/child relationship and the infant's feelings about himself. The infant responds fervently to his mother's sparkling eyes and smiling lips, her loving and strong embrace punctuated by her steady heartbeat, and her melodic voice, all of which are more meaningful than words. The child reflects this loving glance back to the mother. As mother and child reciprocally affirm one another, their special relationship solidifies and the child's status as favorite takes root. Their ongoing mutual affirmation reinforces their importance to one another. The significance of this golden relationship impacts the child throughout life and may impact the child's progeny.

Pregnant couples experience babies' pleasures and displeasures even in utero. Pregnant mothers talk about the impact of their diet or stress at work on the activity of the fetus. Early in my practice, I worked with a male client who wanted to be intimately involved in his wife's pregnancy. The moment the pair learned of their pregnancy, he rested his heart on his wife's stomach, repeating the words "Little One, I love you and your mother more than life. We will always be one, a united family." Throughout the pregnancy, each day began and ended with this ritual. In the seventh month of the pregnancy, the father left town for two weeks of lecturing. Throughout the trip, the fetus kicked endlessly, creating distress for the mother. She endured sleepless nights and struggled through the days, tired and uncomfortable. When Dad returned home and placed his heart over Mom's belly whispering his love for Little One, immediately the fetus calmed down.

Twenty-five years after my first session with this mother and father, I had occasion to meet Little One, now a college senior. She talked about the intensity of the attachment she felt to her parents, while she felt jealous of her younger sister, who "traveled the world" and enjoyed "amazing summer jobs in London one summer and San Francisco the next." She acknowledged that her parents encouraged her "to go and do," but each time she planned to do so, she backed away. As we explored this phenomenon during family sessions, I asked her parents to recount memories of the pregnancy. As they described Dad's heart on Mom's stomach and its calming impact on Little One, all three sobbed profoundly. The moment of awakening freed this treasured child to pursue life experiences requiring more separation from her parents.

THE TWO-PARENT FAMILY

In my thirty years of professional practice, certain themes have emerged regularly. One of the most powerful is the presence of a second parent, strong and involved, countering the impact of the other parent's preference for a given child. One parent functions as a check and balance for the other. This moderates the impact of the dominating parent, enabling the favorite child to grow up with a more realistic set of expectations.

What children want most is for their parents to love and respect one another. This relationship provides secure boundaries within which children can flourish. It is normal for children to fantasize about replacing one parent in the heart of the other. But, if this vision were to materialize, the child would be fearful of the accompanying responsibility. The involvement of strong, confident parents permits children the freedom to feel powerful without burdening them with responsibility beyond their capabilities.

Unique bonds between each parent and each child are inevitable. Feelings—positive or negative—may be especially strong for the child who looks most like a loved or despised grandparent, who was born when the parent most wanted or most feared the birth of a baby, or who has musical skills reminiscent of a beloved or disliked aunt. Feelings stimulated by such associations are translated from the parent to the child, reflecting irrational favoritism or negativity. It is the responsibility of the other parent to monitor the partner's treatment of the child, helping to ensure an objectivity that is in the best interest of the child.

During my recent consultation with a mother, father, and teenage daughter, the mother insisted her husband was too lenient with their daughter, and the husband found his wife too rigid. The daughter enjoyed partying more than studying and using her cell phone more than focusing on the task at hand. In her mother's eyes, this daughter challenged every family rule—about curfews and drinking, leaving her room in a messy state, not fulfilling household responsibilities. The mother imposed limits on the daughter and they fought continuously. The father, exceedingly critical of his wife, sided with their daughter, often giving into her unreasonable demands, for example, driving her places at times that were inconvenient for him and when she could have easily taken public transportation. The pressure intensified within this family triangle as the mother and father became more alienated from one another and their daughter's self destructive, out-of-control behaviors escalated.

The daughter, adopted from South America, physically resembled her adopted father, who was also of Hispanic descent. For him, this physical bond provided a profound association with his roots. The experience of the family consultation awakened this father to a constellation of hidden feelings regarding his ancestry: seeing someone in the family—his daughter—look like him comforted him. His inclination, to reward her for this pleasure and not punish her when she should have been punished, made setting or enforcing boundaries difficult for him. Also, the father became aware of the negative ramifications of his internal beliefs: as the oldest son in his first-generation family, he was brought up to look out for the women in the family, especially his mother, as his father worked multiple jobs. This instinct fed his irrational attachment to his mother and his daughter. He confused his desire for his mother's life to be easier with permitting his daughter's life to be too easy.

As this father became more conscious of the underlying thoughts influencing his responses to his daughter—his favorite child—he became more receptive to his wife's viewpoint. Mother and father realigned, working as an effective team. Their daughter's behaviors gradually moderated. Overall, the tension in the family declined, benefiting all of the members. The family grew stronger as one parent monitored the other, and as the parent who had been misaligning himself with his favorite child became receptive to moderating his behaviors.

A parent who provides a counterforce to favoritism keeps favoritism in check. This benefits all the family members. The parent with the favorite child learns to differentiate between rational and irrational reactions and to make more informed decisions. The favorite child becomes more balanced, growing up with the advantages of feeling empowered yet with scruples emanating from accountability. Each child, then, within the family, is more likely to enjoy the coveted favorite child status at different times, thus increasing the likelihood of each child enjoying its rewards. When the powerful parent remains entrenched in a position or the other parent is uninvolved or weak, the dark underbelly of favoritism surfaces. Children not held accountable for their behaviors grow into adults who are often ethically, psychologically, or morally wounded.

WASHINGTON PERSONALITIES

I have observed closely the impact of being a grown-up favorite child during my work as a psychotherapist in Washington, DC. The city attracts people who are lured by power, who want to "get things done."

In the public arena, this dynamic abounds. For example, Bill Clinton, on track to becoming one of America's great presidents, put his reputation in jeopardy by spinning the truth regarding his sexual liaisons. Why take the risk? Because he did not see his behaviors as risky. His father died in a car accident before his birth, and his mother then married an inadequate man. Bill, very responsible, took care of her and his younger brother. As his mother's favorite child, Bill believed that he could have anything he wanted, without repercussions. He grew up with the confidence required for his political career but, with no adult holding him accountable for his behaviors, he was cocky, believing he could do or have anything.[13]

George W. Bush tainted his presidency by secrecy and apparent misinformation. When he was a young child, his beloved younger sister, Robin, was diagnosed with leukemia. Their mother, Barbara, took Robin from Midland, Texas, to New York City for treatment. Young George was left at home under the supervision of a trusted nurse sent from New York by his grandmother, as well as various caretakers. Family communication was managed to protect young George from the knowledge of his sister's terminal illness. Within nine months, she died.[14]

When Barbara returned home, she surrendered to her sadness while, at the same time, having to comfort her young son George. She snapped out of her emotional state when she heard George tell friends that he could not play; he did not want to leave his mother who was sad. According to family stories, Barbara felt guilty that her young son was so concerned about her. Further, she realized how little attention she had paid to young George's needs. To assuage her guilt, she indulged him. He got away with behaviors that his younger siblings never could have, and escaped the consequences. George grew up pushing boundaries, expecting to get what he wanted, with little accountability.[15]

Barbara parented as if she were a single parent while George Senior was preoccupied with establishing himself as a prominent Texan businessman and politician. George Senior paid little attention to his children. Without his participation, Barbara's parenting of George Junior developed unfettered. Her mothering style, maybe driven by her need to compensate for overlooking George during Robin's illness, provided George with the best gifts and worst traits resulting from favorite child status. Unlike his siblings, George was not frightened by his mother's temper; he did not fear the consequences of her threats. He grew up to be successful in most circumstances, pushing boundaries and limits.[16]

THOSE WHO HEAL

Having been powerful in their families, favorite children commonly seek careers involving fame. Their "can-do-it" attitudes provide the foundation necessary to confront the risks that are necessary for success. The intensity of this drive, while it is required for those who take on challenges, can nonetheless impede interpersonal relationships. Unaccustomed to failure, when confronted by unhappy spouses, alcoholism, or scandal, those favorite children who find their way to psychotherapy struggle with the aspects of their personality that undermine healthy interpersonal relationships. When they heal, their lives become more satisfying. Two clients seeking my guidance were Ed and Gail.

Ed, a preeminent litigator and former White House Fellow (discussed more extensively in chapter 9), began psychotherapy when he was pressured by his wife. Her distrust of him grew as he lied about his drinking and remained unreliable in terms of his commitments to her. Married twice previously, Ed did not want a third divorce. He gave himself to psychotherapy with unwavering focus and determination, as was characteristic of this favorite child. Giving up drinking, growing more comfortable with directness and honesty, and honoring his obligations to others, Ed experienced benefits of his creativity that had previously been unknown to him. With Ed's enhanced energy came enhanced success and gratification, as well as a better relationship with his wife.

Gail, a renowned television reporter, began therapy when working on a closely scrutinized senatorial campaign. Her fear of her own promiscuity and heavy drinking drove her to therapy. She was a brilliant woman with an extraordinary work ethic, but her behavior threatened her competence in that shrewd and competitive world. Gail felt obligated to sleep with every powerful man who propositioned her or to match colleagues drink for drink. In the course of her therapy, she reclaimed her confidence and solidified her ability to set healthy boundaries for herself. Her healing permitted professional achievement without personal risk, and laid the foundation for a healthy intimate relationship.

Though Ed and Gail are members of the Washington power elite, their strengths and life challenges are similar to those of favorite children from all walks of life. The power these people learned from their status as favorite children has helped promote their significant life achievements. Such accomplishments, however, can be undermined by the potential destructiveness of the dark side of favoritism.

FAVORITISM SURROUNDS US

Favoritism is a truism. It just exists. Even when parents deny its existence, children can commonly identify who in the family is favored and why.

Children's growth and development is impacted by the conscious and unconscious attitudes of their parents toward them, even before their birth. The raw feeling absorbed by infants before the development of language skills affects their functioning as adults.

Favoritism taking root before birth, during infancy, or in early childhood is neither positive nor negative. Let us now look at those dynamics in families that help to turn the characteristics of favoritism into a positive resource as well as those that taint the potential gift.

SECTION TWO

THE FAVORITE CHILD COMPLEX

CHAPTER THREE
THE FAVORITE CHILD COMPLEX

When my first child was born, I never believed that I could love another child as much as him. I couldn't get over the wonderment of what my body produced. When my second child was born, I never believed that I could love a child as much as him. He was an easy baby, always smiling and so beautiful. His baby pictures looked just like my husband's. When our daughter was born, I was resolute that she would not be my favorite. I wanted a daughter but loved my sons so much. I didn't want either of them to feel displaced. Now, my children are all grown. I was shocked when we gathered at Christmas and all agreed that my daughter was the favorite. Everyone felt relief as we laughed and talked about this secret known to everyone but me.

—Rose's reflection

Parents have favorite children; they prefer one child to another. This is normal, a fact of life. Sometimes the selection of the favorite child changes daily, while in other families the position lasts a lifetime. Ultimately, parents want all their children to mature with the confidence necessary to succeed in the world. This confidence can be derived from favored status. Growing up as the favorite child empowers children by teaching them some essential skills that are required to tackle life's challenges.

The word *favoritism* evokes strong reactions, as we have seen, often inviting parental rebuttal. "I treat all my children the same," parents respond, feeling challenged by the suggestion that they have favorites. Recently, a mother who read my blog on favorite children e-mailed me, telling me that she was intrigued by the topic, even though she had no favorites. In our e-mail exchange, I questioned whether her children would share her point of view. Not knowing, she readily facilitated my contacting them. Independent of each other, these children agreed: their mother had a favorite, though, outwardly, she worked to treat all children equitably. These children, like Rose's children referred to above, knew the truth, even the unspoken truth, that prevailed in the family.

Children, even identical twins, are distinguishable, so why should they be treated the same? Doing so denies their individuality. Parents are not carbon copies of each other, either. So, of course, their responses to the same stimulus or provocation differ. Failure to acknowledge the differences in personalities and preferences among all the family members, and the differing reactions each person evokes, compromises the mental health of everyone in the family. Family members are forced to function in the terrain of their own Shadow, slowly building family secrets into an unseen but potentially explosive situation.

Whether it is acknowledged or not, favoritism exists in all families. The favorite child is defined as the child who, in the moment, brings pleasure to the parent who matters most to the child. This child becomes the recipient of the hopes, joys, and aspirations of this parent. When these wishes are rational and grounded in the child's best interest, favoritism contributes to positive mental health. When these wishes are irrational or grounded in the *parent's* best interest, favoritism contributes to destructiveness within the family.

Along with parental wishes and ambitions, favored children receive tools that help to foster success, especially confidence and feelings of empowerment. Based on the special relationship with the parent, the favorite child feels entitled to perks that others in the family do not have.

In families with multiple children, the role of favorite may rotate among them. In more rigid families, roles may be tightly designated, with one child being favored while other children are overlooked or unfavored. To be overlooked is to be largely ignored. To be unfavored is to be the recipient of parental disdain, regret, anger, or agitation. For the purposes of this book, we will focus on the favorite child and consider the overlooked or unfavored child primarily in the context of the dynamics surrounding the favorite.

Children without siblings can experience the favorite child phenomenon. When an only child brings pleasure to the parent who matters most to him, the dynamics of favoritism can arise, as they do for children growing up with siblings. Franklin Delano Roosevelt, an only child who was his mother's favorite, was pressured from birth to bestow pride on her. In exchange, he grew up determined to have whatever he wanted. Only children can also be overlooked or unfavored, growing up feeling invisible or not liked, as do some children who have siblings. But our focus here and in the next few chapters is on the dynamics of the favorite child complex and its effect on all of the family members.

THE FAVORITE CHILD COMPLEX

The favorite child complex is made up of those conscious and unconscious behaviors enacted by all the family members in reaction to a favored relationship between one parent and one child. This favored relationship may be fluid, lasting for hours, days, or months, and rotate among all the children in the family. Alternatively, the favored relationship may be fixed, existing between one parent and one child.

A Complex: What Is It?

A complex is a group of mental factors, conscious or unconscious, connected by a central theme. These factors influence the attitudes and behaviors of all the participants in a defined system. The favorite child complex impacts all the people in a given family, often over generations.

In and of itself, a complex is not necessarily negative. It becomes so when potentially destructive attitudes and behaviors converge.

Parents, based primarily on *their* needs, designate a given child as the favorite. The needs can be subtle and not evident to the parent, as when children's personalities or appearances remind parents of revered or deceased relatives. The needs can be concrete, and more obvious, as in response to children's outstanding academic, artistic, or athletic achievements.

The rewards enjoyed by favorite children are given because of their elevated status in relationship to the powerful parent. When parents are unconscious of their motivation in designating a given child as the favorite, usually the rewards of favoritism are not earned and may be confusing to the child. When parents are more conscious of their motivation, then the rewards of favoritism are more likely to be earned and to be more meaningful to the child.

Indulging children because they bestow pride on their parents differs from rewarding children to honor goals they have achieved. For example, parents often indulge children as a reward for outstanding grades. Some mothers or fathers reward their child because the child's achievement reflects well on them, publicly highlighting their outstanding parenting skills. These parents are probably less aware of what really motivates them to treat a particular child as their favorite, simply believing that good grades should be rewarded. Alternatively, parents may reward children for outstanding grades in order to reinforce their children's hard work and tenacity. These parents are probably more aware of what motivates them. In families where favoritism is fluid, parents can operate from either platform, rewarding children for reflecting well on the parents or for having achieved certain goals. When favoritism is fixed, parents are more likely to operate from the unconscious position of rewarding children because they reflect well on Mom or Dad.

The benefits of favorite child status include more privileges and less stringent enforcement of rules than for other children. Favored children are not held accountable to the same standards as are other children in the family in comparable circumstances. There are many ramifications of favorite child status:

(1) Favorite children develop feelings of power and effectiveness and the confidence to take on challenges.
(2) Favorite children often learn to exploit their position, feeling entitled to have what they want.
(3) Favorite children are often not held accountable for their behaviors; they may carry this expectation throughout their lives.
(4) Favorite children's bonds to their favorite parent can inhibit their autonomy and interfere with their mental health.
(5) Favorite children may struggle with issues of intimacy.

Favorite children thus have the benefit of growing up with confidence, believing they can accomplish anything. They often strive for challenging goals and usually achieve them.

The curses of favoritism may include feelings of entitlement and lack of accountability. Those likely to suffer these negative consequences of favoritism are children growing up in families where (1) favoritism is fixed, focused on one child; (2) one parent dominates child rearing; and (3) communication is hidden and dishonest.

VULNERABLE TO SOCIOPATHIC BEHAVIORS

Children impaired by the destructive consequences of favorite child status sometimes exhibit characteristics resembling those of sociopaths. Like sociopaths, favorite children can be self-absorbed. They tend to view rules and relationships as existing to be used to their advantage. As with sociopaths, the behaviors of favorite children are largely predicated on the skills of ingratiation. Not all sociopaths are favorite children, but some are.

Both favorite children and sociopaths can be experts in knowing how to charm people. Charm, an important skill in the art of manipulating people, can emanate from empathy, the ability to identify with someone else's emotional state. Favorite children commonly use their empathic skills to further meaningful connections with others, connections that are not made by sociopaths. Sociopaths employ false empathy as a device to ingratiate themselves with others, not as a foray into relationships reflecting compassion.

The word *sociopath* conveys a potential psychiatric diagnosis, which "favorite child" does not. Sociopaths lack (1) conscience and (2) the ability to emotionally connect with other people. These character deficits enable them to function without remorse or concern for the implications of their behaviors for others. When forced to explain their sordid behaviors, sociopaths justify their behaviors as being driven by someone else—often a parent, a supervisor, or some other authority figure.

Favorite children and sociopaths are inclined to perceive life as a game of getting what they want. But those favorite children who do not grow up to be sociopaths are more likely to develop consciences that guide their pursuit of goals. They are less likely to display behaviors widely judged by others as immoral. For example, a favorite child and a sociopath may both pursue a job promotion and will be skilled in enlisting preferential consideration from the supervisor. The favorite child who has a conscience is likely to honestly represent his ability to do the new job, while the sociopath is not.

In her book on sociopaths, Martha Stout wrote that "in the interest of individual ambitions, [sociopaths] can do anything at all without the slenderest glimmer of guilt."[1] Herein lies a critical difference between sociopaths and most favorite children. Most of the latter do have a conscience.

Throughout this book, close scrutiny is given to determining the family dynamics that can steer the development of favorite children away from potential sociopathic behaviors. Favored children who have a greater regard for the consequences of their behaviors are more apt to positively influence their worlds and live satisfying lives. These children are more likely to grow up in families where communication is open and honest, and where adults, complementing each other, work cooperatively in parenting children. In these families, favoritism is usually fluid, with all the children enjoying opportunities to experience favorite child status.

HOW THE FAVORITE IS CHOSEN

The factors influencing the selection of the favorite child may be obvious to parents. For example, some parents acknowledge their preference for infants, obsessing over their every movement, while overlooking older children in the family. Other parents favor older children to whom parents can teach skills. These parents may overlook children too young to learn the skills, children who do not share their interests, or children whose natural gifts evoke for parents feelings of envy. When parents are aware of their favored feeling for one child, it is possible they will make efforts to be responsive to their other children, though family members generally know who is the favorite.

Often, the selection of a favorite child originates within the unconscious life of the parent and has little to do with the child per se. Usually, these variables driving the choice are irrational, unknown to the parent or other family members. Variables influencing favorite child designation can begin to unfold in utero and continue throughout life. The variables can be conveyed in the mother's chemistry as the fetus grows in the womb. The parents' family histories and their lifestyles at the time of the baby's birth influence the selection process. Parents' views of themselves, perceptions of others, life preferences, and countless other determinants will influence the favorite child designation.

When children make parents feel good about themselves, they are likely to be chosen as favorite. This was illustrated in stories told earlier that focused on the relationships between mothers and infants who responded positively to the mothers, making them feel good about themselves. Among older children, fathers clinging to visions of their own athleticism may favor children who are outstanding athletes. Physically attractive daughters, complimented and acknowledged for their beauty, may elicit feelings of irrational pleasure in mothers who are struggling with tortured feelings resulting from a mastectomy or other characteristics that they perceive as shortcomings. These parents and children are unaware of the lifelong imprint that their bond, stirred by unconscious communication, has on the development of the children.

Frequently, children's behaviors that engender special parental feelings are subtler than the examples described above. Families often remain clueless as to why particular children elicit special treatment. Jane, a fifty-five-year-old client, puzzled over her continued jealousy of her younger sister. As an adult, her sibling continued to carry the childhood nickname of Love Bunny, given to her by her mother because, as an infant, her mother reported, this child loved stuffed bunny rabbits. In the course of my client's treatment, she realized she had no recollection of her sister's attachment to stuffed rabbits; nor did she find pictures in the family album of Love Bunny holding stuffed animals. In her therapy, Jane realized for the first time that her sister was illegitimate, a fact never consciously acknowledged within the family. Yet they all joked that, with her blond hair and blue eyes, she resembled no one in this family of dark-haired and hazel-eyed people. Jane realized that Love Bunny was born when her father traveled excessively and her mother had an affair with the man who, as was known to all in the family, was the love of her life. Jane's mother and father raised Love Bunny as if she had been conceived in their own lovemaking.

The mother's special bond with Love Bunny reflected the mother's unconscious processes. We can only speculate about the mother's attraction to Love Bunny, though the nickname offers clues. Love Bunny may represent to the mother the ultimate reward of her affair. Alternatively, treating Love Bunny as the favorite may have been the mother's effort to alleviate her guilt, unknown even to her, for cheating on her devoted husband and conceiving this baby out of wedlock. My client's mother insisted she loved all her girls equally, though the family knew differently: their mother clung to her youngest daughter as a child clings to a stuffed rabbit that is dearly beloved. My client grew up tense, not realizing that her unease was a consequence of the family secret—their pretense that they did not know of Love Bunny's illegitimacy.

NO FAMILY SECRETS

All children in families know, and usually agree on, who is favored. The child who is favored often denies or minimizes his role, though he secretly relishes the position. As one client said, "I know that I was favored, and everyone else in the family knew it. My mom, though, pretended that she didn't have a favorite. I always felt badly for my brother who didn't get treated as well . . . but not that bad."

The responses of nonfavored children range from relief at not having to grow up in the spotlight to engaging in behaviors intended to provoke a parental response. These siblings sometimes tease the favorite. Other times they praise the favorite, preferring to echo the sentiments of the powerful parent rather than challenge him or her. The nonfavoring parent may be accepting or critical, relieved or threatened, by the partner's attachment to a favorite child. Nonfavoring parents sometimes bond with other children in the family; sometimes they remain silent or isolated.

Family members' feelings about favoritism may change over the years or remain static. Young children, once envious of the favorite, may grow to be adults who are relieved not to be burdened by favorite child status. Alternatively, as adults, people may continue to crave the privileged status of favorite child, feeling injured at not having achieved that exalted position. Favorite children themselves may live their lives coveting their prescribed roles. They may fear altering their roles, not knowing how else to function or not wanting to risk losing their status.

All these reactions, from childhood through adulthood, are normal. They become destructive when they are hidden, concealed deep in the family's psyche, and not expressed.

The pressure to "make believe" that favoritism does not exist creates stress for family members and tension within the family. As family members try to live with falsehoods, they bury feelings that ultimately express themselves in self-destructive behaviors, such as drinking, eating, or drug taking—the hurtful effects of depression, obsessive thoughts, or anxiety. When a family gathers, the requirement to deny truth may trigger hurtful fights, often about irrelevancies, not understood by anyone.

Communicating the feelings generated by favoritism within the family helps to ensure the mental health of all family members. The willingness of each person to respect, not deny, other family members' experiences is crucial. The sentiment can be expressed humorously or seriously, gently or with anger.

One goal here in normalizing the favorite child complex is to eliminate the shame connected to favoritism. In giving permission to acknowledge and discuss the issues it provokes, family members are emancipated from the stressful burdens of living with the secrecy and deception that are evoked by the emotions of favoritism. Reducing the potential destructiveness of favoritism means that the advantages—confidence, power, and determination—can be enhanced.

CHAPTER FOUR
WHO'S THE FAVORITE AND WHO ISN'T

When my first child was born, my mother was as proud as a peacock. It was the first and last time she praised me. I loved this baby in a special way. He represented the only thing I ever did right in my mother's eyes. I held that close to my heart forever. Every time I looked at this child, I remembered her pride. For this, I felt differently about him than I did the others. He was my favorite.

—Susan's reflection

The parent's favorite child can be obvious to all. Some parents blatantly display preference for children of a given gender: "After three sons, mother really wanted a daughter" or "We all wanted a boy, especially Dad, who was overwhelmed by all the women in the house. Even the dog was female!"

The bestowal of favored status on an oldest son may be anchored in religion, culture, or old English law. Sons of Jewish mothers provide endless content for comedians. The powerful status of the oldest son in Italian families was represented in the popular HBO show *The Sopranos*. Scholars debate the drama stoked by the laws of primogeniture in Shakespeare's plays.

Even children's names may predict their favored status. Sara

Roosevelt, the mother of Franklin Delano Roosevelt, determined her child's name before his birth. She committed her life to bringing up a son as great as his name—a name reflecting his descent from two great families, the Delanos and the Roosevelts. I. Lewis "Scooter" Libby, the younger son of his family, was named after his father, putting a favored relationship in place. My colleague Josephine, the youngest of five children, was her father's favorite child. He finally had a daughter named after his mother, whom he idolized.

Each of these examples illuminates parental selection of favorite children that reflects parental needs—needs that are usually unconscious. The selection has little to do with the child but is, rather, due to an accident of birth—sex, birth order, name, or connection with a person significant to the parent. The process of selection can appear spontaneous, just happening, although, in truth, the choice reflects parents' instinct to provide themselves with associations necessary to comfort them in the world.

PARENTAL ATTITUDES TRANSMITTED DURING PREGNANCY

Some scientists speculate that fetuses sense their place in their parents' world.[1]

The description of Little One (in chapter 2) poignantly illustrated the impact of the uterine experience in the life of a young woman. Little One likely lived with the awareness that her attachment to her parents was irrational and limiting, but still she could not modify her behavior. With her parents as willing participants, the three, as a unit, began therapy. In the security of that experience, Little One surrendered to feelings previously known to her only in their most primitive state, the nonverbal, intuitive communication experienced by a developing fetus. The comfort she learned in her mother's womb was transmitted to life outside the womb, in which this comfort manifested itself as an irrationally strong attachment to her parents. This limited Little One's development, challenging her efforts to grow independent from her mother and father. In family therapy, Little One reclaimed feelings she had long understood intuitively and began to integrate them with her conscious awareness.

Prenatal memories formed from rudimentary feelings are buried deep in our psyches and may leave an imprint on our personalities. Yolanda, an accomplished forty-two-year-old, began therapy haunted by feelings of being unliked and unwanted. She understood these feelings as irrational and in sharp contrast to her life experiences, which were affirming and embracing. Yolanda lived with a premonition she could not shake: she feared her demise.

This bright and beautiful woman had achieved the status of a full partner in a prestigious consulting firm many years before her peers. Her dream life was active, often the focus of her therapy hour. When Yolanda felt pressured at work, her dreams were particularly vivid. This was especially true during the time when Yolanda was the lead partner in a complex international negotiation. When the negotiations were going on in Asia, Yolanda functioned at a high level during the day and had terrifying dreams at night. She recorded her dreams, which were powerful and unnerving, and analyzed them with me upon her return.

In the dream that was most frightening to her, Yolanda was horizontal, resting on arms that moved her through water. She trembled and shook; her legs flailed. She feared she would be dropped and sink, or her body would collide with the pool's wall and she would be killed. In her therapy, we explored the dream's possible meaning: Yolanda experienced herself as a fetus, the water as amniotic fluid, and the arms as her mother's umbilical cord, which did not hold her securely. When Yolanda explored with me her feelings that were stimulated by the arms dropping the fetus, she imagined her mother letting her die, not holding her or protecting her. When talking about the feelings experienced as the fetus collided with the pool's wall, Yolanda began sobbing. She imagined her mother as forcefully killing her. Yolanda admitted that she had often suppressed her feelings that her mother had never wanted her and had hoped for a miscarriage.

As Yolanda worked in her therapy to expunge her irrational feelings of vulnerability, she confronted the complexities of her relationship to her mother. Yolanda became aware of her mother as an indulged person, her grandmother's favorite child, who was ill prepared for motherhood. After she married the big man on her college campus, "a good catch," for this twenty-year-old coed with no ambition, her husband, Yolanda's father, was drafted to serve in World War II. He was stationed in the United States, and he and his wife lived together in an efficiency apartment with rudimentary comforts. At the conclusion of the war, he was discharged. The couple moved into her parents' home. Yolanda's mother wanted to be mothered; instead, she became a mother. Within nine months, Yolanda was born.

In her therapy, Yolanda confronted her confusion. While trusting her instinct to be correct—that her mother did not want her—Yolanda did not want to believe it, hoping her thoughts were wrong. No child wishes to be correct in feeling unwanted by her mother. Yolanda spoke to her aunts and uncles as well as her mother's friends to learn more about her mother, hoping to learn about her mother's delight while pregnant with her.

Instead, Yolanda's long-buried suspicions were verified. Her aunts recollected that, when pregnant with Yolanda, her mother had deep and irrational fears of miscarrying. "It sometimes seemed as if your mother wanted to miscarry," an aunt reported. Further, Yolanda learned that when she was two, her mother did miscarry in the ninth month of a pregnancy. The umbilical cord snapped when she strained to open a stuck window. The family lauded Yolanda's mother as heroic. She had not alarmed anyone; she had lived with a dead fetus in her belly for a couple of days, waiting until her regularly scheduled doctor's appointment.

When told this anecdote by her aunt, Yolanda heard a different story: that of a mother killing her baby, or if one wants to be generous, that of a mother not fighting to save her baby. Her mother did not want children. Yolanda lived her life feeling the injury of being an unwanted child. Putting into language this painful truth, while concurrently expressing her painful emotions, freed Yolanda from living with the unease of her free-floating anxiety.

The stories of Yolanda and Little One dramatically illustrate the profound impact of nonverbal communication between parents and their young children. This communication impacts the emerging character of the child. Only after children have grown into adulthood and are aided by therapeutic intervention do they begin to appreciate the power of primitive experiences on their personalities and lives.

Without any therapeutic intervention, people may be largely unaware of the influence on their personalities of maternal attitudes and feelings. Unlike Yolanda's mother, who was frightened to connect, other mothers who have struggled with similar issues may be irrationally attached to their children. In return for staying psychologically connected to their mothers, these children may be designated as their mother's favorites and have difficulty establishing their own identities. Other mothers vulnerable to forging inappropriately close bonds with their children become pregnant to fill their own emptiness as older children move out into the world. In exchange for remaining the baby of the family, such a child is likely to be designated by the mother as her favorite.

We can surmise that fetuses are influenced by communication transmitted by their parents. Chemical and physiological reactions may possibly be woven deeply into their psyches. Thus, pathways to favoritism or rejection may begin prior to the infant's birth.

PARENTAL ATTITUDES CONVEYED DURING INFANCY

The seeds of favoritism or rejection planted during infancy reflect the evolving relationship between mother and child. Some mothers reflect their preference for caring for infants, labeling this stage of mothering as their favorite. Other mothers remain as unconscious as they were during their pregnancies of whether they are treating a given child as the favorite.

The infant/mother relationship that breeds favoritism is influenced by two essential factors: the left side of the infant's brain begins to develop more rapidly only after eighteen months, and the relationship between mother and child becomes more interactive as the infant grows older.

First, after eighteen months, the left side of the infant's brain begins to develop more rapidly. Babies begin developing verbal skills that evolutionary psychologist David Livingston Smith terms "camouflage."[2] Smith believes that language serves the function of camouflage for people, allowing them to utilize words for protection from pain. As was previously discussed, fetuses are vulnerable to emotional injury that is generated from uncensored emotion. After two years, babies, through the use of language, begin the process of moderating the raw power of incoming communication. For infants, as for all children, issues of being selected as favorite, or being pushed aside, generate complex emotions. However, as children mature, the intensity of feelings can be moderated by language. Still, the long process of developing the ability to spin experience, making uncomfortable experiences seem less ominous, likely begins during infancy through the rudiments of language.

Second, the relationship between mothers and infants becomes more dynamic as the infants grow older. Mothers are more likely to prefer babies who make them feel competent as caretakers. Other common variables influencing maternal selection of favorite children are the mother's lifestyle when her child is born, the sex of the child, and birth order. The mother's relationships with her husband and with other family members—children, mother, father, in-laws, grandparents, aunts, or uncles—all have an impact on a mother's attraction to a particular child.

Infants are psychologically scarred for life if their mothers do not physically and emotionally bond with them. This rejection leaves an imprint on their primitive psyche, affecting their ability to build healthy and trusting relationships with people. But all is not lost. Other adults in the world of the emotionally abandoned infant can mitigate the impact of the rejection by reaching out and bonding with the infant. These adults may be fathers, grandparents, adult siblings, or beloved aunts or uncles.

Maternal Bonding with Baby

The interactions reported earlier between two mothers and two infants in a bookstore demonstrated the impact of mother-child dynamics and mothers' and children's influence on each other. In the first example, the child reinforced the mother's feelings of competence, and, in the second, the child heightened the mother's feelings of inadequacy. If the pattern perpetuates itself, we can project favoritism taking hold in the case of the first mother and child, but not in the case of the second.

The first mother conveyed more loving feelings to her child than did the second mother. Both children reacted to their mother's stimulus with pure, unfiltered honesty that was appropriate to the mother's stimulus. One mother was calm and invited the baby to be calm, while the other mother was agitated and her baby responded in kind.

Mothers are less likely to perceive themselves as "good" or "bad," and more likely to perceive their babies as "good" or "bad." Good babies don't cry. They sleep well, and, when unhappy, they are easily calmed. In contrast, mothers describe infants who are not easily calmed as "fussy," which is shorthand for "difficult."

Mothers, delighted with happy infants, tend not to recognize the influence of their calm on their babies. Good babies, often referred to as "easy babies," get disproportionate credit. Similarly, in fretting about unhappy infants, mothers tend not to recognize the impact of their stress and frustration on their babies' agitation. These babies receive disproportionate blame.

Mothers, associating themselves with "good" infants, feel positive about themselves. As this relationship continues, it reinforces itself and enables the roots of favoritism to grow. Babies absorb feelings of well-being from their mothers. Mothers who parent more difficult babies generally feel negatively about them and want to minimize their attachment to their infants, the objects of their discomfort. If this relationship continues without modification, mothers end up emotionally distancing themselves from their babies.

Infants are vulnerable to absorbing their mothers' feelings of favoritism or rejection. Babies, lacking language skills, are receptacles, absorbing their mothers' mental and physical state—positive or negative. The roots of favoritism planted during infancy can have a strong influence on the child's developing character.

Distant Mothers

When a mother is unavailable to nurture her newborn, because of the mother's emotional or physical problems, a father or other loving adult sometimes bonds with the infant. This maternal surrogate may treat the baby as his favorite out of sympathy or because the infant fills a void for the caretaker. While the attachment dilutes

Inconsolable Babies

Calm, patient mothers can have agitated babies. Defining the source of their babies' distress is sometimes difficult, even for sensitive mothers or experienced pediatricians. Adoptive parents may struggle with infants who fuss inordinately or refuse eye contact, the babies' way of conveying distress at having been rejected by their birth parents. Unable to comfort their infants, mothers may feel frustrated and are often tired due to sleep deprivation. The challenge to a mother of an unhappy baby is to achieve clarity as to what is her responsibility and what is not.

When assuming inappropriate responsibility for their babies' distress, mothers become unhappy with themselves. To protect themselves from feelings of frustration or incompetence, these mothers are vulnerable to distancing themselves from their babies, emotionally hurting themselves and their babies. Babies, as emotional sponges who lack the language skills necessary to understand or moderate the experience, absorb their mothers' anguish and imitate their emotions. The feelings of inadequacy that babies absorb from mothers become wired into their young brains and woven into their personalities.

Unhappy babies can breed unhappy mothers. While attending to the infant lays the essential groundwork for the child's development, preoccupation with a baby's unhappiness can blur the boundaries between mother and child. As the boundaries become less clear, the objectivity demanded of the mother is to make healthy decisions for her infant and herself may diminish. A prerequisite for effective parenting of difficult infants is for the mothers of these children to care for themselves and value their efforts to make their infants more comfortable.

Ultimately, mothers want children to live productive, fulfilling, gratifying lives. Mothers who trust their competence when responding to their infants can have a positive impact on the mental health of their children. These children have the opportunity to mature with the confidence gleaned from knowing that they are favorite children.

the negative repercussions of maternal rejection, the scars caused by this rejection may never disappear completely.

Charles, a thirty-eight-year-old with an enviable career as a political analyst, began therapy because of his many failed relationships with women. During his first session, he reported, "My mom and I have never been close. But it doesn't bother me. I have the best father in the world. My dad more than made up for anything I didn't have with my mom."

As Charles recounted the family story, before he was conceived, his father, Tony, lived a lonely existence. His mother, Dorothy, long preoccupied with pleasing her father, focused on him with greater intensity in his old age. When Dorothy became pregnant with Charles, Tony's excitement contrasted with his wife's apparent indifference. She remained focused on her father's welfare.

After Charles's birth, his mother's involvement with him, as he described it, was perfunctory. The family album lacked pictures of Dorothy holding him, while it bulged with pictures of Tony holding him. Their loving eyes fixed on one another and they both grinned from ear to ear. Their attachment to each other grew stronger through the years.

As an infant, Charles offered his father the pleasure that had eluded him, and Tony offered his son the consistent love required by children. This father and son bonded, finding in one another the affection and affirmation that was not provided by Dorothy. In return for offering companionship, Tony indulged Charles, treating him as the favorite child. Charles, having few memories of his father saying "no," grew up believing he could have and do anything. This personality trait contributed to his developing confidence, fostering a successful career and a growing sense of entitlement to anything he wanted. These traits served Charles well in his professional world, though he remained lonely, longing for an intimate partner. His relationship with his father enriched his life but did not ameliorate what was probably a primitive wound sustained due to maternal rejection. (This mirrors Bowlby's findings as summarized in chapter 2.)

Yolanda, my client discussed earlier, illustrates the dynamics generated when a grandmother fills the psychological void created by an emotionally removed mother. Through conversations with aunts and uncles and old friends of her mother's, Yolanda's understanding of her mother grew.

Yolanda and her parents lived with her grandparents, Gigi and Pa, until Yolanda turned three. Gigi, who had a long history of indulging Yolanda's mother as her favorite child, encouraged her daughter to "go and have fun" and happily looked after her infant granddaughter. Yolanda's mother, not wanting to assume the responsibilities of motherhood, readily complied.

Over time, however, the repercussions were significant. Yolanda's mother grew increasingly uneasy around her baby. Her parenting skills did not develop, nor did she bond with her infant. Yolanda's attachment to her mother diminished, while her attachment to her grandmother increased. Yolanda's family members reported that, as an infant, she cried when her mother picked her up, only to be calmed when Gigi held her.

Yolanda's mother's confusion in her relationship with her own mother, Gigi, grew after Yolanda's birth, according to lifelong friends of Yolanda's mother. First, they explained, Yolanda's mother wanted more distance from Gigi, yet resented being displaced as her mother's favorite by Yolanda. Second, Yolanda's mother felt inadequate in comparison to Gigi. Third, as time progressed, Yolanda's mother felt publicly shamed when Yolanda cried when held by her mother and calmed down when held by her grandmother.

Yolanda continued to recount her story. When she was three years old, her parents moved to their own home. There, her father replaced her grandmother and embraced Yolanda. Yolanda's relationship with her father continued the special feelings kindled by Gigi. As an adult looking back at her parents' relationship, Yolanda remembered her mother as commonly rejecting her father's hugs or turning her head away when he tried to kiss her hello. Yolanda's mother seldom went with Yolanda and her father for ice cream, or to the zoo or the circus. Yolanda surmised that she and her father filled the void for each other created by her mother's rejection.

Yolanda grew up appreciating the advantages of being Gigi's favorite grandchild and her father's favorite daughter. Due to these relationships, she felt powerful in her life and so her confidence flourished. As an adult, she moved up the ladder of her prestigious consulting firm at an accelerated pace and maintained a reputation as the person most likely to succeed in any challenge. But her grandmother and father were limited in their abilities to defuse Yolanda's pain as she struggled to cope with her mother's rejection. Even when she was an adult, Yolanda's spontaneous reactions were a beaming smile when talking about her grandmother and a grimace, with tension in her voice, when talking about her mother.

Mother's Lifestyle When Baby Is Born

The story of Scooter Libby revealed the importance of lifestyle as a variable in a mother's choice of a favorite child. Over many years, my mother-in-law told me that when her first child was born, she was without resources: she did not have the skills required to care for her infant, the extended family to assist her, nor the financial resources to hire a caretaker. Uncomfortable in the presence of her infant, who triggered her feelings of inadequacy, she distanced herself from him and took him to her family home in Louisiana to be cared for by others.

In contrast, when Scooter was born, his mother had the financial means to hire people to help take care of her son. When he fussed, she handed him over to a caretaker to comfort him and was not confronted by the negative impact of her anxiety on her infant. Her lifestyle during Scooter's infancy provided her with the resources to allow her to hide from her inadequacies, resources that were not available to her during her older child's infancy.

Yolanda's story speaks to the challenges of an adult daughter with a child who lives in her mother's home, not independently. Apparently, Yolanda's mother competently managed living on her own, keeping house for herself and her husband while he served in the army. Upon his discharge and their moving back home, Yolanda's mother reverted to being the child her mother indulged. Reclaiming the life she had lived as a favorite child, she gave up functioning as an independent, successful adult. Mothering a child was difficult for a woman who was being mothered herself.

Some mothers seek to have babies to fill a void created in their lives when their children go to school or when their marriages are unfulfilling. The issues presented by Klara and Alan mirror those of many couples.

Klara and Alan began couples therapy when Klara was six weeks pregnant with their third child. Alan was unhappy. With his business struggling and their children in school full-time, he had anticipated Klara's returning to work to augment the family income, as they had agreed. Instead, Klara became pregnant when Alan thought their sexual activity was protected. Klara, distraught, held Alan's anger to be unfair, insisting that the pregnancy was an accident.

In the presence of a therapist, Klara's deception quickly emerged. She was enraged by Alan's lack of financial success and had no interest in working "to help him out." She bellowed, "He bought these businesses with our savings. *He* has to make it work." Klara acknowledged the depth of loneliness she experienced in the marriage, resenting his round-the-clock preoccupation with work. "Even our vacations are related to work—a convention, a buying trip, or something like that," she complained. "Nothing is just for us."

Klara felt Alan had taken on work as his companion, and she looked to a baby that would be hers. With two older children in school, who no longer required as much attention as they had earlier, Klara's estrangement from Alan emerged. She acknowledged to me that she enacted her rage by luring him into unprotected sex.

The first four weeks of their couples therapy were intense. Klara and Alan came in two or three times each week to examine whether they could raise this unborn child with loving involvement and not further jeopardize their already fragile marriage. Acknowledging shared joy in parenting their older two children, and committing to ongoing therapy for themselves, they decided to have the baby, raising the child collaboratively as they raised the other children.

Klara and Alan accomplished their goals. By the time the baby was born, Alan had worked through his resentment about the pregnancy. He joined Klara in showering the infant with love. The couple continued in therapy, learning to engage with each other so that their resentments were not reenacted. Hence, they avoided the risk and drama of a contentious pregnancy. The infant grew into a confident young woman, flourishing as her parents' favorite child. Klara and Alan credited her birth with their improved marriage, and this was reflected in her privileged status.

This story is not unique or uncommon. Rather than cope with the life changes demanded when their youngest child begins school, some women fill the void and uncertainties surrounding their lives with another pregnancy. Mothers' attachments to these children are usually special. Other family members frequently view "the baby" as mother's favorite child, a position awarded by the mother to the child for having given her a focus other than her ill-defined life goals. In exchange for protecting the mother from fears generated by having a limited focus or being lonely, this child gets to grow up indulged as the favorite.

Unlike most couples, Klara and Alan availed themselves of professional guidance as soon as their divergent reactions to the pregnancy surfaced. Their marriage not only survived, but also grew stronger. Klara did not cling to the baby to fill her emptiness, permitting the child to grow without irrational constraints imposed by her. Alan did not resent the baby; a loving man, he developed his own profound feelings of love for the child.

The HBO series *Tell Me You Love Me* dramatizes stressful interactions between a husband and wife provoked by issues surrounding pregnancy.[3] Carolyn and Palek, the couple portrayed, began counseling because of the stressfulness of infertility. Ultimately, Carolyn became pregnant through fertility treatments, and Palek acknowledged his resentment at the impact of the infertility and then the fertility on their marriage. Unable to resolve his resentment and fearing its poisonous repercussions in their lives, he wanted the fetus aborted. He offered Carolyn the option of abortion or divorce. Carolyn chose to have the baby, believing that if she chose abortion she would never forgive him. That, too, would corrupt their marriage.

At the conclusion of the season, Carolyn miscarried, and Palek offered comfort. She rejected him, not trusting his responsiveness. She believed his affections were rooted in having what he wanted: no baby complicating their lives. The season ended with the viewer not knowing whether or how Carolyn or Palek reconciled their complicated emotions.

What would Carolyn do with her feelings of loss? What feelings would she bury deep inside herself, complicating her relationships, not only with Palek but potentially with other men as well? How difficult would it be for Carolyn to access and resolve these feelings later on? After her miscarriage, would Carolyn's attachment to her unborn infant make this child her favorite child even if she had others? How would this impact her relationship with a subsequent child?

A mother's lifestyle when her baby is born impacts her emotional, psychological, and physical abilities to care for her infant. Mothers who feel well cared for are more likely to be more responsive to their infants' needs and to be more loving.

BORN TO FILL A ROLE

Susan, whose reflection introduced this chapter, received the reward she craved with the birth of her son and the concomitant affirmation by her mother. Her mother's accolades generated more euphoria for Susan than did holding her newborn, Bert. His birth and her mother's affirmation became linked together, in a connection Susan "held close to [her] heart forever." Bert, symbolizing her mother's approval, secured favorite child status, a position he enjoyed throughout his life.

Bert's coveted status was awarded, not earned. The factors influencing his position as favorite child had little to do with him. At birth, he was blessed with good health, having no medical issues that were distressing to the family. Susan's mother wanted this grandchild, her first, to be a boy, to honor the memory of her deceased husband. In his grandmother's eyes, Bert looked exactly like Susan's father. According to Susan, her mother told all who would listen that "the shape of their eyes, pointed chins, adorable ears, and thin lips make them look more like father and son than grandfather and grandson."

With the birth of this boy, Susan's mother pretended that the son was hers, the child she wanted to have for her husband but could not. After Susan's birth, her mother had been unable to have additional children. Susan's mother longed for a son and had difficulty accepting her daughter. Susan grew up sensing her mother's distance. With Bert's birth, Susan's mother experienced vicarious fulfillment. This made Susan finally feel accepted by her mother, dissipating her lifelong pain. For Bert, being male and being the first grandson were accidents of birth for which he carried no responsibility. Yet Susan rewarded him with the favorite child designation.

The Role of Greatness

Like Bert, Franklin Delano Roosevelt enjoyed the privileges of the favorite child for reasons having little to do with him. The second wife of her husband, James, Franklin's mother, Sara, believed her ticket to honor was to raise a son to be more successful than her husband's son from his first marriage. While this older son was honored with his father's name, James, Sara honored her son, as noted earlier, by combining the names of two prominent families, her own "Delano" with her husband's "Roosevelt." From the moment of his birth, Sara Roosevelt devoted her life to her son.[4]

Franklin Delano Roosevelt, the only child born to Sara and James, grew up as his mother's favorite child. Sara's special treatment of Franklin reflected her needs, not anything that was intrinsic to him. She looked to her son to assuage her insecurities, first, in relation to her own father, and second, as her husband's second wife. One of ten children, Sara believed that she could cement her relationship with her adored father by bringing up an accomplished son. And, fiercely competitive with her husband's first wife, Sara was driven to help Franklin surpass his half-brother in all endeavors. Franklin's father, James, was fifty-four when Franklin was born and is reported to have been an aloof man. It is possible that Sara also looked to Franklin to provide her with a relationship filled with the vitality that was missing from her marriage.

Rewarded for being the son she required, Franklin was indulged by Sara, he was given essentially all that he desired. Further, Sara believed that because Franklin was the son of two great families, the world should indulge him. She pressured schools in which he was enrolled, and later his wife and the White House staff, to treat him as she saw him: as a man entitled to have all his whims met.

Bonnie Angelos, author of *First Mothers*, describes Sara Roosevelt's commitment to her son as unwavering—from his birth in upstate New York to Sara's death in the White House: "When he was a student at Harvard, she rented an apartment in Boston to oversee his social life. When he and his young wife needed a larger house, she provided it. When he was stricken with polio, she pampered and cosseted him, against his wishes. When he was president, she schemed to bring the White House to her standards. And when he was contemplating divorce, she threatened (so it was whispered) to cut off his funds from the family fortune."[5]

This mother and son, Sara and Franklin, remained entwined throughout their lives, and their relationship interfered with FDR's freedom to make personal decisions as an adult. When he wanted to divorce his wife Eleanor, Sara cajoled him with bribes and threats. Ultimately, she won. He could not say "no" to his mother.

FDR mirrored his mother's temperament: "He was confident, determined, and pleasantly stubborn when it came to getting his own way."[6] As her favorite child, he occasionally pushed her to get his own way. However, he rebelled against Sara in two major decisions: marrying Eleanor and entering politics. Not wanting to forfeit her special relationship with her son, Sara ended up acquiescing.

The destructiveness imposed by Franklin's status as his mother's favorite child wreaked havoc upon the lives of Franklin, Eleanor, and their five children. Among these five children, there were nineteen marriages, fifteen divorces, and twenty-nine children! Two of Franklin's children were elected to the House of Representatives but, in spite of repeated attempts, none were elected to higher office. The relationship between Franklin and his mother not only undermined the quality of their lives and those of people surrounding them but undermined the lives of the subsequent generation as well.[7]

General Douglas MacArthur, also a renowned American, grew up as the favorite son of his mother, Pinky. His life, especially from college and beyond, was fused with hers. Until Pinky's death, their lives remained entwined.[8] As her favorite son, MacArthur believed he was entitled to get what he wanted, to get his own way. Consequently, MacArthur's first marriage ended disastrously. His career ended in shame. His own son, Arthur, was so uncomfortable with Douglas's pressured involvement in his life that Arthur changed his name and moved to a place where he could live in obscurity.

The daughter of a prominent Virginian family, whose brothers fought in the Civil War, Pinky married a young hero of the Union Army. She committed her life to supporting the military careers of her husband and son, determined that they should excel. When Douglas MacArthur entered West Point, Pinky moved to a hotel room overlooking the parade grounds. Under her watchful eye, Douglas succeeded at West Point, graduating first in his class and winning the award as the outstanding all-round cadet. At West Point, Pinky's life had purpose and meaning while her husband served as an officer on battlefields in the Philippines and her older son served as a naval officer.

After Douglas's graduation and until her death, Pinky followed Douglas from base to base to oversee his career, determined that he should be successful. Douglas's father died about ten years after Douglas's graduation from West Point. His brother was killed shortly thereafter. Pinky, already inseparable from Douglas, became even more obsessed with the success of her son's career. She was determined that he should follow in the footsteps of her deceased husband and have opportunities befitting the son of a general. She used connections, engaging colleagues of her deceased husband, to help advance her son's career. For example, during World War I, she lobbied the War Department to promote MacArthur to brigadier general. Although the usual protocol of obtaining General Pershing's consent was not followed, MacArthur received his appointment.

As MacArthur's career advanced, he was criticized as being arrogant, first when serving as commander in the Philippines at the beginning of World War II and then as commander of the international forces during the Korean War. MacArthur was ordered to take offensive and defensive action in the Philippines immediately after the bombing of Pearl Harbor. He ignored those orders and the Japanese gained air superiority in the Philippines. In Korea, MacArthur issued statements supporting the war while President Truman prepared to engage North Korea and China in peace negotiations. Ultimately, President Truman fired MacArthur for insubordination, an ignominious ending to his stellar career.

The stories of Roosevelt and MacArthur are noteworthy because they provide insight into the characters of men and families who have influenced history. But there are many lesser-known mothers and fathers who have looked to their children to live out their dreams.

The Role of Scholar

Karen, the oldest daughter in a first-generation family of Korean immigrants to the United States, began therapy because of depression generated by the burdens she felt as the favorite child who was expected to live out her mother's academic and professional dreams. As the oldest child, she was anointed the "smart one," who would bring honor to the family through academic excellence. Karen was expected to excel academically: to graduate first in her class in the competitive science magnet school that she attended, become a Westinghouse scholar, and receive a scholarship to MIT or Caltech, all of which she had the ability to do.

Her brothers and sister, also smart and good students, were expected to achieve, but the expectations for them were not as high as they were for Karen. Therefore, their parents believed they had time, which was not available to Karen, to complete household chores. No one challenged the myth of Karen's total unavailability to participate in household work. The parents, working long hours at their convenience store, depended on their children to maintain the house. Karen's siblings competently fulfilled their responsibilities to the family and in school. But their excellence, expected by their parents, was not acknowledged.

Karen enjoyed the freedom that came with having no household responsibilities. When she took a study break, rather than help prepare dinner or fold laundry, as did the other children, she sat in her room chatting on the phone or listening to music. Alienated from her siblings and feeling guilt for exploiting her position as her parents' favored child, Karen began therapy as a senior in high school. Unable to put language to her feelings, Karen sensed the unfairness of her parents' treatment of her in comparison with the other children. She knew she was fully capable of doing her fair share around the house and that her siblings were as bright, hardworking, and motivated as she. Karen thus struggled with an incapacitating fear of failure generated by the pressure to succeed.

Unfulfilled Dreams

An only child, Dean lived the life that his father craved, as an artist. But this career was not satisfying for this forty-year-old man. He buried his unhappiness in bourbon and drugs, pretending they were aids required for his creativity. An internationally acclaimed painter, Dean was in Washington for an opening when he collapsed. As a part of a comprehensive medical evaluation, he was referred to me for a psychological evaluation, which clarified that he had, in fact, suffered a mental breakdown. Single, Dean remained inordinately attached to his parents, and they came to Washington to oversee his care. They participated in his evaluation.

Dean grew up encouraged to pursue any dream he had. His parents had amassed great wealth through hard work. "I want you to take advantage of the freedom our wealth gives you. You can to do with your life whatever you want," Dean reported his father as saying more than once. During Dean's evaluation, the inaccuracy of this statement surfaced.

Dean's father, Malcolm, projected onto him the hopes and aspirations Malcolm himself had had as a young man. During Malcolm's adolescence, teachers praised him for his artistic talents. Malcolm remembered his pleasure as an artist as being countered by his father calling him a "sissy." Malcolm walked away from painting, focusing on sports in high school and business in college. He lived his life regretting the decisions he made that distanced him from the passion of his youth. Being a benefactor of museums did not satisfy him. He encouraged Dean to pursue painting. He wanted to love his son as he had hoped to be loved, as an artist. Dean, not wanting to disappoint his father, passively complied.

During the evaluation, Dean recalled his father's pleasure as Dean's artistic skills matured. Good grades and athletic achievements received pats on the back, but accomplishments as a painter received resounding praise and elaborate gifts, such as two cars—one big enough for large canvases and a second for fun. Enjoying the rewards, and gratified by the pleasure he brought his father, Dean pursued his career as a painter. It was only during his evaluation that

Dean began to acknowledge that he had pursued a career he did not like because he did not want to disappoint his father.

When I met with Dean's father, Malcolm, he was confused and upset. He had not intended to pressure his son into pursuing a career as his own father had pressured him. Malcolm had difficulty accepting that the heaping of inappropriate rewards on his son grew from the older man's desire to have Dean live out Malcolm's dreams. Dean was indulged as a favorite child, giving his father something he profoundly wanted—vicarious pleasure in his son's artistic accomplishments and the affirmation of his son as the artist.

The psychological evaluation prompted by what turned out to be Dean's mental breakdown exposed a family with good intentions that went awry. Dean's father wanted his only son to have the golden opportunity he, himself, did not have—to be a painter. Dean enjoyed his father's various forms of encouragement, such as unending praise and attention, lessons with the best teachers, and cars that were envied by his friends.

The psychological boundaries between this father and son broke down through their unconscious communication: Dean's father projected onto Dean his hopes and dreams. Dean internalized his father's wishes. This relationship formed the basis of the family system, respected by Dean's mother. She reported, "I felt loved by both my husband and son but I also understood there was something special between them." Not questioning this "something special," she colluded in fostering what proved to be a destructive relationship.

Dean, a favorite son and an only son, unconsciously carried the burden of living out his father's unrecognized dreams. If Dean had had siblings and had still been the one child carrying out his father's aspirations, it is possible that this would have created a competitive atmosphere, destructive in its own way to family functioning. As an only son, Dean felt the burden of what he referred to as his father's "last hope to achieve his dream."

Just as Dean tried to live out his father's dream, Audrey, another client, tried to live out her mother's dream. A thirty-eight-year-old attorney, Audrey lived the life her mother could not live but had hoped that her daughter would live. Evelyn, Audrey's mother, sacrificed herself and molded her daughter to be professionally successful and not dependent on a man.

After graduating from high school, Evelyn worked full-time as a secretary, helping to support her mother and her younger siblings. Within a few months, she met a navy pilot, fell in love, and eloped. During the next five years, three children were born, two daughters and a son. Shortly thereafter, the marriage fell apart. Evelyn's husband had affairs, and he started drinking heavily. With three young children, little money, and no extended family to assist her, Evelyn felt trapped.

Audrey, the oldest child, became the vessel holding her mother's hopes and dreams—to be financially self-sufficient through a secure profession. Her mother struggled, scrimping and saving extra money so that Audrey could take additional classes or participate in new experiences that might help to further Evelyn's ambitions for Audrey. These opportunities were often provided to Audrey at the expense of her sister and brother, who were deprived of experiences important to them. This provoked in Audrey feelings of guilt.

Evelyn's words rang in Audrey's mind throughout her life: "If your father was good for one thing, it was his mind. He was as sharp as a tack. At least he gave you that." Audrey understood that she was her mother's favorite child because she had her father's mind and, thus, the ability to excel academically. Audrey received straight A's in high school and received a full scholarship to Duke. She majored in physics and again achieved straight A's. Audrey was awarded fellowships to both law and medical schools. She became an esteemed constitutional lawyer, financially secure and not dependent on a man. This favorite daughter lived the life that her mother wanted.

While her professional life differed from her mother's, her personal life mirrored her mother's. Audrey was distrustful of men. She could not sustain a healthy relationship. She began psychotherapy, wanting help in modifying those parts of her personality that precluded intimacy. While appearing social to the world, she spent many weekends home alone, isolating herself from women as well as men. Underneath her engaging exterior was a depressed and uncomfortable woman. Audrey had just begun therapy as I wrote this book, working hard at becoming more comfortable with me and more trusting of me. She has much self-discovery to do in her journey ahead.

Dean's father and Audrey's mother are parents from two different families who looked to their children to correct childhood experiences that they themselves had endured. In exchange for taking on this responsibility, each child enjoyed the rewards given to the favorite child. But, having grown up enmeshed with the powerful parent, as they did, they suffered negative repercussions. Dean had a mental breakdown, and Audrey was severely depressed.

THE OVERLOOKED CHILD

Some parents, like Evelyn, favor children who have the skills necessary to achieve, which the parents may have lacked. Other mothers and fathers, like Malcolm, embrace children as favorites who are like them, and, if there are other children in the family, may overlook those who are different. These parents may struggle when relating to the different children, distancing themselves rather than learning to be more comfortable in their presence.

Muriel came for a psychological consultation because, in spite of living a life that should have been happy, she found little pleasure in it. She teemed with resentment, envious of the close relationship that her sister Maya had with their mother. Muriel's husband's and children's impatience with her ranting pushed her into therapy.

When engaging with her mother and sister, Muriel complained of feeling like an outsider. Her mother solicited Maya's advice and ignored Muriel's. Her mother praised Maya for orchestrating luncheons at a restaurant or navigating Walmart, while demonstrating no interest in Muriel's thriving accounting practice. When Muriel declined invitations to be with her mother and sister, she was equally miserable, hating the fact that they were having an experience without her.

Maya, Muriel's younger sister, was a carbon copy of her mother, small and petite, with fair coloring. Both concerned themselves with yoga, healthy eating, and volunteer work. Neither showed the intellectual curiosity that drove Muriel to excel in school and in her career. Resembling her father, tall and statuesque, with freckles, Muriel had no memories of her mother ever praising her appearance. Rather, she remembered her mother's criticism of the length of her hair, the color of her sweater, and the fit of her jeans. Muriel vividly recollected her mother's pressuring her to wear makeup, at twelve years old, to conceal her freckles. Though Muriel was an adult, her envy of the relationship between her sister and mother felt childlike. Her thoughts and feelings, unchanged since childhood, belied the logic and competence that marked many years of her life experiences.

As Muriel's therapy unfolded, she grew to understand her mother's overwhelming sense of inadequacy and her complete dependence on her husband. When Muriel's mother was quite young, her parents were killed in a car accident. Raised by a loving aunt and uncle, who suffocated her with protection, she grew up unsure of herself and lacking confidence. In marrying Muriel's father, who was twenty years older than she was, Muriel's mother married a protector, a caretaker, someone to replace her aunt and uncle.

Muriel's mother had little appreciation of her own contributions to the marriage. Both she and her husband took for granted her excellence as a traditional wife and mother—raising children, making meals, maintaining the house, and arranging an active social life. The praise that was forthcoming focused on her beauty. Muriel's father enjoyed his wife's appearance, joking about his trophy wife or child bride.

Muriel's mother devoted her life to being beautiful. Maya, whom strangers often thought to be her mother's sister rather than her daughter, served as a visual reminder to the mother of her beauty. She perceived Maya as an extension of herself. In contrast, Muriel's mother could not relate to Muriel, who was driven by her mind, not her appearance. In contrast to Maya, Muriel represented to her mother those traits that accentuated her mother's insecurities —intelligence, self-sufficiency, and the courage to take the risks that are necessary for success.

Through her therapy, Muriel grew to understand that in her parents' marriage, functions were rigidly delineated: her father was the intellect and her mother the beauty. By an accident of genes inherited at birth, Muriel embodied her father. Her mother could not relate to Muriel, a woman with business savvy. Muriel's mother favored the daughter who was most like her.

WHY SO MUCH ABOUT MOTHERS?

While this chapter has explored the potential bonding between fathers and children, it has focused more intensely on the bonding between mothers and children. Favoritism that arises during pregnancy or infancy can reflect a mother's unconscious needs, which she wants her infant to fulfill. This type of preference is rooted deep in her psyche; it is not subject to modification and is conveyed to the baby through the primitive communication of raw feeling. Babies, pliable like soft clay, absorb these visceral emotions, growing up knowing that they are their mother's favorite child. The infant's identity becomes entwined with the mother's, and the implications for the child's development are profound.

Fathers, like mothers, are vulnerable to bonding with children, which evolves into favoritism. Fathers can look to children to fulfill their unsatisfied needs: unrealized ambitions or the deep emptiness of living a lonely existence. Fathers can also be sensitive to the needs of infants that are dismissed by their mothers. The dynamics between fathers and infants developing into favoritism are similar to those described between mothers and infants.

This chapter has focused on the relationship between parents and favored children that originates from parental needs that are usually unconscious. With its roots deep in the parent's psyche, the favored relationship remains focused on a child who fills the parental needs, and in exchange, this child is designated as favorite.

We will next explore fluid favored relationships, in which all the children in the family have the experience of being favored by both parents.

CHAPTER FIVE

THEY'RE ALL MY FAVORITES

Kent Ravenscroft admits that, for the moment at least, both he and his wife prefer their seven-year-old son to their daughter. "She's four years old and is going through a normal stage of being thin-skinned, throwing wild tantrums and pouting. But our favoritism will probably shift in the other direction in a few months," said Dr. Ravenscroft, a child psychiatrist and an associate professor of psychiatry at Georgetown University.

—Lawrence Kutner, *New York Times*

These remarks by Kent Ravenscroft reflect what all parents know: kids go through various stages, challenging parents in different ways. Parents, based on their own personalities, have preferences for particular ages.

Here we will focus on favoritism that is "fluid," flowing from child to child, from parent to parent. In these families, the awarding of favorite child status is less likely to originate from deep inside the parent's unconsciousness to meet the parent's needs. Rather, we will find two parents commonly alternating the role of important parent. We will also find all the children in the family having turns as the

---

Epigraph. Lawrence Kutner, "Parent and Child," *New York Times*, April 5, 1990, http://www.nytimes.com/1990/04/05/gst/fullpage.html.

favorite of both adults. Here, we will discover the relationship between the adults to be loving and respectful: the parents will communicate openly, confronting one another when witnessing inappropriate displays of favoritism, and they will fight with the intention of resolving differences, not to be right.

The changing designation of favorite child will be based on behaviors anticipated by predictable life stages, exemplary achievements, shifting family dynamics, and individual idiosyncrasies. Optimally, all children should experience the rewards of favoritism, and all parents should experience the pleasure of that relationship with each child. Adults, as well, enjoy the pleasures of being declared "the favorite parent." In selecting one parent over the other, children feel powerful as they affect their parents' feelings.

The declaration of favoritism can be an expression of an honest feeling as well as an expression of manipulation. Expressing pride in children's accomplishments by affording them special rewards can convey honest parental feeling. But such statements can morph into manipulation when the behaviors of the honored child become the standard by which other children in the family are judged.

One mother tried to cajole her younger daughter, Angie, to be more like her sister, the favored child. In a family therapy session, fifteen-year-old Angie complained it was unfair that her sixteen-year-old sister had a much later curfew. Angie maintained that her strong academic achievements, in contrast to her sister's average grades, should earn her at least equal treatment. Her mother maintained her position: "If you'd dress the way Cecily does and not wear such short skirts, I would trust you more. You'd have a later curfew."

The connection between skirt length and curfew was specious, fostering a sense of dishonesty. The issue was *not* the length of this fifteen-year-old's skirt but the fact that her skirt length made her mother uncomfortable and her sister's skirt length did not. Cecily protected herself from her mother's unease by waiting to shorten her skirt, rolling it up after leaving home, while Angie, more defiantly, wore her skirts short in her mother's presence. In holding Cecily's behavior as the absolute standard, the girls' mother tried to manipulate Angie by offering a later curfew. Ironically, she was unknowingly encouraging Angie to behave deceitfully, as her sister did.

Children, too, use the words "you are my favorite," both lovingly and manipulatively. When a parent buys a child an unexpected toy, like a new bike or headset, or takes him on a special outing, like to a professional football game or to play paintball, the child may lovingly embrace that parent as the favorite. In contrast, when a mother sets limits on the behavior of a child and the child shouts, "Dad is my favorite," the child uses the status of favoritism manipulatively, setting up one parent against the other. Though the mother grasps the child's irrationality, the child may accomplish the intended goal—to hurt the mother for having enforced the rules. In a healthy family, parents are not seduced by children's declarations, whether they are intended to be manipulative or not, with regard to the favored parent.

The dynamics of favoritism in families are complicated. Open communication among family members that focuses on issues of favoritism helps to ensure that all family members experience the varied rewards of favoritism within a healthy framework.

PREDICTABLE LIFE STAGES

Human development is predictable. Adults expect infants to be cuddly, two-year-olds to be terrible, and adolescents to be defiant. Children, when young, expect their parents to be playful; when they are adolescents, they expect parents to offer advice; when they are much older, they expect parents to require caretaking. Social scientists codify these predictable stages of development across the life span, basing their categorizations on the "work" or skills required for people to grow physically, mentally, psychologically, morally, and socially. Mastering the work of one stage provides the necessary foundation for progressing to the next stage.

Each adult relates differently to each child at each stage, reflecting the uniqueness of the adult and the child. While the work of infants is learning to trust primary caretakers, the work of adolescents is learning to establish independence, separate from their primary caretakers. To succeed in their work, infants engage lovingly, with smiles and coos. In contrast, defiance within a healthy range is required of adolescents if they are to succeed. Some parents prefer taking care of a dependent infant over a rebellious teenager, while other parents experience the baby stage as boring and uninteresting. Adolescence is a preferred stage for some parents, stimulated by the engagement and challenge. Others resent the demands of parenting a teenager or are threatened by the child's need to create psychological distance. Parents, preferring children who are working on mastering the skills of one developmental stage or another, favor each child as that child passes through the desired stage. In these families, all children benefit from experiencing the advantages of being the favorite.

Developmental Stages

Developmental psychology is the scientific study of the psychological changes that occur in people over the life span. Normal development and change are systematically defined in terms of diverse aspects of human development, ranging from motor skills to moral development. Also studied are cognitive understanding, including problem solving and conceptual understanding; language acquisition; personality and social and emotional development; and self-concept and identity formation.

Psychologists codify the skills that it is necessary for people to master during each developmental stage. Successful completion of the "work" or skills of each stage is required to advance to the next stage.

The developmental stages and the work of each stage are as follows:

Infants (to eighteen months) The physical work of infants is learning to crawl, eat, and talk. The psychological work of infants is learning to trust and bond with family members. The mental work of infants is stimulating their brains to grow, especially the left side, which is the center for cognitive learning. How infants learn to trust others and how their bodies and brains are stimulated to grow affect how infants will learn to control themselves as toddlers.

Toddlers (to three years) The physical work of toddlers is learning to walk, climb, explore, and play. Toddlers learn basic lessons in caring for themselves—feeding, dressing, and using the toilet. In mastering these skills, children accomplish their psychological work—building confidence in themselves in developing control over their bodies and learning that they are autonomous from their mothers. The mental work of toddlers is learning to communicate through language and continuing to stimulate their brains. How toddlers learn to control their bodies affects their preparedness for impacting their world as preschoolers.

Preschoolers (to five years) The physical work of preschoolers is exploring the world outside the home. The psychological work of preschoolers is learning to socialize, to initiate, and to feel effective in the world. This is accomplished as the young child carries out projects successfully while working within boundaries. At this age, children start learning about feelings of guilt. The cognitive work of preschoolers is developing their creativity and imagination through play. How preschoolers learn to socialize and feel effective in their world impacts their readiness to begin mastering the tasks of latency, the time period before entering puberty.

Latency-Aged Children (to 11 years) The physical work of latency-aged children is learning to adapt to the realities of the world, primarily through play. The psychological work of latency age children is building self-esteem through mastering the world outside of the family and learning from their own mistakes. The cognitive work is developing their intellectual framework for complicated thought, which requires more abstract thinking. How latency-aged children develop trust in their own competence affects how their identities will emerge during adolescence.

Adolescents (to eighteen years) The physical work of adolescents is adapting to the realities imposed by their developing sexual bodies. Their psychological work is establishing an identity, separate from their parents, leading the adolescents on the path to living an independent life. The cognitive work is developing the mature thinking and judgment necessary for independent functioning. How adolescents embrace their own character affects how they will tackle the challenges of young adulthood.

Young Adults (to forty years) The psychological work of this stage is committing to a relationship and a career. Young adults learn to be intimate with another person, without jeopardizing their sense of self. Cognitively, young adults develop the thinking and skills necessary for the pursuit of a satisfying work life. How young adults master their commitment to relationships—intimate and professional—impacts their readiness to be fully productive members of their families and society, which is the work of middle age.

Middle-Aged Adults (to sixty years) The physical work of this stage is adapting to the body's changes—menopause and reduced sperm production, decline in muscular strength, and decline in reaction time. Also important is learning that the body takes longer to recover from illness and injury. The psychological work of middle-aged adults is committing to their essential roles as contributors to the future of society; these adults are responsible for passing along knowledge to the next generation. The cognitive work of this stage is continuing to be productive in work and creative in transmitting information to younger people. The success of middle-aged people affects their preparedness for meeting the challenges of old age.

Older Adults (over sixty years) The physical work of this stage is continuing the work started during middle age, adapting to the body's slow decline. The psychological work is primarily introspective, examining the integrity of one's life. If older people feel satisfied, then they continue to work and create, maybe in ways differing from those in which they worked and created at other times in their lives. If they are unsatisfied, they struggle with issues of self-acceptance and the meaning of life. The cognitive work of older people is to keep their minds active, working to diminish possible mental deterioration.

Parents, directed by their own developmental stages and personalities, have differing preferences for children during given developmental stages. Children, directed by their developmental stages and personalities, have differing preferences for parents.

FAVORITISM BASED ON DEVELOPMENTAL STAGES

Parents of four-year-old and seven-year-old children easily understand Ravenscroft's preference for his seven-year-old son over his four-year-old daughter. In the course of successfully accomplishing her work of learning to function within boundaries, Ravenscroft's four-year-old daughter comes up against her parents' boundaries. The child has to learn to accept them and work within them. Her willingness to do so varies and is influenced by many factors, such as her innate personality, her mood in the moment, her exhaustion or hunger level, and the presence or absence of siblings, friends, or grandparents. Also impacting on the child's response is her parent's mood. A stressed, tired, or pressured parent is more likely to convey impatience with a four-year-old's insistence than is a relaxed, rested, or calm parent.

The work required for Ravenscroft's seven-year-old to grow is less demanding of parents than the work of his younger sister. The young boy's developmental tasks are focused inward, requiring him to mentally envision the skills and steps required for mastery of given goals. While he may be bristling with questions for his parents, it is unlikely that he will be as obstreperous as his younger sister.

Critical to appreciating Ravenscroft's relationship with his daughter and son is the concept of fluidity. First, each child passes through all the developmental stages. Second, each child enjoys the advantages of each parent's preference for a given stage. Third, as each child moves to the next developmental stage, parental responses differ. Fluid favoritism in a family recognizes that children grow and change, and, as they grow and change, different responses are evoked in each parent. Each child enjoys the rewards of being mother's favorite, and of being father's favorite, when passing through the developmental stage preferred by each.

Children's responses to their parents are fluid, reflecting children's unfolding interests, developing skills, or emerging personalities. Children pull toward the parent they perceive as particularly well suited to help confront specific physical, psychological, or educational challenges. For example, in some families, children wanting to develop confidence as competitors or skills as athletes may favor fathers. Children may push away from fathers and favor mothers when seeking to organize their social lives or to be soothed when sick.

The preference for same-sex or opposite-sex parents fluctuates, reflecting the child's work of forging a sexual identity at different developmental stages. As pubescent bodies emerge, children favor same-sex parents, identifying with them and finding more comfort in expressing uncertainties and asking questions. To accomplish later developmental goals, children may push away from the same-sex parent and toward the opposite-sex parent. Children's fluidity in anointing mother or father as favorite reflects the complexity of the developmental work of girls becoming women and boys becoming men.

As alliances reflecting favoritism change within a family, the entire family is affected. My daughter, usually docile, was much easier to parent than was my very active son. She seldom challenged the rules. Her demands were reasonable, so she usually got what she asked for. In contrast, my son challenged the rules and his behavior required constant monitoring. When my daughter observed me permitting her younger brother to play before completing his homework, a privilege she did not think he had earned but was given because of favoritism, she was furious with me. In response, she manipulated my husband to allow her to stay up much later than normal, getting an unearned reward for herself.

My husband and I, of course, enacted the family tension: he challenged my decision, allowing our son to play before completing his homework, and I challenged his allowing our daughter to stay up late. In these moments, I told myself that I had been my daughter's favorite parent, so I felt competitive with my husband, fearing permanent displacement. My husband relished the experience of being "the good guy" in her world. Within a day or two, when our daughter believed my husband had indulged our son and not her, the entire process was replayed, only in reverse!

Our son was equally a player, resenting our daughter when we set limits on his behavior. He insisted she was our favorite. "You never punish her," he hollered. True, but that was not driven by favoritism. Unlike him, she seldom got into trouble. When she did, her response was not to behave combatively and defiantly, as he did. Rather, she was overcome with shame and anxiety. My husband and I had to be vigilant, so that our concern for her tension did not preempt our displeasure with her behavior. In those moments when my husband and I communicated well with one another, the family benefited. When we relied on each other, we had more confidence that our responses were equitable and our treatment of our children was fair.

Favoritism in a family is more likely to remain fluid when parents are honest with themselves about their own temperaments and receptive to their partner's moderating input. Parents accepting the unevenness of their own temperaments are more likely to accept the unevenness of the temperaments of their children and be appreciative of each child's uniqueness. For example, one client reflected that she favored her younger son when she was tired or anxious. This son, an aspiring stand-up comic, made her laugh and helped her to achieve a perspective on her day. She favored her older son, whose seriousness and thought patterns reflected hers, when she hungered for an intellectual partner.

The two stories told below illustrate families coping successfully with the stresses imposed by favoritism as favoritism shifts from one parent to the other. In both stories, children's changing developmental needs spur them to gravitate away from one parent and toward the other. In fluid families, this movement impacts the relationship between mother and father, as well as between each parent and each child.

The first vignette focuses on the tension created for Jennifer and Damon as their young children gravitated away from one parent and toward the other. The impact of this movement on the family dynamics is powerful but less stressful than with older children. When children are younger, their developmental tasks are more basic and, as they move from one developmental task to another, their impact on the family is less dramatic. As children grow older, their developmental work becomes more complex, stimulating more dramatic family dynamics. The second vignette, focusing on the triangle composed of Phyllis, Robert, and Marissa, exemplifies the complications of fluid favoritism in a family's response to the developmental needs of a young adult.

Jennifer and Damon: Parenting Preschoolers and Latency-Aged Children

Jennifer and Damon sought couples counseling. They struggled with balancing two careers and parenting. Shortly after the beginning of their counseling, competitiveness between them emerged for their sons' affections. Quickly, they acknowledged that those issues that brought them to counseling had less to do with juggling the demands of their lives and more to do with being uneasy when enforcing limits with their boys. Each parent preferred parenting tasks more likely to engender positive feelings from the children. Jennifer and Damon each wanted to be the favored parent who was adored.

Jennifer, a college basketball player, thrived when participating in high energy, competitive sports. As an adult, she played tennis with the same determination that she had exhibited when playing college basketball. Damon, in contrast, was a professional chef, which reflected his lifelong interest in cooking and artistry. When their children, Eric and Alan, were young, they relished creating "masterpieces" with their father. At eight years old, their older son, Eric, pulled away from Damon, declaring, "Cooking is for sissies," and gravitated to his mother. He preferred to shoot hoops or hit tennis balls with her. Damon was devastated, feeling rejected by his favorite son.

Working with Eric in the kitchen, Damon had developed a special affection for his older son. They had established a routine before the younger son, Alan, was old enough to participate. Those initial feelings bonded Damon to Eric. When this son first left the kitchen, Damon was heartbroken, feeling abandoned. Though he knew it was irrational, Damon felt personally attacked by Eric's declaration that cooking was for sissies. Damon felt ashamed of his reactions. Though he told himself that the attack was not personal, his misery did not subside.

In therapy, as Damon grew to understand his feelings, he flourished. He realized that, as the husband of an athlete and father of sons, he feared that his sons would reject him as his own father had. Damon was the son of a father who believed cooking to be effeminate, blatantly preferring his other sons because they were athletes. In describing cooking as an activity for sissies and choosing their athletic mother, Eric stirred up Damon's painful memories. Attending to his childhood memories, fraught with feelings of rejection, Damon grew to depersonalize Eric's shift in focus from cooking to sports, and his gravitation toward his mother. With Eric out of the kitchen, Damon began reveling in spending time exclusively with Alan, getting to know this son as he had not done previously.

A few years later, Alan followed Eric out of the kitchen and onto the court. Damon appreciated the special time he had had with each his sons before they turned to focus on friends and the world outside the home. Each son treasured the experience of feeling favored by his father. Damon, accepting the changing interests of his growing sons, appreciated their participation with their mother in activities that were meaningful to her and instructive to them. Damon laughed when reporting to me that, after Alan left the kitchen, Damon found his way to the basketball court, shooting hoops with the rest of the family—and enjoying it.

Phyllis and Robert: Parenting an Adolescent

Appreciating the ebb and flow of favoritism is more complicated when factoring in the vicissitudes of children's emerging sexual identities. At one moment, the same-sex parent is treated with special affection, eliciting from that parent feelings of favoritism. At other moments, the same-sex parent is the villain and the opposite-sex parent, now revered, responds to the child with special feelings of love.

In chapter 2, the tension created by a misalliance between a father of Hispanic descent and his adopted adolescent daughter, together with the boundaries set against this daughter's troublesome behaviors by the mother, was explored. Here, the same triangle is examined in the context of a daughter's emerging sexual identity. As a young child, Marissa, an only child, demanded extraordinary attention from Phyllis, her mother. As Marissa was vulnerable to colds, ear infections, and sore throats, her frequent visits to doctors made working outside the home difficult for Phyllis, and ultimately, she quit her job. Years later, in therapy, Phyllis acknowledged that she had never wanted to be a working mom and she had latched onto Marissa's illnesses as a reason to quit.

When young, Marissa was indulged by Phyllis. Doctors' visits were followed by purchases at the toy store. Seldom did Phyllis refuse Marissa's requests, whether to be given something extra from the store or to stay up late. When Marissa's behavior required punishment, she managed her mother well. First, Marissa apologized. Then, she hugged Phyllis. Ultimately, she talked her mother out of punishing her.

As an adolescent, Marissa pushed against her mother, following an instinct essential for her healthy development. This normal process was dramatized because of Marissa's status as her mother's favorite child. First, as favorite child, Marissa had excessive freedom as her mother seldom set boundaries or limits. Therefore, to provoke her mother's engagement, Marissa escalated her behavior to attract more attention. For example, Phyllis usually ignored the smell of alcohol on her daughter's breath until Marissa would came home dead drunk, maybe throwing up on the living room carpet or puncturing the tire of her car on the curb in front of the house. Only then would Phyllis engage with Marissa, ultimately punishing her.

Second, Marissa was in a psychological bind, as she generated intensified anger within herself. On one hand, she did not trust her ability to survive without being her mother's favorite child. On the other hand, her closeness to her mother limited her. This fueled anger, which manifested itself in provocative behaviors that served to distance her from Phyllis.

Third, Phyllis's husband, Robert, felt a long-standing tension regarding his wife's preferential treatment of their daughter. Though Phyllis and Robert had a loving and trusting relationship, Robert was ineffectual in conveying his concerns. As Marissa pushed away from her mother, she pulled her father closer to her. He delighted in the feelings of being the favorite parent. As her mother's favorite child, Marissa had mastered the art of getting what she wanted. With these skills, she captivated her father.

Marissa fought heatedly with her mother about everything, whether it was hot outside or very hot, whether her jeans were too tight or skin-tight. Marissa's ultimate weapon was to flirt with her father. While girls learn to flirt in their relationship with their fathers, Marissa acknowledged in family therapy sessions that she did so with determination and intensity, calculating her mother's hurt.

Marissa was an exceptionally beautiful young woman, her appearance mirroring that of a fashion model. In contrast, Phyllis saw herself as boyish, flat chested, and without hips. She disliked her dull, thin hair. When she complained, her husband Robert responded lovingly, "Honey, I had to fight off enough guys for you. If you were any sexier, I would have never won." Clearly, he had no issues with her looks.

Phyllis, however, was uneasy with her appearance, and it was in this arena that Marissa exploited her mother's vulnerability. Unconsciously, in flirting with her father, Marissa struck at her mother in the area where she was most defenseless—her appearance. Marissa knew how to injure her mother, how to reject her.

As Marissa came into favor with her father, Phyllis was pained. Her daughter, her favorite child, pushed her away with anger, replacing her with the man who was the love of Phyllis's life. Phyllis and her husband, Robert, talked in therapy about their complicated feelings stemming from how each favored Marissa and from Marissa's response, pulling toward one parent and pushing away from the other. The couple came to understand that while the issues in the family focused on Marissa, she was not the cause of the tension between them.

Troublesome issues in their marriage—competition and feelings of resentment—had been dormant since Phyllis quit her job to become a stay-at-home mom. These old, uneasy feelings between the couple hindered their ability to respond effectively to Marissa's normal developmental task, the task of psychologically pulling away from her mother as she worked at creating her own identity as a woman.

In marrying Phyllis, Robert believed he was marrying a woman whom he would not have to take care of financially, as he took care of his mother. When Phyllis quit her job, he felt betrayed, resenting her dependence on his salary. And Phyllis, for her part, resented the preferential treatment Robert gave to his mother. One aspect of her quitting work was the enactment of competitiveness with her mother-in-law: Phyllis wanted Robert to take care of her financially as he did his mother. Their relationship with Marissa became the focus of their dispute; unconsciously, they enacted their competitive fury with one another.

Issues with children challenge relationships between parents, and feelings emanating from favored relationships accentuate the reactions. As children grow older and the requirements of their developmental work become more complicated, tension within families mounts, bringing to the surface old and unresolved resentments between their parents. Perceiving the ensuing conflicts as the fault of the child leads to scapegoating, unfairly blaming the child. The issue between Phyllis and Robert was not Marissa's angry behavior directed toward her mother, the preferential bond between Robert and Marissa, or Marissa's only-child status. The issue was the unresolved anger between Phyllis and Robert, lying dormant and percolating for years. They projected onto one another the psychological discomfort generated by years of unresolved tensions, and they scapegoated their daughter, unfairly blaming her behaviors for causing the tension between them. Rather, the tension between Phyllis and Robert probably contributed significantly to the tension Marissa enacted in her errant behaviors.

SCAPEGOATING

When scapegoating occurs in a family, the family's health and vitality are threatened, and the family's ability to maintain the fluidity of favoritism is impaired. The child's provocative behaviors are not the root causes of the tension, though the behaviors may elicit uncomfortable feelings in family members. Family responses to provocative children are influenced by deeply buried resentments and tensions held by each parent, resentments that are rekindled in their marriage. Marissa's attacks on her mother, described above, and her father's inability to hold her accountable for her behaviors generated family tension but did not cause it.

The family tension had its roots in Phyllis's hidden resentment of Robert's treatment of his mother. Phyllis, unable to express this tension in language and talk it through with Robert, reenacted the tension by quitting her job under the guise of taking care of her daughter. Robert's experience of helping his mother financially was upsetting to Phyllis. And when Phyllis quit her job, she provoked similar feelings inside Robert that he was unable to resolve satisfactorily with her.

The issues stimulated by the triangle of Robert, Marissa, and Phyllis replicated those from an older triangle, that of Robert, his mother, and Phyllis. Robert and Phyllis, unable to resolve the complicated issues generated by the first triangle, reenacted those issues in their second triangle. Phyllis's competitiveness with her mother-in-law, her desire for Robert to take care of her, influenced her response to Robert's taking care of Marissa. Robert's resentment at having to take care of his mother spilled onto his resentment of Phyllis's retirement from work.

In my work with college-aged men and women and their parents, issues related to scapegoating often emerge. Parents believe that if their children had followed their advice regarding careers,

The Scapegoat

A scapegoat is a person who is made to bear the blame of others. The concept originated in the Old Testament: Aaron confessed all the sins of the children of Israel over the head of a live goat on the Day of Atonement. The innocent goat, symbolically bearing the people's sins, was punished unfairly in being sent away into the wilderness. In modern-day psychology, a person is scapegoated when he or she is blamed unfairly, by family, friends, colleagues, or society, for tension or anger within the group. The group uses the scapegoat unfairly to absolve its members from responsibility for the group's malfunction.

The psychological ramifications of scapegoating are profound:

1. It is hostile. It inappropriately moves blame and responsibility away from those responsible.
2. It is unfair. Angry feelings are projected, through inappropriate accusations, onto others.
3. It vilifies the target. Feeling wrongly persecuted, blamed, and criticized, the person scapegoated suffers rejection.
4. It obscures truth. Usually unconsciously, those who blame others hide from personal awareness of their roles in creating group unrest.

Scapegoating is a mechanism employed to defend people against bad feelings, such as shame and guilt. Rather than confront these unpleasant feelings, those who scapegoat displace onto others these dreaded, negative feelings.

lifestyles, and significant relationships with others, then the family would function smoothly. While some tension is inevitable as children in their late teens and early twenties forge their own lives, other tensions may reflect parental unease generated by the fact that their children are becoming more independent. If children successfully move on, the parent/child relationship has to be renegotiated. No longer caretakers as they once were, parents struggle to redefine their roles. This is complicated in families where parents are invested in the belief that it is desirable to treat all the children the same.

The parents in one family, not understanding their anorexic daughter's complaints of feeling overlooked and her jealousy of her sister, insisted that they loved both their daughters equally and treated them the same. The anorexic's mother and father had difficulty understanding that treating both daughters the same denied each their individual needs. "We treated Eve the same as Wendy. Wendy was successful. We don't understand why Eve isn't."

Eve, my client, is the younger of the two daughters. Eve was a high school senior when one parent accepted a prestigious, highly visible presidential appointment. Wendy, three years older, was a college junior in Boston when the family moved to Washington. That year was jarring for Eve: a new school and new friends, one parent consumed with forging new professional opportunities while the other parent continued working long hours as a high-level executive.

The routine that the family had in place before the move was inadequate in helping Eve adapt to life in DC. Eve was always different from her sister: Eve was an introvert and Wendy an extrovert. Eve was an artist and Wendy an athlete. Eve liked to make her own decisions while Wendy was more solicitous of her parents' opinions. The issues provoked by the move accentuated Eve's differences from Wendy. Treating Eve as Wendy had been treated in high school overlooked Eve's needs.

At dinners, Eve's parents talked nonstop about their exciting days and Wendy's successes. Eve spoke timorously about her day, only to be reassured by her parents that with time, life would improve. Eve ate little at dinner, often feeling sick to her stomach. This average-size young woman began losing weight. Soon weight loss became a game she played with herself. She grew thinner and thinner.

In family psychotherapy sessions, Eve's mother and father related their shock that relocating to DC was stressful for Eve, because it would not have been for Wendy. They defended themselves over their lack of acknowledgment that Eve's anorexia was a call for help, because that was not what Wendy would have done. Eve's parents insisted the problem rested with the fact that Eve had not approached them for help, because Wendy would have done so. They thought it "crazy" that Eve felt pressured by their frequent reporting of Wendy's achievements, while Eve was struggling.

Eve's parents wanted to discuss their distrust of their daughter. They believed she had lied deliberately, telling them everything was "fine" when, in fact, her life was not "fine." They wanted to punish her for having lied by grounding her every night for an undetermined period of time. We talked for several hours about the reasonableness of the punishment. What emerged was that living in Washington was difficult for everyone, and only Eve expressed this truth.

Eve was being scapegoated for challenging the family's false representation of reality. Further, her parents were fearful that Eve's anorexia would damage the appearance of their all-American family. Ultimately, her parents realized how little thought had been given to moving Eve during her senior year in high school. They blamed the family tension on her rather than acknowledge the destructiveness of treating her as they had treated Wendy.

With time, both parents explored their role in contributing to their daughter's eating disorder. The parents continued working with her therapeutically, stretching themselves psychologically as they learned to parent her very differently from the way they had parented Wendy. They grew to understand that treating their daughters equally denied what made each of them special.

It is easy to embrace the idea of every child as the favorite; it is harder to hold on to that idea when children such as Eve challenge the family members' idealized view of themselves. To resolve the underlying issues, parents are often forced to confront the issues of their own growth, the challenges of their own developmental stages.

"THEY'RE ALL MY FAVORITES"

Hearing of my interest in favoritism, I received the following e-mail from Roberta: "I'm sure that my kids think we have a favorite child, but I agree with my husband that they are all our favorites. True, some are 'easier' to raise than others, but we feel fortunate that our kids each have special traits that make them stand out from one another. It's impossible to be perfectly evenhanded in raising four different individuals. One can only try to be fair."[1]

In contrast, in "The Dirty Little Secret of Motherhood," an article published online in the *Daily Beast*, author Laura Bennett admitted that she had a favorite child, yet the particular child who was the favorite changed.[2] Everyone in the family knew who was the favorite, talked about it, and laughed about it. Many bloggers responded to Bennett's article, emphatically echoing Roberta's sentiments. They believed, unlike Bennett, that they favored all their children, not one in particular. The bloggers and Roberta agreed that, as parents, they tried to be fair and appreciate their children's individuality.

In her e-mail to me, Roberta highlighted three considerations critical to fluid favoritism, favoritism that rotates among children in a family. First, each child is different. Second, some children *are* easier to raise than others. Third, fairness, *not* perfect evenhandedness, drives healthy parenting.

After I received Roberta's e-mail, she asked her children if they would communicate their thoughts to me regarding favoritism in the family. Three of her four children agreed; her fourth child, in the throes of moving, was unavailable.[3] The contrast between Roberta's perceptions and those of her children was striking. The children, who as adults had little contact with one another, perceived favoritism in the family similarly.

First, Roberta said there were no favorites, but her children disagreed. Without communicating with one another, they agreed upon who was the favorite of which parent, and why: the third child, who was a super-achiever and extraordinarily good looking, was favored. The oldest child, struggling with ADHD and weight problems, was not favored until adulthood, when the individual was properly medicated and the weight issues were controlled. At that time, the beloved third child fell out of favor, in connection either with physical distance or with tension created by the child's expressed disappointment over a lingering issue with Roberta. The mother's favoring of the youngest child was unwavering, either because the child was the only one of the given sex or because of the child's inherent charm. The age differences between the oldest and youngest, the difference in their sexes, and the time of their birth in relation to the mother's divorce were understood by the children as leading to the existence of two favorite children in the family (that is, the third and the fourth) when the children were younger.

Second, Roberta wrote that some children are easier to raise than others. Her children appreciated the impact of their personalities on the bestowal of favorite child status, agreeing that the oldest sibling was most challenging for the parents. Through e-mails, I explored with this child the impact of being the oldest child. This child did not experience pressure related to birth order: "I think my feelings of unease related to being most like my mom in those ways she didn't like herself and to being the kid that generated for Mom the most memories of her failed marriage."[4]

This third child explained that the oldest child remembered the fighting between the parents leading to the divorce, and that her sibling found little relief after the divorce. "I sensed that my oldest sibling remained angry with Mom for staying in that awful situation as long as she did," the third child wrote.[5] While this child did not recall fights or family tension predating the divorce, the loss of the father after the divorce was painful. The fourth (and youngest) child had no recollection of family life prior to the divorce or of the ensuing relocation.

In my communication with the family members, all agreed that the oldest child was most like Roberta in personality and body type. In raising this child, Roberta was forced to confront those characteristics of herself that she liked least. In raising the third child, Roberta engaged with a person reminding her of her father, the person whose warmth she craved. Roberta projected onto this child the positive traits that she saw in her father. In raising the youngest child, Roberta enjoyed experiencing the personality of someone very different from the others, in part because this child was the only child of the gender. All the members of the family agreed that the fourth child was the least demanding and most mild mannered, which was effective in getting this child's needs met in a style that was not offensive to others.

Third, Roberta's children, as adults, agreed that she tried to be fair, though while growing up, they felt differently. One incident concerning caramel apples stood out. Roberta purchased one treat for each child. She gave one to her three younger children but froze one for the oldest, who was not to get the treat until ten pounds was lost. From Roberta's perspective, this was fair, and it acknowledged the differences among her children: three of her children did not have weight issues and should not be deprived of the treat. She did not want her oldest child treated differently, being denied the treat, but feared that giving the treat to this child was not in the child's best interest. By freezing the apple until the weight goal was achieved, Roberta tried to be fair to her four children. As an adult reminiscing, the oldest child remembered the pain generated by the experience. As an adult, this child reflects with compassion on Roberta's struggle to be fair.

No Two Children Are Identical

Roberta's story dramatizes how the differences among her children—in personality, appearance, and age relative to her divorce—impacted her treatment of each of them. Her third and fourth children were her favorites. Both were further removed than the first two from the unhappy dynamics surrounding her first marriage. The personality of her third, physically attractive child allowed Roberta to engage in a fantasized relationship with her dad—the relationship she wanted. For that reason, this child received excessive praise. The personality of her nice-looking youngest child, who was calm and embracing, permitted Roberta to feel appreciated and successful as a parent. For that reason, this child was rewarded with relaxed behavioral standards.

The oldest child felt unfavored until adulthood, believing it took that many years to mature and for Roberta to overcome her own demons that were stirred by this child. Less is known about the second child, who did not communicate with me. The siblings who did communicate with me agreed that the silent sibling was always "the most independent of us," though they never sensed that Roberta treated this child differently. One way of understanding the second child's nonparticipation in this exploration is that this child continues to operate somewhat removed from the family. Roberta, because of her personality, reacted differently to each of her children, and, in turn, each of her children reacted differently to Roberta.

While Roberta, in her communication with me, and Laura Bennett, in her column for the *Daily Beast*, voiced different positions on the existence of favoritism in their respective households, they agreed that each child differed. Bennett wrote that "Children are born with the personalities that they have. And some personalities are just easier to get along with than others. I have kids who operate like me, and I understand them better. I am better able to get along with them. These are the ones who are not so intellectually gifted, so they work hard to succeed."[6]

The desire to appreciate children's individuality is reflected by many people who responded to Bennett's column. Trentsky, J9tigger, and RavensNana were three of those who responded.[7] Trentsky wrote, "Each of my kids bring a very special quality to our relationship, and it's up to me as their parent to nurture those that are positive." J9tigger wrote, "I love both of my boys, and for completely different reasons. On different days one will strike me as more of whatever I am craving than the other." RavensNana wrote, "My son is more like me emotionally, but my daughter is someone I have lots of fun with, so it's more like I'd pick one of them to shop with, one of them to watch movies with, et cetera."

No children are carbon copies of each other, even identical twins. While such twins share the same genes, their environmental experiences differ, even from the beginning. Scientists believe one fetus may receive the first run of nutrients if its position in the womb is more advantageous, closer to the placenta. Some scientists speculate that the child receiving preferred nutrients is larger at birth, influencing personality differences. Other scientists speculate that the fetus closest to the placenta may have a closer attachment to the mother, and that these feelings are held onto throughout life.[8]

Parents may intend to treat children the same, but children, like Roberta's oldest child, do not always view it that way. The following anecdote describes the experience of a mother whose belief in her fairness was challenged by her daughter, whom we discussed earlier.

Frances, the mother of two daughters, believed she treated her two daughters fairly until Angie, the younger daughter, challenged her treatment of Cecily, the older. "Why do you favor my sister?" Angie asked one afternoon. Frances knew deep down in her heart that Angie spoke the truth. "I remember the moment vividly," Frances recounted. "I felt like I had been exposed, found out. That I was standing there naked." Frances's overwhelming shame drove her decision to begin therapy, requiring her to curtail the extensive international travel that was required for her work, thus potentially jeopardizing her lucrative career as a lobbyist.

In our first family psychotherapy session (described at the beginning of this chapter), Angie questioned her mother about the disparity between the curfews imposed on her and on her sister. Frances became defensive, insisting she had to protect Angie: the length of her skirts made her look too sexy, so an earlier curfew was appropriate. Upon further reflection and with time, Frances grew to appreciate that presenting herself as protecting Angie was a pretext necessary to defending herself against uncomfortable, long-forgotten memories from her own childhood.

Frances, the second daughter of four, grew up as the favorite. She excelled in school; she was a super-achiever in academics and extracurricular activities. Her mother, cold, aloof, and anxious, offered little praise but turned to Frances for advice and counsel. In this way, Frances was distinguished from her siblings, being honored by her mother more as a peer than as a child. Because Francis was aligned with her mother and therefore not with her sisters, her sisters had something Frances wanted. Her siblings had warmth, fun, and companionship in each other.

Frances lived her life feeling left out and resenting her mother for singling her out. As an adult with her own children, she vowed she would never single out one child. She would treat all her children equally, encouraging them to be close to one another. Now, as the mother of adolescent daughters, Frances was confronted by one child for preferring the other. This touched Frances's deepest fears.

In her therapy, Frances identified the complicated feelings that motivated her behavior. When exploring old childhood feelings that continued to haunt her, Frances first identified the shame she carried due to her mother's attention. Second, she recognized her resentment at having worked hard to maintain her favored position. She described herself as monitoring her behavior, doing nothing that might make her mother uncomfortable, and becoming and remaining a super-achiever. Third, she was angry at not having been as central to her sisters' lives as they had been to each others'.

The feelings driving her relationship with her daughters were more complex. First, in exploring the complexities of her relationship with Cecily, Frances acknowledged that Cecily reminded her of her sisters. Like her sisters, Cecily had to work hard for good grades and had to curtail extracurricular activities to achieve them. Cecily stayed home studying while Angie was out in the world achieving. Having Cecily around the house more often than Angie offered Frances opportunities to establish the warm, fun-filled relationship she had craved with her sisters.

Second, Frances identified that her treatment of Angie reflected feelings about herself. Frances felt ashamed that success came easily to her and so she minimized Angie's success.

Third, Frances accepted that Cecily was the recipient of her projections of happiness while Angie was the recipient of her projections of her unhappiness. In essence, her unconscious associations with Cecily were positive and those with Angie were negative.

In confronting Frances with her resentment, Angie offered her mother the opportunity to grow emotionally, to tackle the developmental challenges of middle age. Frances, open to hearing the painful truth expressed by her daughter, accepted the challenge of confronting long-buried feelings. Honest communication in the family opened up and, with it, Frances grew closer to accomplishing her lifelong objective—treating her daughters equally, favoring both.

STRUGGLING TO BE FAIR

Treating all children with fairness requires extraordinary parental skills and patience. No two children are the same and, because no two parents are the same, all children affect all parents differently. To achieve the desired outcome—treating all children the same, holding each as the favorite—requires parents to be honest with themselves and receptive to feedback from others. The communication can be difficult to absorb, whether between husband and wife, as represented by Phyllis and Robert, or between parent and child, as represented by Frances and Angie. Once the message is heard, the family requires profound self-exploration to modify the dynamics. Doors then open, permitting parents to tackle the work of their own growth.

This chapter, along with chapters 3 and 4, has explored the dynamics of designating a child as the favorite. This chapter has investigated favoritism where the intention is for all children to have opportunities to feel chosen. When the system falters, however, parents can work cooperatively to solve the problems.

Next we will explore the rewards permitted by fluid favoritism and the dangers imposed by rigid favoritism.

CHAPTER SIX

REWARDS AND RISKS OF BEING THE FAVORITE

My brother James had it all. He was the oldest son in our Irish Catholic family. He had our grandfather's name and knew he'd inherit the family business Grandpa had started. He was expected to be a star, and as long as he produced, my parents gave him anything he wanted—cars, clothes, and an allowance bigger than the rest of ours. My brother succeeded. He was the star running back on his high school football team and shattered all school records. In college, he was president of the student government. After graduate school, he took over the family business, and, against all odds, turned a small but successful business into a business with a national presence.

—Annemarie's reflections

Annemarie, sister of James and client of mine, recalled her brother's treatment in the family. Her story parallels that of Ruth, a colleague, who recollected similar dynamics surrounding her brother, Nate. James and Nate were favorite children in their respective families.

Like James, Nate was the oldest child in his family and was expected to take over the family business. He did. From early childhood, his skills were cultivated. He grew up with confidence and leadership skills. In high school, Nate was a star tennis player, and in college, he was editor of his college newspaper. Here, the similarities between these two brothers end. One exploited his role as favorite son. The other did not.

James restructured the family business to financially benefit himself. He alienated his sister and five brothers, in essence robbing them of their inheritance. James's smooth style often obscured his manipulations until he achieved his desired end, making it difficult for his siblings to challenge the repercussions of his maneuvers. When he was confronted, his aggressive responses intimidated his siblings. They were no match for James, who was driven by raw feelings of entitlement. He expected to get his own way, not relenting until he succeeded.

In contrast, Nate was confident but not arrogant. He engaged cooperatively with siblings, friends, and employees. He embraced his mission as oldest son, to develop competencies necessary to oversee the family's well-being, as adroitly as his father, and prepared himself to replace his father in the business one day. Nate matured into this role. As an adult, he took over the business. It prospered, and he ensured that his sister and brother received their fair share of the profits. He also employed his nieces and nephews who wanted summer jobs or more active roles in the business.

Why the differences? Why did one favorite son turn the blessings of being an entitled oldest son into a family debacle? Why did another favorite son use the skills he gleaned from his status to benefit his siblings as well as himself? We will explore, first, the family dynamics contributing to each outcome and, second, the advantages inherent in favoritism and the risks incurred.

REWARDS OF FAVORITISM

To be favored is to be preferred to *all* others. Favorite children mature knowing that the people most powerful in their lives, their mothers or fathers, have selected them for this coveted status. Having been chosen, these children quickly learn the requirements—the interactions with their parents that are required to retain their position. This special parent-child bond, often unconscious, affords children enhanced favors and treatment that is not available to other siblings. Favored children learn to get what they want, expecting no less.

Growing up as the favorite imbues children with emotional requisites for success—determination and confidence. They grow up with additional benefits:

(1) *Favorite children are likely to be socially astute.* Having learned to cultivate relationships with powerful parents, favorite children apply these skills to significant adults in their broader world. They ingratiate themselves with coaches, teachers, or advisors, adults in positions of authority who can promote them in their future.
(2) *Favorite children are likely to be resolute.* Having learned to get what they want from powerful parents, favorite children approach the world with doggedness, believing they are entitled to what they want. Not accepting "no," they are skilled in getting what they wish for.
(3) *Favorite children are likely to be effective.* Having learned that they are powerful in the lives of their parents, favorite children grow up feeling confident. This feeling cultivates a "can do" attitude and drives them to succeed.
(4) *Favorite children are likely to be optimistic.* Having learned that they are effective in getting what they want, favorite children are hopeful. This attitude enables them to tackle difficult challenges.

As children who have developed the life skills necessary to get what they want, favorite children mature into confident adults. They are not daunted by challenges and are driven to succeed by the exhilaration of achievement.

Traits characteristic of favorite children—social astuteness, determination, effectiveness, and optimism—drive their powerful personalities. These traits, giving rise to confidence, prepare favorite children to tackle challenges. My clinical practice is filled with men and women coming to Washington to do just that, to solve important social and political issues. They come as elected officials or high-level appointees, as journalists determined to reveal the next scandal, or as lobbyists pushing legislation for powerful special interest groups. Overwhelmingly, these people grew up as favorite sons and daughters.

RISKS OF FAVORITISM

Favoritism, rooted in the unconscious needs of parents, is fraught with complexities. The difficulties are magnified when one parent engages, essentially unchallenged by the other adult, with the favored child. The result is that growing up for the favorite child is fraught with risk.

(1) *Favorite children are likely to be manipulative.* Having learned behaviors necessary to get what they want from the powerful parent, favorite children often approach the world calculating how next to get what they want.
(2) *Favorite children are likely to feel entitled.* Having been indulged by powerful parents, favorite children often expect to be given what they want.
(3) *Favorite children are likely to grow up without feelings of accountability.* Having their behaviors overlooked by indulgent parents, favorite children often grow up believing they can do what they want with no consequences.
(4) *Favorite children are likely to be robbed of the freedom necessary to forge their own identities.* Having grown up enmeshed with powerful parents, favorite children can grow up not knowing where their boundaries start and their parents' boundaries end.
(5) *Favorite children are likely to be frightened of knowing themselves.* Having grown up protective of their status, favorite children often learn to conceal from themselves and others personality traits that are disliked by their powerful parents. If these traits become visible, the favored status is threatened.
(6) *Favorite children may resemble sociopaths.* Having grown

> up self-absorbed, favorite children, like sociopaths, may lack a conscience. They are usually slick, expert at both seducing and blaming people. (This is not to say that all or most favorite children are sociopaths.)

Favorite children may mature into adults with few scruples. This is a byproduct of having grown up believing they can have and do whatever they want without consequences. Favorite children often give little thought to the potential repercussions of their behavior and may be impervious to the potential implications for others.

The curses of favoritism—dishonesty, entitlement, inadequate conscience, lack of accountability, and identities fused with parents—undermine the favorites' ability to make decisions based on moral principles. Political scandals often derive from attitudes harbored by favored children: feeling entitled to getting what they want, believing they can get away with whatever they do, and having no sense of accountability. They approach life as if they can do anything without consequences. Elliot Spitzer and Bill Clinton are recent examples of politicians who, in their own way, betrayed public trust. They tried to talk their way out of the consequences of their objectionable behaviors, a skill they perfected while growing up as favorite children.

Elliot Spitzer, former governor of New York State, was an esteemed former prosecutor with a future some people speculated might lead to the White House. His reputation was that of a driven and ethical public servant who would not permit any misbehavior or corruption. Knowing the criminal system and the law as well as anyone, why would he jeopardize his future for a night, or a few nights, with a call girl? Simply because, as a favorite child, he thought he could get away with it. He did not believe there would be consequences for his actions.

As president, Bill Clinton permanently tarnished his reputation by his liaison with Monica Lewinsky, and, when confronted with his behavior, he spun the truth. Why? Because that is how favorite children behave: they believe they can have whatever they want with no consequences. If confronted, they believe they can convince others of their version of truth, talking their way out of any possible repercussions.

Scooter Libby, though not elected, as were Spitzer and Clinton, is another public servant whose reputation for hard work and brilliance was tarnished by the appearance of impropriety, because he lied to federal investigators and he lied during grand jury hearings. Libby, an esteemed litigator when working in the private sector, knew the possible pitfalls of perjury. To guide his appearance before the grand jury, Libby could have had access to legal counsel experienced in representing high-profile public officials in such matters. Why did he risk his career by not taking seriously the repercussions of lying and not being represented by such counsel? Libby, having grown up as the favorite son, imagined he would not be held accountable for his spinning of the truth. And so he jeopardized his future.

Not all favorite children behave in questionable fashion. Some, like Nate, mentioned above, do not. The differences between the upbringing of Nate and the upbringing of James illuminate the family dynamics that invite healthy moral development of favorite children, as well as those that do not. As a favorite son, Nate had his own identity. He was not fused with either parent, and both parents worked cooperatively, as checks and balances for each other, in raising him. He was brought up in a family that honored the firstborn son, and in return, expected him to honor the family.

In contrast, James's father was passive in the upbringing of his child. Family dynamics centered on the dyad of James and his mother. She believed his success to be a reflection on her. Others in the family were trivialized.

JAMES: THE FAVORITE CHILD WHO PUTS HIMSELF FIRST

Annemarie, James's only sister, grew up feeling overlooked by both her parents. As an adult seeking solace, Annemarie investigated the family history with a passion. She spoke at length with her parents, siblings, aunts, uncles, cousins, and friends of the family. She pieced together the following story.

Before James was born, their father, Paul, had just taken over a business started by his father-in-law, Jim. None of Jim's sons, Paul's wife's brothers, were interested in owning this small company, which demanded long working hours. Though the business was lucrative, no financial rewards were sufficient to compensate for working with their critical father.

James's mother and father, Mary and Paul, had moved far away from their families, trying to make their own way in the world. They found themselves unhappy, living 862 miles from their families, and still struggling financially. Mary and Paul grabbed the opportunity to take over the family business. They were confident that Jim's difficult personality would not impede their ability to run the business

Families Reenact Their Histories

Carl A. Whitaker, a pioneer of family therapy, believed the ghosts of past generations impacted the here and now, and that what transpires in the present impacts the family legacy into the infinite future. Current research in neuroscience and sociobiology validates the experiential wisdom of this sage.

Whitaker, beginning his medical career as a psychiatrist doing individual therapy at Emory University, ended his career working with families at the University of Wisconsin Medical School. This progression reflected his professional development as he realized that the individual is but an isolated piece of a complex puzzle. He believed it is absurd to attempt to envision a completed jigsaw puzzle by studying just one piece and equally absurd to attempt to improve the quality of life of an individual without seeing the family in context.

When working with families, Whitaker required the participation of as many members as feasible, including infants and great-aunts, dogs and parakeets. He respected the fact that each family member filled designated roles, that modifying the function of one—even slightly—impacted everyone else. "A family is like a well-oiled tractor," he said. "You tinker here, and the whole system is affected."[1]

"History repeats itself" was a Whitaker mantra. He understood the profound way in which family behavior repeats itself from one generation to the next. He found intriguing the influence of new variables, such as a spouse with her own family history, on the family of focus. He appreciated the family symphony: each person's unique sound, he contended, integrates into the overall melody. The score is replayed in each generation, and the sound of the orchestra modifies itself to integrate the unique style of all the musicians present.[2]

because Mary, an only daughter, was the apple of her father's eye. She could do no wrong. According to Annemarie, Paul was teased relentlessly by her mother's brothers. They chided him, saying that their father paid Paul well to take care of his beloved daughter and to bring her back to the area.

The teasing of Mary's brothers, a reflection of their instincts, was riddled with truth. Mary was her father's favorite daughter. What they did not know was that Jim, Mary's father, in his relationship with Mary, was reenacting his relationship with his mother.

Family History: James's Grandparents

Mary was named after her father's mother, a woman whom Jim adored. According to family stories, Jim's father, though successful professionally, was an alcoholic who gambled when drunk. As the oldest son, Jim looked after his mother, at times shielding her from the abuse generated by his father's drinking. When Jim was a young adult, he worked in the family business, driven less by professional interest and more by concern for his mother. Not trusting his father, and concerned that his father might have siphoned off money from the company, Jim believed that working in the company helped protect his mother's financial well-being.

When Jim's father died, his mother was a woman of financial means, maybe because of Jim's oversight of the company. Or maybe Jim's father was not as bad a man as portrayed by family legend and would have secured Mary's future without Jim's oversight. Regardless, upon her husband's death, Mary was wealthy and the sole owner of the business, which Jim predictably took over, ran, and eventually inherited. One of Jim's siblings worked briefly for the business. Apparently, that ended disastrously with the brothers not speaking to each other for years.

Family stories are rich with anecdotes about Jim's father's behaviors when he "had one too many." What is unclear, however, is whether his heavy drinking was independent of Jim's birth or in response to the loneliness he may have felt as Mary emotionally turned away from him and to her son. Alternatively, Mary may have turned to Jim to fill the void created by her husband's affair with liquor.

Whatever the psychological details, Jim was his mother's favorite son. He was the focus of her attention and her hero, saving her from the antics, alleged or real, of her alcoholic husband. And she generated for Jim powerful feelings about himself: he replaced his father as the fulcrum of his mother's life. Throughout his life, Jim felt protective of his mother. His reactions to her were spontaneous: sensing his mother's discomfort from the subtlety of her hand movement or a change in her breathing pattern, he rushed to comfort her. Instinctively, he knew what to do. The protectiveness Jim felt for his mother was replicated in his protectiveness toward his daughter, his mother's namesake.

James, His Mother, and His Father: An Unhealthy Triangle

Paul's wife, Mary, revered her father, Jim, and trusted him to make life easier for her. Her first child, a son, was born a year after she and Paul became involved in her father's business. Just as Jim named his daughter after his beloved mother, Mary named her son James in honor of her beloved father, Jim. Mary gave birth to five more sons and a daughter but held none as precious as she did James.

Paul grew increasingly invisible to his wife. He lived in his father-in-law's shadow, never as important to his wife as he wished. After he took over his father-in-law's business, the business flourished, becoming prominent in the community. He received little recognition of his accomplishments from Mary. She dutifully attended ceremonies acknowledging his achievements but seldom displayed exuberance. There were photographs of her alongside him at these events with her hands folded, never smiling or looking happy.

According to Annemarie, her father was unable to secure her mother's affections. Paul never effectively challenged Mary's unyielding attachments, first to her father and later to her son. The family dynamics involving young James, his mother Mary, and his father Paul replicated the dynamics of the previous generation, involving Mary, her father, Jim, and her mother.

James lived his life according to his mother's expectations. He did not question her preferences. She strongly influenced his choice of friends, the sports he played, whether he wore blue shirts or yellow.

He wanted to go to Michigan State but she preferred the University of Michigan, so he went to the University of Michigan. He fell in love with one woman but married another, the woman whom Mary believed was better suited for him. As recounted by Annemarie at the beginning of this chapter, James was expected to be a star, to bring pride to his grandfather's name, and he did. He was expected to take over the family business, and he did. James expanded the business from a local venture to a business of national prominence.

The identities of James and his mother Mary became fused, often preventing James from knowing if his decisions reflected his preferences or hers. He worked at developing those personality traits that his mother endorsed, such as socializing with "the right people," and suppressing those traits she did not like, such as expressing a political viewpoint that was different from hers. The relationship between Mary and James, who were so focused on each other, prevented either from building meaningful relationships with the others in the family. Though the outward appearance of the family was that of a model family, going to church together and enjoying family meals, the internal workings were far from ideal. The children appeared exemplary, good students and athletes who participated in church activities. As James followed in his mother's footsteps, feeling entitled and special, his siblings followed in their father's footsteps, hard working but feeling minimized and lonely.

James and His Siblings: Contentious Relationships

Mary fulfilled her responsibilities to the other children, doing for them what mothers did, volunteering at school, supervising homework, and arranging for doctors' appointments and tutoring. The children experienced her as impatient to fulfill her obligation so she could move on, having little interest in them. None of the children felt her warmth or caring.

James's attitude toward his siblings replicated his mother's indifference. Self-absorbed, James showed little interest in their lives. While they were expected to attend his sports events, he never attended theirs. The alienation between James and his siblings deepened as they grew older. The disparity between them grew larger.

James felt more privileged and they felt more marginalized. He and his mother were a closed unit. The other children in the family craved entry.

James constructed for himself a life replicating his childhood experiences, which looked good from the outside. He married a beautiful woman with good pedigree. They had poster-like children who attended desirable schools and played the right sports. James expanded the business and it attained national stature.

James also carried into his adult life self-absorption and arrogance, attitudes he had learned as his mother's favorite son. These traits created tension in his marriage. According to Annemarie, when her sister-in-law challenged James, vicious, unproductive fights ensued. Over the years, her sister-in-law learned to go along with her husband. In observing her brother's family, Annemarie noted the reenactment of her and her siblings' childhood: in his special bond with one child, James overlooked the others.

The events surrounding Mary's death highlighted the depth of James's selfishness, and maybe his unscrupulousness. Annemarie and her other siblings assumed they would inherit an equitable portion of their mother's stock in the company. Instead, all the stock had been signed over to James, the transfer occurring when Mary's lucidity was questionable. The stock transfer was staged with such finesse that the evidence was insufficient to allow a legal challenge to the action. The siblings, exclusive of James, inherited the family home, which had to be sold to pay taxes.

The lives of James's six siblings were plagued with suffering. As children wanting attention, they grew up depressed, acting out their unhappiness. As teenagers who smoked and drank excessively and pushed the envelope of teenage pranks, they got parental attention, but it was attention that pushed them further away from their idealized brother. They carried into their adult lives addictive behaviors used to mask their depression. Two of Annemarie's brothers drank excessively and never had permanent, intimate relationships. Another brother allegedly had affairs, ruining his marriage and alienating him from his children. Annemarie, aware of difficulties in sustaining meaningful relationships, became committed to a long path of healing.

With Mary's death, the family connections disintegrated. James believed he had sacrificed his life to be the obedient son. He honored the family by expanding the business, bringing pride to his mother, and overseeing her welfare. Inheriting the family business was his reward for having lived a predetermined life. He believed that he had no responsibility for his siblings' anguish.

The reactions of Annemarie and her five siblings differed dramatically. Four of her brothers wanted to challenge the inheritance and were angry that Annemarie and their youngest brother were unwilling to participate. Her youngest brother was enraged with Annemarie. He believed that, since Annemarie had spent more time with their mother, Annemarie should have known the legal maneuverings that transpired and intervened. In directing his anger toward Annemarie and not James, this brother demonstrated that, even in her death, their mother protected her favorite son. Annemarie dealt directly with James, confronting him with her pain at his betrayal. In the months prior to Mary's death, Annemarie spent considerable time with her mother, struggling with painful feelings derived from having grown up as an overlooked child. After her mother's death and her fight with James, Annemarie moved on, away from this dysfunctional family.

Benefits and Costs of Favoritism for James

As the favored child, James was taught throughout his life to learn the skills required to be successful in his mother's eyes. First, from birth, Mary conveyed his special role in her life. As we have seen, infants absorb nonverbal communication. The impact of this experience is profound, influencing the development of the child's personality. Second, as his mother's favorite child, James believed he was special and entitled to what he wanted. The words "can't have" were unknown to him. Third, James believed he could reach any goal he aspired to. The words "can't do" were not in his vocabulary. Having learned about competition as a football player and in classrooms, he never accepted coming in second. He was super-confident in his abilities. Fourth, he knew how to please people and gain their trust. He mastered this art in his relationship with his mother and employed these skills in relationships with others.

James's need for his mother's approval interfered with his learning to make independent judgments and decisions. His psychological closeness to her interfered with his developing an identity separate from hers. As outlined in chapter 5, developmental stages provide the framework within which children accomplish given developmental tasks. Successful completion of these tasks at each stage is required for progression to the next. Not having mastered the developmental work of a toddler—beginning to define himself as separate from his mother—James grew up hampered, lacking emotional and interpersonal skills. When he was an adult, his insular emotional world reflected his developmental immaturity. Those close to him, such as his wife and children, lived with verbal abuse and tantrums when he did not get his own way. The smoothness with which he financially exploited his six siblings—his blatant immorality—was an outgrowth of his favored child status as well.

NATE: A FAVORITE CHILD IN BALANCE

Nate's upbringing, like James's, reflected his family history. Nate's family honored the position of the oldest son and prepared him for the role of family caretaker. According to my colleague, Ruth, this tradition was handed down from her grandparents, Zaide and Bubbie, to her parents, Abe and Ethel. Ruth believed her brother was raised to emulate the biblical statement, "To whom much is given, much is expected."

Ruth acknowledged that Nate's activities and achievements were the focus of more family attention than her own or those of her brother, Noah, and she sensed that Nate felt more pressure to excel than they did: "Nate was so focused on what he needed to do, whether it was writing a paper, interviewing for a summer job, or modifying his tennis serve, it made the rest of us tense."

As he grew up, Nate's path was clear: do well in high school to get into a good college, so as to get an MBA or go to law school. Then he would work in the family business, gradually taking over from his father. Ultimately, the business would be his, along with the responsibility of overseeing his siblings' inheritance. While her brother said this was the path he wanted for himself, Ruth observed he had little choice. Unlike Noah and Ruth, who grew up with the freedom to forge their own lives, Nate found his life was largely predetermined.

Family History: Nate's Grandparents

Nate's grandparents, as single people, emigrated from central Europe in the late nineteenth century. According to family stories, Nate's grandfather, Zaide, was among the first in his family to come to the United States and was expected to help the sisters, brothers, and cousins who followed. He quickly learned English, saved money, and started his own business, wholesaling machine parts. The business provided jobs for family members needing employment.

Nate's grandmother, Bubbie, who was about eighteen years old when she arrived in the United States, followed her older brother to this country, and she lived with him and his family. Within months, Zaide and Bubbie met, fell in love, and married. Abe, their first child, was born nine months later. Three more children were born in

First-Born Sons

Across cultures, oldest sons have had favored status, governed by the laws of primogeniture. These laws were created to protect the father's legacy and to provide economic and military security for his family.

The laws of primogeniture, brought to England in 1066 by the Normans, influenced European-based cultures. Designating the oldest son as family leader provided safety. Military strength was the prerequisite for survival, and sons, not daughters, were warriors. The oldest son was designated as leader because fathers did not know how long they would live and the life expectancies of children were uncertain. Therefore, as soon as sons were old enough, fathers began their training. By virtue of their age, oldest sons were the first to share meaningful experiences with their fathers, providing opportunities for bonding before younger siblings joined in the training. As the oldest, these sons received the most training and were best prepared to lead the family in fighting off attackers.

Preventing family lands from being subdivided into small parcels afforded both strategic safety and economic security. Bigger buffer zones between the borders of property provided people with greater safety from their enemies.

Economically, working larger parcels of land was more efficient, and this was especially important in areas where the amount of rich, tillable soil was limited. Primogeniture, by ensuring that an estate would remain intact, was intended to protect a father's legacy, in terms of both people and property.

Primogeniture is not limited to cultures with European roots. Similar laws influence African and Asian cultures as well. In Southern Africa, the culture of Tswana tribes influenced family culture.[3] Men were honored, and women were treated like children. The oldest son inherited privileges, such as the religious and political leadership of the tribe. He inherited the family wealth, traditionally measured by the number of cows. Since the oldest son had no responsibility to look after his widowed mother, the youngest son inherited the family house with strings attached—that he provide his mother with shelter. This ensured the widow a home if the oldest son took his inheritance and left. In some Tswana tribes, women defined the lines of inheritance, though men still inherited the wealth: the oldest sons of the oldest sisters inherited the cows.

In many Eastern cultures, influenced by the precepts of Confucius, sons were more highly valued than daughters. The family name and lineage were passed through men. The oldest son, in particular, received preferential treatment as well as more responsibilities in the family.[4] Some Southeast Asian cultures even dictate that if the father dies, everyone in the family, *including the mother*, obey the oldest son.[5]

In writing about modern Japanese families, Theodore Bestor and Helen Hardacre highlighted the vast influence of primogeniture across cultures. They wrote that "the multigenerational family organized around primogeniture, that is to say, passing the entire estate of the family, the social role, the financial assets, the occupation, the profession, from father to the eldest, usually the eldest son—is a distinct characteristic of [the] Japanese kinship system. But, it's not unique to Japan by any means. Many... societies in Western Europe have similar kinship systems. And, indeed, one explanation for the colonization of the United States is that eldest sons were inheriting family farms in Europe and younger sons were being sent off to settle the 'New World.'"[6]

Throughout the world, the laws of primogeniture have an impact on the dynamics of individual families. Oldest sons—by virtue of their gender and birth order—receive preferential treatment. However, their treatment, in individual families, affects the functioning of families differently.

rapid succession. Abe remembered his home as a place with an open door, where his parents invited in extended family members or friends who needed food or shelter. Abe reported to Ruth that when he came home from school, he never knew who, or how many people, would be sitting around the big kitchen table, sharing in meals his mother prepared. On cold days, the mailman would be there, sipping hot chocolate.

Nate, His Mother, and His Father: A Healthy Team

When he was born, Nate was the first child and a son. His role as the child to whom much was given and much was expected was predetermined by the family's cultural expectation that he would follow in the footsteps of his grandfather and father.

Nate's father, Abe, ran the wholesale company started by his father, Zaide. None of Abe's siblings chose to work in the company: one brother became a doctor, the other a lawyer, and his sister became a university professor who married a doctor. According to Abe, when his brother completed law school, he pressured Zaide to incorporate the business, issuing shares of stock, and talking openly with the family about his plans for the business. At that time, Abe worked alongside Zaide, and Zaide wanted Abe to have the authority required for running the company, earning the financial rewards he deserved. Also, Zaide wanted his other children to enjoy financial benefits from his life's work. When he talked with Bubbie and his children about his objectives, a plan was derived that the family accepted as being fair: Abe would inherit 51 percent of the company and the remaining 49 percent would be divided among his three siblings. Abe was entitled to 80 percent of the earnings from future spin-offs from the company. His siblings would be entitled to invest in the ancillary businesses.

Abe ran the business successfully and it prospered. He provided well for his wife and children, and his siblings also enjoyed financial benefits from the business. Following the patterns in traditional families, while Abe worked, his wife Ethel tended to the children and the house. According to Ruth, Ethel made minute-to-minute decisions governing the lives of the three children, but significant decisions were made in collaboration with Abe. When Ethel and Abe disagreed, the children could not predict which parent's position would prevail. Ruth believed this reflected the earnestness with which her parents struggled to arrive at decisions both could embrace.

Ruth remembers her parents' love for one another. She describes her father coming home from work and kissing her mother immediately, even before taking off his hat and coat. "It was as if they had to connect with each other after having been apart all day," Ruth commented. Ethel and Abe looked to one another for intimacy and fulfillment. They depended on each other for constructive criticism regarding the treatment of the children. As a loving couple, they trusted each other for advice, ensuring that their children were not forced into the unhealthy role of meeting mom's or dad's needs.

While Ethel and Abe worked to be evenhanded in raising their three children, the expectations for Nate were greater than for the other two, and he was offered more resources to live up to those expectations. While all the children were expected to do well in school, Nate was subtly pressured as the others were not. If Nate did not do well on a single test, his parents immediately directed him to review the test with the teacher. Because his parents were actively involved in the details of his life, they quickly intervened to assist him, increasing the likelihood of his achieving an A. As Nate got older, he learned to expect an A and, if he struggled with a course, he advocated for himself. He initiated the request for extra help, expected it, and received it.

Ethel and Abe were attentive to the schoolwork of Ruth and her brother, Noah, but they did not attend to the details of their lives with the same scrutiny that they gave to Nate. Questions regarding consulting with teachers were not asked until midterm grades were posted. At that time, if Ruth or Noah required tutoring, they received it, which helped them to obtain a B rather than a C, not the A that Nate received through earlier intervention. Ruth and Noah seldom thought about asking for extra help unless they felt desperate and worried they might flunk a course. The two younger siblings did not expect to achieve as much as Nate; nor did they expect others to be as responsive to them. Ruth and Noah grew up not knowing how to advocate for themselves as well as their brother did.

His parents' expectations ensured that Nate would receive extra privileges. For example, all the children were rewarded, usually monetarily, for making the high honor roll. Nate, of course, often made the high honor roll while his siblings seldom did. In some courses, if students had an A at the time of the final, they did not have to take the final. Nate was often in that position, allowing him to go to a movie or watch television as his brother and sister studied in their rooms. Technically, Nate did not receive these extra privileges, consisting of money and freedom, because he was the favored son, but, as the oldest son from whom the most was expected, he was directed down the path that offered him these benefits.

Ruth recalls that as a child she and her younger brother would occasionally be jealous of Nate's success. The younger siblings would tease Nate relentlessly for studying so hard and achieving so much. In protest of his excellence they would call him "Mr. Parent Pleaser" or hide his favorite tennis racket. When fighting among the children erupted, family discussions predictably ensued. The parents understood that the younger children were expressing jealousy and that their older son, in his seriousness and eagerness to please adults, elicited more intense teasing. The discussions routinely ended with a lecture about treating each other respectfully.

Nate and His Siblings: Working It Out

When he was an adult, Nate's assumption of the presidency of the family business was thoughtfully orchestrated. Initially, Nate worked alongside his father. Gradually, Abe gave more responsibility to Nate. Eventually, Nate took over the running of the business, though his father and mother remained the major shareholders.

Wanting to secure the future of the business while being fair to all his children, Abe embarked on the same course as his father—speaking openly with everyone in the immediate family. Abe wanted Nate to have the authority required to successfully run the company, as Abe had had, yet he wanted all his children to enjoy the fruits of his financial success, as his siblings had done.

Ruth reported that the family engaged in lengthy conversations, everyone speaking with everyone else. No discomfort was overlooked or trivialized. Disputes were talked about until amicable resolutions were reached. Eventually, the strategy derived by Abe and his children replicated the formula worked out between Zaide and his children: Nate received controlling stock in the business and a guarantee that he would own all future business ventures evolving from the company. Ruth and Noah received equitable portions of the existing business and opportunities to invest financially in their brother's future business ventures. Nate, Ruth, and Noah each felt respected in this process and embraced the plan. Over the years, closeness among the three siblings grew, and so did their respect for one another. Many nieces and nephews had summer jobs in the company, and, after graduating from college, one of Noah's children chose to work for Nate, aspiring to run a subsidiary of the company.

As adults, Ruth reported, she and Noah trusted Nate. They were not jealous of his prominent role in the family. Ruth said, "I grew up with the best of both worlds. I had the freedom to live my life as I wanted and the security of knowing that my big brother would always look out for me. My life is a lot easier because of his success. I don't envy the pressure to excel that drives Nate's life. Noah and I talk about this. I know he agrees with me."

Benefits and Costs of Favoritism for Nate

Under Nate's leadership, the business flourished. Nate had objectives and was certain he would accomplish them. Nate recruited respected people to work with him, men whom colleagues had cautioned were too important to meet him. Nate arranged meetings and won them over with his optimism, focus, and charm.

Nate felt enormous pride in his achievements in developing the business. Ruth recounted his delight when he distributed profit checks to her. The day after she received her check, predictably he would call to verify its arrival. "His voice always sounded like it did when he was a kid, delighted that something wonderful happened." When she commented to him about the thrill in his voice, he talked about his joy in fulfilling his responsibilities to the family. He knew his parents would be proud.

As reflected in Ruth's comments, Nate grew up with more pressure to excel than his siblings and with no alternatives with regard to his life's path. Yet he seemed comfortable with his life, gratified that his family and siblings shared the benefits of his success.

Abe and Ethel worked cooperatively in bringing up Nate; both were actively involved in his life. It appears that they talked through disagreements, reaching decisions that both could support. Though Nate was unquestionably the favorite child, Ruth and Noah felt loved and valued by their parents, not overlooked by them. The openness of discussions contributed to their feeling of safety and their trust in the family.

Abe and Ethel believed the oldest child to be special, which also meant added responsibility, and they saw their role as parents as that of giving him the tools he needed to successfully perform his duties. Their perception of Nate did not preclude conveying their love to Ruth and Noah. The dynamics of this family provided an environment in which Nate developed with the advantages of favoritism and did not fall prey to its corruption.

FAVORITISM INFLUENCING MENTAL HEALTH

The stories of James and Nate begin with similar themes but end with dramatically divergent outcomes. Recalling chapters 4 and 5 helps to explain this disparity.

Chapter 4 detailed the selection of favorites based on neurotic parental needs. In that chapter, we saw that being the favorite was based on a relationship exclusive to one parent and one child. This was the relationship that James had with his mother, and it was not challenged effectively by his father. Chapter 5, "They're All My Favorites," explored the selection of favorite child status when parents more competently meet their own needs and help moderate each other's needs. Nate grew up in such a family.

Children growing up in both types of family environment are likely to enjoy the benefits of being the favorite, but children growing up in families where favoritism is limited to one parent and one child are more likely to be plagued with negative repercussions as well.

Victims of Favoritism

Children selected as the favorite to fill the void in the life or psyche of a parent grow up with their identities fused with those of their parents. These children lack the experiences required to establish their own identities. Their lives are driven by behaviors necessary to court their powerful parent and to ensure the preservation of their favored status. Without this status, many favorite children lack confidence in their abilities to function successfully in the world. While reaping the benefits of favoritism, these chosen children are also victims of their elevated status.

To summarize material that has already been covered in chapters 2, 3, and 4, the selection of favorite children can begin as early as in utero or at birth. Mothers' verbal and nonverbal communications, their gestures and demeanor, profoundly affect the personalities of their children before the development of the children's language skills. After a parent has designated a child as his or her favorite, the interplay between the two reinforces their importance to each other. This entire process reflects the unconscious activities—the satisfaction of parents' needs, the selection of children, the communication between parents and children—that reinforce the relationship.

The relationship between favorite children and their parents, in an unhealthy family dynamic, is noteworthy for its exclusiveness: in the mother-father-child triangle, the role of the "other" parent is usually that of being invisible. The connection between the powerful parent and the child drives the child's development and dominates the family dynamics. These favorite children grow up like the children referred to by Freud, cited earlier in this book: the children, who, as unquestioned favorites, grow up with confidence emanating from their perception that they have succeeded in pushing aside one parent to win the heart of the other. This belief, generating feelings of raw power and complicated tension, profoundly influences their personalities.

Tension is created by the grandiosity of favorite children. These children are likely to confuse being "the indisputable favorite" with believing they have *replaced* the absent parent. This belief, unconscious and therefore usually unchallenged, permits children to grow up with a false sense of self. In reality, children do not usually replace parents as sexual, social, intellectual, or financial partners, and if they do, other complicated psychological problems emerge.

No one is perfect. Healthy psychological development requires children to learn this lesson: to accept the "good" and "bad" parts of themselves. Favorite children believe they are perfect because that is what adoring parents have taught them, and wanting to ensure their status, favorite children feel pressured to maintain views of themselves as beyond reproach. The need for perfection, to be "good" at all times, breeds tension that is eventually expressed as self-defeating behaviors—depression, deception, loneliness, and addiction.

Some favorite children grow up not knowing about being whole, which is an important lesson that should be learned from family relationships. To be whole is to accept the good and bad parts of yourself; this is a lesson learned by accepting that each parent is both good and bad, loving and hateful. Favorite children are deprived of this critical lesson. They grow up believing the distortion that the favoring parent is all "good" and the invisible parent is all "bad." Identifying with favoring parents and distancing themselves from invisible parents, favorite children grow up with the distorted belief that they themselves are only "good."

Favorite children, needing to court "good" parents, work at being "good" in the eyes of these parents. In rejecting the parts of their characters that are unattractive to favoring parents, these children grow up estranged from parts of their own selves. Consequently, favorite children live with the tension of never fully knowing, loving, or accepting themselves. The experience of being unconditionally loved eludes them.

Growing up, children naturally experience tension in developing their gender-based identities. To help resolve this developmental tension, healthy relationships with parents of both sexes are required. An exclusive relationship with the parent of one sex deprives children of learning about themselves in relation to the other sex. This is true for a daughter, regardless of whether she is favored by a mother or father, or for a son, regardless of whether a father or mother favors him. In either case, children are robbed of the experience of experimenting with gender-appropriate behaviors in the safety of a relationship with both parents. As young adults, many favorite children search for elders, of the sex of the absent parent, to teach them lessons not learned from the man or woman who has been missing from their psychological lives.

Loneliness also fosters tension for favorite children. When they are growing up, their attachments to their parent can interfere with the development of close relationships with others, both inside and outside the family. Close relationships are further impeded by their belief that they are entitled to what they want and their insensitivity to the impact of that on others.

Containing anger creates tension for favorite children. These children may harbor anger at the adoring parent, feeling resentment at the obligation of filling their void or frustration at the impossibility of the task. Favorite children are often unhappy with the invisible parent, resenting his or her absence or inability to rescue them from the requirements imposed by the powerful parent. Favorite children often dislike the fact that so much about their lives has been predetermined, that they have been robbed of finding their own way in the world.

Seldom is this anger expressed directly. How could favorite children be angry with parents who adore them and have indulged them? Instead, favorite children may displace their anger on siblings, treating them cruelly. Eating disorders, drinking, or chronic physical illnesses may also be expressions of the masked rage of favorite children.

Others in families are victims of the dynamics surrounding favoritism between one parent and one child. While the first victim is the favorite child, another victim can be the "other" parent, whose relationships with the spouse and the child are challenged. Even if adults have unsatisfactory marriages, when one adult uses a child to cover over the unhappiness, both parents are deprived of opportunities to struggle with each other and grow. Additionally, the "other" parent is not only excluded from loving involvement with his or her spouse's favored child but may also be the recipient of that child's hostility. The hostility may reflect the powerful parent's attitude, which has been absorbed by the child, or the child's anger at having been abandoned by the absent parent.

Other children in the family are additional victims. Not having had the advantages of favoritism, these children grow up lacking confidence and resolve, often feeling they are second-class citizens. Even as adults with meaningful lives, these siblings struggle with the scars of not having been chosen, desperately longing for affirmation from the powerful parent. The scars may become exposed around holidays, when painful memories of being overlooked emerge, or around family visits. The pain can be expressed by irrational fighting with spouses or children, sleep issues, or other unpleasant changes in behavior.

The relationship among the nonfavored children varies. When one child receives disproportionate attention, other children may compete fiercely for the crumbs, feeling hostility toward each other. Witnessing the pain suffered by a sibling who is also unfavored may ameliorate the pain of being rejected by one parent. In other families, children feeling rejected or overlooked comfort one another, banding together and creating their own family unit.

The story of James dramatically illustrates the tragic situation generated by the exclusive relationship of favoritism between one parent and one child. Mary, his mother, grew up as her father's favorite daughter. The father protected her, overseeing her life. Involved with him, she did not mature into adulthood with the skills required to establish adult intimacy, boundaries, or self-awareness. She looked to her son James to care for her as her father did. In doing this, James was rewarded with the confidence of a young man who believes he has replaced his father. With that confidence, he grew into a focused, determined man who excelled professionally in the world.

The cost of his success was enormous. He lived a life pressured to be "perfect," denying those parts of the person he was that were unattractive to his mother. He devoted his life to impossible tasks, trying to fill his grandfather's shoes and his mother's void. No one can fill anyone else's shoes or fill anyone else's void. James lived his life robbed of opportunities to choose his own path: where he went to college or whom he married. His tension, amassing over the years, was probably unconscious. Ultimately, his tension imploded in the dynamics surrounding his mother's death, blowing the family apart. James could not understand the family's reaction, believing it to be everyone else's fault. He grew up as the favorite child, feeling entitled to what he wanted with no concern for its effects on others.

BENEFICIARIES OF FAVORITISM

Infants are receptacles of their parents' hopes and dreams. Recently, an e-mail arrived in my inbox entitled, "The Most Important Baby of All Time (to Me)," announcing the birth of a relative's baby. The baby is proudly described as reflecting both him and his wife, "having [his] blue eyes and [his] wife's delicately arched nostrils." The challenge ahead for my nephew and his wife is reflected in chapter 5, "They're All My Favorites": bringing up children with the gifts of favoritism while minimizing the risks. Parents want children to mature with focus and determination, confidence and power. Parents do not want children to become adults who behave with entitlement or self-centeredness, deceptiveness or indifference to consequences.

As was said earlier, all children can enjoy favorite child status, reaping its benefits and developing strong moral fiber, if they grow up in families where favoritism is fluid. In these families, favorite child designation flows from child to child, from parent to parent. Both parents have a strong, positive presence in the family and respect each other. These parents work cooperatively, supporting the healthy growth of their children.

Chapter 5 also challenges the belief that there are no favorite children, that parents treat all children the same. Many parents hold that position, though their children contest it, easily identifying the favorites. What is significant is that favored children exist in all families and that, in families aspiring to treat children similarly, favorite child status can rotate from child to child. This fluidness reflects the changing needs and preferences of both parent and child. The ability of families to talk through the difficult issues posed by favoritism are crucial for the well-being of the entire family unit.

Nate's story, recounted earlier, exemplifies that of a favorite child growing up in a family where the parents met their own needs, and, as appropriate, each other's needs. They collaborated in raising children, openly discussing issues. In this fluid family, the status of favorite child was not fluid; Nate's status was that of the favorite, but the other children did not feel overlooked or minimized. Mirroring their parents' open communication, these siblings felt safe enough to tease their favored brother about his status. They matured into competent, effective adults, even if they were not as driven as their oldest sibling or as determined to succeed at his level.

Nate's brother and sister, Noah and Ruth, had their own memories of feeling special to each parent. Ruth smiled from ear to ear as she talked about being "a daddy's girl," remembering her father's eagerness to take pictures of her when she dressed up for a dance. The family joked that often he cut her date out of the picture! Ruth recalled the cold, blistery evenings when her dad would take her for an ice cream cone to satisfy her craving: "He would smile and say to me, 'Ruth, I wouldn't do this for anyone but you. Driving in this weather is sheer madness.'" Ruth had loving recollections of special times with her mother, days when her mother would let her stay home from school and the two of them would spend the day doing a jigsaw puzzle.

Noah had similar memories of his parents: "Mom had a sense of when I needed extra time with her, alone time. Some days she would surprise me, appearing at school to pick me up early. We'd just hang out. How special the time was." The only one in the family to like baseball, Nate remembers fondly how his father would reward him by taking him to a game: "When I'd ask, 'Why?' my dad would smile and say, 'Just because I love you.'"

Tracking this family, we can see that Nate's emergence as a favorite son with scruples is understandable. First, neither parent looked to him to fill their needs. This permitted him to grow up unencumbered and with the freedom to forge his own identity. Second, accompanying his role as favorite son was the expectation that people in addition to him, his sister and his brother, would benefit. Third, his parents jointly made decisions regarding his welfare. Fourth, there were no secrets about his role as favorite child. His siblings could complain or tease him. Fifth, there was open dialogue in the family. With no secrets, trust among family members emerged. Sixth, even though Nate's role as favorite was prominent, his sister and brother each benefited from the occasional experience of favorite child status.

To conclude, the rewards of growing up as the favorite child are enormous, while the potential risks are disturbing. Favorite children are less likely to be encumbered by the pitfalls of favoritism when growing up in families where favoritism is openly discussed or fluid among children and parents. Children are more likely to fall prey to the treacheries of favoritism when they are awarded the position in exchange for filling the needs of the powerful parent.

SECTION THREE
CHILDREN'S STORIES

CHAPTER SEVEN
FATHER'S FAVORITE SON

Every woman's dream guy, John resembled a model at 6'2" with toned muscles and red, wavy hair. His blue eyes sparkled. His body retained the fitness of the well-known college lacrosse player that he had been. At forty, his financial success reflected national recognition for his profound accomplishments. John envisioned an ideal Saturday as riding a bike with an infant secure in the baby seat, his adoring wife riding alongside, and concluding the afternoon with baby's napping while [John was] making passionate love to his partner. So why wasn't he married? Why did a committed relationship elude him?

—Dr. Libby's clinical reflection

Frustrated by his personal life, John began psychotherapy. After his third relationship with a married woman ended disastrously, he recognized that he, on his own, was unlikely to find the loving and satisfying relationship he desired. John acknowledged that his relationships began and ended similarly: each woman initially showered him with accolades, insisting she wanted to leave her husband for him. Each relationship ended with the woman enraged, feeling as if John had manipulated her into a relationship she did not want.

JOHN AND HIS FATHER: AN ENTWINED RELATIONSHIP

John explained he was the youngest of four children. Alex, his father, fought continuously with John's older brother, Tim. Their dad wanted Tim to play football but Tim's short, weak physical frame made the sport an unrealistic possibility. Alex had no respect for Tim's musical talents and ignored John's sisters, Betty and Carole. This reflected their father's lack of interest in women. John's docile mother, Joan, unobtrusively washed, ironed, shopped, cooked, dusted, and vacuumed.

The interactions between John and his father sharply contrasted with his father's interactions with all the others in the family. John escaped the humiliation that Alex inflicted on Tim, Betty, Carole, and Mom. In contrast, Dad's responses to John were affirming and validating, infusing John with feelings of competence and self-worth. Alex organized his life around John's to help ensure this son's success.

Genetically, John embodied the physical traits and intellectual acumen required for this idealized position. His muscular body and outstanding coordination offered a body type begging for training as an athlete. Intellectually facile, John absorbed all that his father taught—from strategies for scoring goals on the lacrosse field to those for achieving A's in calculus.

Alex based all major decisions affecting the family on John's needs and interests. Decisions about the neighborhood in which the family lived, as well as decisions about when they moved, depended upon which school Dad determined to have an academic program or athletic coach advantageous to John's development. Alex insisted that family mealtime be set according to John's schedule, with no regard for the scheduling demands of John's brother, sisters, or mother. In his concentration on John, Alex invested himself in cultivating a protégé who could create psychological distance between his impoverished immigrant background and his vision of an American success story.

Alex dismissed his wife Joan with a contemptuous tone and indifferent treatment. He viewed her as hired help, providing her with a weekly allowance. She had no voice in running the family.

Alex's attitude toward his wife reflected his anger at his own mother, who had abandoned him as a child. When his family emigrated from Hungary during the revolution, his mother chose her mother over him, staying to care for her mother rather than emigrating to raise her infant son. Alex never again saw his mother. Rarely did he speak of her; he behaved as if she had died when she remained in Hungary—and to him she had died. Alex's treatment of women reflected anger at his profound loss, though he never acknowledged his deprivation or anger.

John sensed his special position in his father's life and energetically fulfilled the requirements of his role. He delighted in the hours his dad spent throwing a football, instructing him on the art of running and kicking. He absorbed his father's advice on how to play sports and how to approach a teacher. Alex felt effective in this relationship: he had something to teach this son, who learned quickly and eagerly and would then implement what he was taught.

Craving his father's adoration, John worked actively to perpetuate it. When honored as an athlete or scholar, John religiously acknowledged his dad's contributions. Seldom did John's name appear in the press without his father's supportive role being acknowledged. John cemented his favorite child status in subtle behaviors as well. When looking at his father, John's eyes glowed like sparklers. When talking to his father, John's voice had the gentleness of a mother cooing over her baby. When smiling at his father, John conveyed the contentment of a satiated infant.

The relationship between John and his father was important to Alex as well. Alex trusted John's loyalty and devotion as he had trusted his own father's. Alex experienced intimacy with John that he could not permit himself with women. Alex lived a lonely life, and John filled the void.

Because of his relationship with his father, John distanced himself from four people he viewed as losers—his mother, sisters, and brother. John had the important parent, the powerful parent, all to himself. John absorbed his father's love and attention as a dry sponge soaks up water. He lived a life structured exclusively for his benefit. He was recognized for his achievements, and he enjoyed his fame and power.

The Oedipus Legacy

Oedipus's story is powerful, living on as an expression of a universal human experience. Over 2,500 years old, the story illustrates human discomfort with normal childhood fantasies—young boys envisioning themselves as strong enough to kill their fathers and victoriously claim their mothers. The illusion of winning this ultimate competitive struggle is the unconscious expression of the father/son/mother tension, the Oedipal triangle. Denying the attraction and competitiveness between parent and child, not putting language to it, can lead to tragedy.

As a six-year-old, Freud saw his mother nude. This experience stimulated an awareness of his fantasies that stayed with him over a lifetime. In elucidating his theories of human development, he termed the experience the "Oedipal Complex" and talked about the complex as gender specific, sons wanting to kill their fathers to win their mothers.

Many psychologists now believe the Oedipus legacy to be gender neutral. Oedipal issues can also emerge from relationships between fathers and daughters, and between parents and children of the same sex.

The themes of the story are as relevant to human experience now as when Sophocles was writing in 450 BCE. Oedipus did not intend to kill his father or to sleep with his mother. When an oracle first told Laius, Oedipus's father, that he would be killed by his son, who would then marry his mother, Laius, to protect himself, directed a servant to leave the newborn to die on a lonely mountain. Oedipus was found and rescued. Many years later, as an adult, an oracle related the prophecy to Oedipus; he structured his life to avoid the predicted events, keeping the oracle's prophecy a secret.

Feelings of desire and competition between parents and children are inevitable. When these fears are kept secret, tension generates behaviors that undermine the relationships among mothers, fathers, and children. While children fantasize about replacing one parent in the heart of the other, the fulfillment of their dream would be their worst nightmare, as it was for Oedipus.

According to the version of the story told by Sophocles,[1] a shepherd found Oedipus in the mountains and gave him to the king and queen of Corinth. They adopted the child, naming him Oedipus. They loved him with all their hearts and never told him he was adopted.

When Oedipus learned from the oracle that he would kill his father and marry his mother, he left Corinth to protect the parents he loved. On the road, he and a man fought; the man struck him and, in response, Oedipus killed him.

A year passed and Oedipus tried to enter the city of Thebes, but he was blocked by the Sphinx, a monster with the body of a lion and the head and torso of a woman. The Sphinx would not let anyone enter or leave the city who could not answer the riddle: what walks on four legs in the morning, two legs at noon, and three legs in the evening? Over the many months that the Sphinx guarded the city entry, no one successfully answered the riddle, so no one entered or left the city. Thebes was cut off from the outside world.

Oedipus correctly answered the riddle. "Man," responded Oedipus. "He crawls on all fours as a baby, walks upright as an adult, and uses a cane in old age." The monster, in a fit of fury, threw herself from the city wall and died.

Oedipus freed the city from the tyranny of the Sphinx. He entered Thebes as a hero. The queen of Thebes had been alone for a year. Her husband had never returned from a journey and was presumed dead. Oedipus married the queen as the reward for causing the death of the Sphinx and emancipating the city. The two were happy in their marriage and had children.

Then Thebes suffered a severe drought. Trying to determine what was to be done, Oedipus consulted the blind prophet Tiresias, who instructed Oedipus to find the king's murderer and punish him. Investigating the death, Oedipus deduced that he had been the murderer, and the details of his birth, abandonment, and adoption unfolded. Queen Jocasta quickly understood that Oedipus was not only her husband but her son. Immediately, she hanged herself. Oedipus gouged out his eyes with a brooch from her gown. He exiled himself as punishment for his action.

The tragedy of this play is the innocence of the characters. Fear of the oracle's prediction—normal, unconscious feelings pushing toward awareness—drove Laius and Oedipus to enact behaviors that proved the oracle correct. The silence of each man precluded the possibility of finding safety in the truth of words. The king and queen of Corinth did not tell Oedipus that he was adopted, since they loved him as a son; thus, when Oedipus heard the words of the oracle, he felt forced to leave Corinth to protect himself from harming those he loved. When Oedipus killed his birth father, Laius, he believed he was defending himself against a criminal. Jocasta married Oedipus, knowing him as the hero who had overcome the monstrous Sphinx. Oedipus suffered shame in living out the prophecy that he had tried so hard to avoid.

John believed that he had accomplished the impossible—replacing his mother as his father's intimate. Though some have derided Freud's description of the Oedipal Complex, it has revealed itself again and again. John's grandiosity obscured a fundamental truth—no child can replace one parent in the heart of the other parent. The loving feelings that adults feel for one another differ from those felt between adults and children. Yet, believing that he had achieved the impossible, John grew up believing he could do anything. His determination and self-confidence resulted in professional achievement but limited his ability to forge intimate relationships.

Rewards of Being Favored

John thrived in his entwined relationship with his father. This favorite son, schooled in the tools for success, developed confidence, screaming, "I can do anything." His attitude projected, "I am the best." His belief in himself conveyed "I can get away with anything." His confidence derived from believing himself to be his father's intimate morphed into his profound conviction that no test could be too daunting for him. Throughout his life he excelled in sports and academics, as well as in his professional life.

On the athletic field, no defender, playing any position, came between John and the lacrosse net. Sports announcers described John as "unstoppable." "Go John! Go John!" rang out from the stands as his play stirred the crowds. The adoration from the bleachers, as well as from his teammates, mirrored his dad's. John responded to this praise by playing harder and striving for even greater success.

John's success in the classroom duplicated his success on the lacrosse field. His achievements, fueled by his resolve to be further admired, reflected his dogged determination to be "the best." Plaques citing his academic excellence rivaled the number of those he earned in sports. When he was in high school, colleges pursued John with both academic and sports scholarships. Ultimately he selected Dartmouth over Stanford. John's high school record replicated itself in college; for graduate school he selected the University of Pennsylvania over Yale and Stanford.

Since John had mastered the art of being mentored by his father,

John's talents translated effortlessly into professional settings. Senior attorneys believed John to be *the* exemplary protégé: brilliant, hard working, tenacious, appreciative of supervision. In these relationships, John felt the security of familiarity, nurturing harder work and greater achievement. His career was quickly catapulted to extraordinary heights, his achievement respected throughout the legal community.

By the time he was forty, John's reputation as a highly esteemed public servant was secured by his critical role in three cases, which set important precedents. He parlayed this success into a lucrative private practice. The qualities required to ensure favorite child status—an iron will to succeed and the art of expressing appreciation for his enabler, Dad—secured success after success in his professional life.

Costs of Being Favored

Despite his many successes, intimate relationships with people other than his father continued to elude John. He had no internal compass to direct honest self-appraisal. His self-aggrandizement, fused with his father's unabashed praise for him, left him no room for self-reflection. No one's praise equaled what John believed he deserved. His development, motivated by his eagerness to be admired, left John blind to the needs of others. John's overinflated views of himself made it impossible for him to accept his wrongdoing when he was confronted with uncomfortable issues in relationships.

Unresolved feelings emanating from the Oedipal triangle influenced John's psychological growth. His mother, remaining invisible, did not challenge the intense relationship between Alex and John. John grew up psychologically scarred, a victim of her neglect. His shame at not being loved by his mother cloaked his profound pain caused by her abandonment. He deluded himself by believing his father had replaced his mother as the significant nurturer in his life As discussed in chapter 4, while fathers can mitigate the pain of maternal neglect, the injury caused by a mother's neglect is indelible, not to be eradicated by anyone. John's difficulty in establishing intimate relationships with women evidenced the breadth and depth of his wounds.

John and Mom

The character of John's mother remains obscure and is detailed more by her behavior than her words. She conveyed her anger at John indirectly, seldom arriving on time for important athletic events or academic gatherings honoring him. She offered little enthusiasm for his accomplishments. John had no memory of her hugging or kissing anyone in the family; nor does he recall her praising anyone, especially him.

We know nothing of her response to John's role as Alex's intimate: was she relieved that John replaced her as the focus of Alex's attention? Did she sense the impossibility of filling Alex's void, created by his absent mother? Was Joan happy to be freed from the pressures of intimacy? Alternatively, did she live with unexpressed rage as she witnessed the close relationship between her husband and her son?

John's pain resulting from his mother's neglect was masked by the thrill of his father's attention. A lie, "Mom isn't important," allowed John to repress his profound feelings of injury. A spin, "I am important. The world revolves around me. I can get whatever I want," obscured John's simple truth: without his mother's loving affirmation, he would never feel whole and fully valued.

John and Dad

Alex and John accepted as undisputed fact that John could fill the cavernous void in his father's heart, a void created, in part, by his mother's rejection and later reenacted in his empty marriage to Joan. Alex and John accepted this truth without conscious thought, ingesting it whole. John lived his life trying to accomplish an impossible feat. Obviously John could not cure his father's profound pain. In reality, John could only distract Alex from his unhappiness.

In marrying Joan, a woman who simulated the aching experience of rejection, Alex selected a mate who generated familiar feelings within him, and so John came to know similar feelings of rejection. In John's therapy, he grew to realize the profoundness of his identification with his father. Both grew up feeling unloved by their mothers. Both denied their anguish, burying their suffering deep in their Shadows. Their repressed pain strained their abilities to forge intimate relationships with appropriate adults.

John and his dad colluded in claiming that their relationship could alleviate the emotional havoc created by their own experiences of maternal deprivation. They held this claim as an unquestionable truth. Since their bond with each other was so gratifying, each professed other relationships to be inconsequential, which muted the suffering created by their unresponsive mothers.

It was important to maintain the dynamics established between father and son. If either grew closer to any woman, including Joan, then their relationship with each other would be in jeopardy. This father/son relationship fueled John's unhappy relationships with women:

- John tried to duplicate with women the relationship he had with his father. If his behavior was what drew his father's love, he believed that that same behavior would give him the love he wanted from women. This delusion generated false hope for John. No woman wanted him to be the center of her existence as his father had, and no woman could adore him the way his father did.

- Children want to be loved by the rejecting or disapproving parent. Even as adults, they continue to work for this approval. Scooter Libby seemed to work for a mentor's approval as a possible substitute for what he experienced as insufficient approval from his father. In his female companion, John unconsciously sought a substitute for his mother. No woman could successfully fill that void.

- No Herculean effort can produce a mother's love when the problem resides in the mother, not in the infant. As explored in chapter 4, many believe there are good and bad babies, not good or bad mothers. Children who feel unloved by their mothers work throughout their lives to be the person their mothers will love. Patty, a client of mine, was a daughter of physically and sexually abusive parents. Even when Patty was in her sixties, she wrestled with whether or not to tend to her elderly mother, who continued to involve Patty in a sadomasochistic relationship. John, accustomed to success, met his challenge in his mother. He could not get from her the affirmation he wanted.

- Fear of accepting the truth of maternal rejection or of a mother's lack of affirmation can be devastating. Deep down, John feared that accepting the truth of his mother's rejection would trigger unbearable pain, killing his spirit, generating uncontrollable rage in him, and jeopardizing his self-esteem.

- John, on some level, believed he had accomplished the impossible, healing his father's psychological injuries, which were caused by his own mother's abandonment, and reenacted in his relationship with Joan. John deluded himself by believing he could ameliorate the anguish created in him by his rejecting mother. Maybe, *he*, in fact, had rejected *her*.

- Alex, wed to the feelings generated by his relationship with his mother, married a woman who kept alive those feelings. John, mirroring his father, repeated Alex's relationships with women, and was most comfortable with women resembling his mother, women who seemed to have their own issues with closeness and intimacy.

- John was driven by conflicting emotions. He unconsciously hungered for his mother's love. On the other hand, John loathed women, especially his mother, mirroring Alex's attitude. John's confused feelings and attitudes complicated his efforts to cultivate relationships with women.
- John could not challenge his father's judgments: if Alex's perceptions about Joan were wrong, then Alex's perceptions about John could be wrong as well.

John and His Sister

John's relationship with his sister Carole exemplified his difficult relationships with women. A visit he paid to her at her home in Arizona resulted in his making some important insights through psychotherapy.

John extended a business trip to spend a weekend with Carole. When he called to suggest the visit, she welcomed him, suggesting he participate in her weekend life of shopping, taking the dog to obedience class, and maybe catching a movie with friends. John felt offended, thinking Carole should center her weekend around his visit. Ultimately, Carole complied, inviting her friends to a dinner party, to be celebrated with vintage wines. John returned to DC, reporting to me that the weekend was a huge success.

A few nights later Carole called him, upset and angry. She complained that John had not complimented her once all evening—about the food or the drink or her wonderful friends. "Instead, you held court, working to impress everyone," he remembered her saying. Carole was even more furious that he had succeeded in winning over her friends, which John reported to me in amazement.

As we explored the weekend in greater depth, John's distortions about the weekend proliferated, skewed by his self-absorption. He minimized his desire to see Carole, portraying himself as having responded to her request. "She begged me to come," he told me. "She sounded so lonely. I felt I had to." John exaggerated the effort he exerted to arrange the visit, minimizing the fact that it took place on a weekend and that it was easy for him to make transportation arrangements. John took credit for the party's success, not understanding Carole's hurt that he had not acknowledged her. He believed that without him, Carole would have denied herself the gratifying experience derived from the dinner party.

As John and I delved more deeply into the disparity between his perceptions of the visit and his sister's, I encouraged John to consider the possible benefits of joint therapy sessions with Carole. Genuinely wanting a better relationship with her and increasingly interested in her perceptions of their childhood, John's enthusiasm for therapy with his sister grew. After many discussions with her, John, who could better afford the air travel than she, sent Carole a plane ticket. They each eagerly and openly participated in several therapy sessions over ten days.

John and Carole identified that during John's short visit, they instinctively reenacted their familiar roles in the family dance. The weekend assumed profound personal meaning for both in bringing to the surface the underlying tension in their relationship:

- Carole recognized that nothing she did over the weekend seemed to satisfy John. In therapy, we identified that John could not be satisfied because it was impossible for her to fill the void inside him created by his emotionally absent mother.

- Carole and John witnessed each other expressing emotions, an experience neither had had prior to that day. Carole sensed John's depression, and John sensed Carole's rage. "When we were alone," Carole told John, "you seemed down in the dumps. You didn't put a positive spin on everything about yourself. That was a first." John sensed Carole's rage. "Every time you spoke to me, I felt attacked," John told her.

- Carole grew to understand that, during the fateful phone conversation after John's visit, her anger with her brother expressed a lifetime of pent-up feeling intended for her dad and other men who evoked a similar emotion. The rage John sensed mirrored feelings she had had throughout her youth. She tried desperately to please her dad, and she failed. She approached the weekend with John consciously trying not to worry about pleasing him. But, as soon as he challenged her weekend plans, she succumbed and lost her determination. From then on, Carole's mindset changed to the expectation that anything she did would not be good enough for John. She reenacted her pained relationship with her father. John, of course, dutifully played his role by overlooking her as he maneuvered to become the center of attention.

- Carole and John acknowledged that the pain of their childhood impeded their daily functioning as adults. Carole complained to

> John, "Since your visit I keep crying. And I have visions of smashing things." John acknowledged that "Since our visit, all I have wanted to do is work and hide at the office."

In their therapy, Carole and John grew to appreciate how both were injured as children growing up in a family where the dynamics between their parents were harmful to all. They were gratified that the dynamics surfacing during their weekend in Arizona offered possibilities for both to find more happiness and fulfillment in their respective lives. Carole returned to Arizona and began intensive psychotherapy for herself. John continued his therapy with renewed fervor.

The events of the weekend and the ensuing joint therapy helped John grasp the factors that had poisoned his relationships with women: manipulation, dismissiveness, disrespect, and lack of appreciation.

John and Women

His relationships with women hampered John professionally and personally. His career glitches inevitably involved women. Due to his overinflated ego, John could not take responsibility for the negative ramifications of his behavior. While female supervisors perceived John as boorish, female supervisees reported him as dismissive and disrespectful. Several women risked being fired rather than working with him. John's spin: women quit because of intellectual incompetence. In addition, attorneys other than John achieved consistently better working relationships with female judges. He mocked his colleagues, saying they were too pliable, unable to consider himself as arrogant.

John's failures in intimate relationships replicated his struggles with his sister and his professional colleagues. Married briefly, he resented his bride's expectation that her career ambitions should be as important as his. When dating, John claimed to be respectful of women, though they experienced him as disrespectful, feeling offended when he turned away as they talked. With men he maintained eye contact; with women he did not. He passed over their comments, returning to those made by men, or worse, he attributed their insights to men.

Though disdaining women, John also craved their love and approval. In relationships, John searched for adoration that would duplicate his father's. Further, John's conflicting emotions regarding his mother—guilt at having displaced her and longing for her love—conveyed contradictory messages. To assuage his guilt, John tried behaviors that had worked with his father. John invited women whose adoration he craved to prestigious dinners. He hoped that if he shared the limelight with them, they would adore him as his father had. This strategy was successful with his dad, but not with these women. However much he cared for these women, the relationships never lasted. Their affirmation of him was never great enough to fill the void created by his mother's absence and could never equal his father's elevation of him.

John hungered for intimacy, for a wife. He longed to parent a son as his father had parented him. He was attracted to married women, but none left their husbands for him. As John's age advanced, his female companions became younger and his entitled persona became more acceptable to them. But, in their youth, they lacked the worldly acumen to be intellectual companions, as required by John.

As John struggled in relationships with women, his friends' lives expanded to accommodate dual careers, children, and pets. He felt envy when he witnessed the richness and chaos in their lives. He tired of being "Uncle John" to so many children. John also resented not being an honored godfather or guardian to any of them. John's friends trusted his love for their children but not his ability to be nurturing. Directly confronted by his friends, John learned that they experienced him as arrogant and dismissive in the presence of women. They did not want their children to witness such sexist interactions and, therefore, spent less time with him.

Encouraged by his friends and believing that any goal was achievable, John began therapy. He stated his objective: "I want you to help me find the right woman. I want to be married within a year."

ROAD TO HEALTH

Complications evolving from his position as his father's favorite child surfaced during John's intense therapy over years. The developmental and interpersonal factors molding his personality were addressed in his individual and group psychotherapy sessions and in his joint session with his sister Carole.

Three fields of modern psychology guide an understanding of John's psychological growth. An understanding of these three areas helps to demystify the process of change enabled through psychotherapy.

(1) Interpersonal neurobiology guides our understanding of the impact of John's family history on his DNA and brain.
(2) Sociobiology sheds light on the importance of language in protecting John emotionally, permitting his self-deception and lying.
(3) Family systems theory explains those dynamics within John's family that nurtured the favorite child syndrome.

Interpersonal Neurobiology

According to old wives' tales, a violent or despairing temperament belongs to the child conceived in anger or sorrow. How amazing that science now backs up the truth of this bold statement.

Advances in science prove that the brain is a dynamic entity, growing and changing; its biochemistry responds to social cues. At the moment of conception, the man and the woman transmit to the fertilized egg DNA encoded with their genetic blueprint. As the infant's brain develops, complex pathways emerge, forging the individual's spontaneous response to a given stimulus.

It is difficult to imagine passionate lovemaking at the moment of John's conception. Neither John nor his siblings have any memories of physical contact between their parents, not even an occasional hug or kiss. They slept in separate beds and maintained physical distance. The mother dressed to appear asexual, in loose-fitting, drab clothes that revealed nothing of her neck or arms. Her subservient profile suggests that sex with her husband was probably an obligation, making it unlikely that she would expect sex to be pleasurable.

It is out of his parents' empty relationship and the convergence of their different emotional states that John was conceived. Alex hungered for a son he deemed worthy to carry on the family name. In his therapy, John wondered if his older brother, Tim, had been the son his father craved, whether other children would have followed. Since Tim was not this child, other children did follow, each born almost exactly two years apart, to the day. John believed this reflected his father's deliberate approach to having children.

Alex distrusted women throughout his life. Distrust bred more distrust, imprinting it ever more deeply. He suffered profound abandonment, which was especially damaging because of his youth and

The Brain: Negotiator between Our Inner and Outer Worlds

The limbic system of the brain rests between the brainstem, which is the most primitive part of the brain, and the cerebral cortex, the most advanced part of the brain. Consistent with its position in the brain, the function of the limbic system is to negotiate between the primitive needs of the organism and the requirements of the outside world. The amygdala and the hippocampus are central to the limbic system. The amygdala is a key component in the neural networks involved with fear, attachment, early memory, and emotional experience. The hippocampus organizes explicit memory in collaboration with the cerebral cortex.

The amygdala functions as an organ of appraisal for danger, safety, and familiarity with approach-avoidance situations. In association with parts of the cerebral cortex, the amygdala connects emotional value to the objects of the senses, based on both instincts and learning history, and translates these appraisals into bodily states. For example, the amygdala is vital in translating the sight of danger into preparing the person to fight or flee.

The hippocampus functions to slow down neural processing in order to appraise ongoing behavior. This is vital if behavior is to become more conscious and deliberate. It permits healthier social interactions.

The interplay between the amygdala and hippocampus is central to normal functioning. The amygdala, representing the primitive functioning of the infant's brain, instinctively senses danger or discomfort and directs the brain to react lack of language skills. Leaving Hungary, losing home and familiarity, compounded his suffering. We know nothing about Alex's mother but wonder about the personality of a woman who made the choice that she did—the choice of her mother over her child. Was she looking for a path out of a bad marriage and willing to sacrifice her son? Was nurturing a child so repugnant to her as to be unbearable? Was her relationship with her mother such an entwined one that she believed she could not function without her mother?

Alex reenacted the trauma of his abandonment by marrying a woman whose treatment of him reminded him of his mother's behavior toward him. Each day, the imprint on his brain deepened as he relived his loss. Alex's unease around women showed in his relationships with his daughters; sensing his discomfort, they did not embrace him and

quickly. The hippocampus, representing more mature brain functioning, works to evaluate the complexities of imminent threat and directs the brain to slow down and strategize.

In infancy, the "fast system" with the amygdala at its core makes rapid, reflexive, and unconscious decisions necessary for immediate survival. This system develops first and organizes the learning that is necessary for the development of mother/child attachment and the infant's regulation of emotions. Anxiety, fear, and depression experienced later in life can be rooted in traumatic sensory-motor experiences and affective memories of early life rooted in the amygdala.

Early trauma, such as prolonged exposure to stress, can impair the hippocampus and generate long-term psychological difficulties. Hippocampal impairment decreases the brain's ability to inhibit, or slow down, emotions triggered by the amygdaloid memory systems. This can cause deficits in the individual's short-term memory and ability to test reality. Balancing the brain's need to respond quickly against the need to respond thoughtfully becomes more difficult.[2]

In people like John and Alex, who suffered early maternal deprivation, it is likely that the amygdala's functioning was impaired. Further, it is likely that the functioning of Alex's hippocampus was impaired by his physical separation, as a young child, from his mother. Thus, the process of building a therapeutic relationship with John, and clients like him who suffer early and prolonged maternal deprivation, may be long and difficult.

the cycle of pained relationships with women deepened. He became more self-protective against relationships with women.

The drama reenacted by John's mother is less clear. She remains obscure, succeeding in maintaining her invisibility in the family. In John's psychotherapy, we were unable to forge an understanding of her. According to John's view, which was confirmed by Carole, no one in the family experienced her as mean, just as inadequate and as a non-presence. Without knowing more, we cannot speculate about the predispositions that were encoded in the DNA she transmitted to John.

John's infant brain, the recipient of his parents' hard wiring, responded instinctively to stimuli—internal and external—moment by moment. The amygdala, located in the limbic system of the brain, probably sensed his mother's physical and psychological discomfort in caring for her infant. This deficient bonding translated into danger to the infant brain. And as, in all species, survival needs prompted the infant to protect itself, to withdraw from the threat. As an infant, John likely retreated from forming a relationship with his mother, by rejecting eye contact, refusing to smile, or crying.

During John's intense psychotherapy, our task was enormous: to challenge the primitive instincts housed in his amygdala as well as the belief systems of at least two generations of men in his family regarding women. The primitive pain of mother/female abandonment that resided in John's core nurtured instinctive behaviors of self-protection—choosing women who were married or otherwise unavailable, distancing himself from women, and behaving in ways that made women push him away. Integral to John's therapy was the task of retraining his brain pathways so that the hippocampus could function more effectively, slowing down the reactions of the amygdala to permit more flexible thinking.[3]

Language: A Tool for Survival

The brain governs survival. Regions of the brain communicate with one another to coordinate the responses throughout the body required for individual safety and the ultimate survival of the species. In humans, our complex brain reflects evolved systems nec-

Language: Man's Camouflage

The science of infant brain development is young. An understanding of the infant brain is growing through animal research, electronic/magnetic observations of the infant brain, and well-controlled observation studies. These methods provide direction for psychotherapeutic insight into the avoidance of pain and the seeking of pleasure. In utero, the most primitive portions of the brain develop first: the fetus reacts to internal and environmental stresses by waving its appendages and sucking. Mothers know the physical discomfort caused by a kicking fetus in the middle of the night. At birth, the right side of the brain, the site for affective and emotional expression, dominates. Infants express their emotions by crying and flailing. Only later, as the left side of the brain develops, does the center for cognition and language begin to develop. With this growth, language begins, permitting more elaborate communication among regions of the child's brain as well as between the child and the world.

When faced with a threat, primitive animals either annihilate the threat or physically hide. People do the same thing, annihilate the threat or physically hide. But to accommodate a world that has evolved in complexity, the human brain has adapted with the evolution of more complex strategies. Language is fundamental to human sophistication.

From infancy, parents teach children about physical and emotional safety. As children get older, acceptable reactions to endangerment change. "Acting out" is scorned. It is not acceptable for a five-year-old to kick and flail like a baby. Adults expect the child to "use words." Children are expected to protect and comfort themselves through the use of language.

Language permits psychic safety by providing those skills required to minimize fear: self-deception, lying, distortion of reality. The telling of comforting stories or spinning reality permits security—real or imagined.

essary for our survival, the development of language being central. Sociobiologist David Livingston Smith, as noted earlier, describes language as sophisticated camouflage permitting us the personal self-deception that is necessary for survival.[4]

As a newborn, John experienced the world in its raw form, with no language to modify the intensity of emotions created by a rejecting mother. By the time he was two and a half years old, as language developed, John could begin to modify uncensored emotions and gain increasing control over his experiences. As language develops, people's behaviors become less governed by their powerful emotions. The emotions do not evaporate, but they become a part of the unconscious world, stored in unconscious memory.

John's childhood taught him the art of self-deception. His father, through both words and action, conveyed falsehoods to his favorite child. Alex taught John that the world revolved around him. In the words of the young child, he learned, "I am important. When Dad comes home from work, I am the one who gets all his attention," which developed in the world of an eight-year-old to mean: "I am important. I am my teacher's favorite. She smiles at me and sends me to the office as her messenger." John's memory of his teacher's adoration may be an example of spin. Did the teacher smile only at John and not at other children in the class? John thought so, but we do not know. Did John remember only her smile, not her scowl? Maybe. Was John, in reality, the only one in the class who got to be the messenger, or is this what John told himself? Was John her messenger because he was the favorite or because he was the only one in the class who had completed the work?

As an adult, John's forte, self-deception and self-absorption, further impeded his ability to establish healthy relationships with women. As described earlier, John thought the visit with his sister Carole was a huge success, while for her, it was a psychological disaster. Early in John's career, young female associates risked being fired rather than working for him; he told himself they hesitated to work for him because intellectually they could not keep up with him. He rationalized his strained relationships with female judges as reflecting their inability to challenge his brilliance, rather than reflecting his arrogance. When a woman with whom he was romantically involved dumped him, he was often shocked, believing the relationship to have been going well.

John and his dad colluded to foster the ultimate lie, that John had the ability to replace his mother as his father's intimate. As Alex focused on John, ignoring Mom, John told himself that he was more important to Dad than his wife was. By the time John was a young adolescent, he had come to believe that he and Dad were a twosome. John told himself, "I matter to Dad, not Mom; and Dad matters to me, not Mom." Dad and John *did* matter to one another, but Mom's absence from each of their lives mattered profoundly. Lying to himself to avoid pain, John negated the importance of Mom and the injury created by her absence.

In adulthood, John's visit to his sister exemplified his use of language to protect himself from emotional injury. To camouflage his feeling that he was not lovable to a woman, John spun his visit to his sister to convey his greatness: his visit was an act of extraordinary generosity. In actuality, John repressed a familiar feeling, his hurt that women did not pursue him. His spin brought into play the familiar family dance, leaving both John and his sister injured and unhappy.

The Family Dance

Family members relate to one another as a well-greased, closed system. They dance the dance choreographed and re-choreographed by prior generations. John's story poignantly demonstrates the power of reenactment.

Carl Whitaker, a family therapist whose influence was discussed in chapter 6, revolutionized the psychotherapy of schizophrenics by challenging the notion that families supported their healing: "Maybe the family really doesn't want the crazy one to heal. Who then would fill that role, a role no one else wants? Every family has to have their crazy member."[5] Whitaker held that families resisted change and change was most likely to occur when families were forced to integrate new people, such as infants and spouses, or even new pets.[6]

In John's family, each member had prescribed roles: Alex was "the Admiral" and Joan "the Mouse." John was his father's favorite son, and Carole, attracted to her father's power, was the workhorse, emanating energy as she worked futilely for his approval. Betty, as her mother's clone, remained innocuous, and Tim, the recipient of his father's contempt, remained angry. Alex, the most powerful family member, had an interest in maintaining the status quo. It allowed him to navigate his repressed childhood pain, finding a path that provided him with comfort. John, the golden boy, had no interest in changing roles with Tim. Carole had no interest in being as invisible as Betty; nor was Betty interested in being as visible as her sister. Each person's role not only steered behaviors within the family but also had an impact on the personalities of the family members. The influence of these roles, as outlined previously, governed John's and Carole's adult relationship.

The parents colluded with one another to perpetuate the distortion of John's importance in the family, his father treating John as if John really could replace his wife as his intimate, and his mother allowing the deception to occur. Joan's inability to place boundaries on Alex's inappropriate treatment of their son left John's grandiosity unchallenged.

The mother/father/son triangle negatively impacted the lives of John's siblings. Motivated by preservation and self-protection, they attempted to inoculate themselves from the profound injury inflicted by their father's contempt. Tim enlisted in the military and volunteered for dangerous missions, probably to reassure himself and prove to his father that he was a man, not a wimp. Having served in Vietnam, he left the military suspicious of people, and thus far is not capable of sustaining intimate relationships. Betty and Carole left home upon graduation from high school. Betty married a man as strong willed as her father, a man who, out of his disdain for Alex, supported her minimal contact with her father. Carole moved across the country, and supported herself through college and graduate school. She established herself professionally, so as never to be as dependent and vulnerable as her mom.

The Rewards of Healing

John began psychotherapy realizing that, as he approached forty, fame and fortune were insufficient for his happiness. He wanted to move out of the life that had imprisoned him, replacing his lifestyle with a loving marriage and children. His journey to health required distancing himself from the lure of the benefits derived as his father's favorite child and healing the scars created by his mother's inattention.

The depth of John's unconscious disrespect for women created a powerful tension in his relationship with me. In selecting a female therapist, John fantasized that I would cure his unhappiness by offering him the motherly love and affirmation he craved. Wrong! As John could not fill the void in his father created by his absent mother, I could not fill John's void. Throughout the early stages of John's psychotherapy, our relationship was difficult as I confronted him with his dismissive attitude to me. He avoided eye contact and credited psychological insights to passages he read in self-help books rather than to our work. He was irritated that I would not give him what he insisted he needed—praise and adoration.

The work of his psychotherapy was tedious. The healing he desired required John to become more conscious of his contribution to his failed relationships with women. Old neuro-pathways, firmly entrenched, responded quickly, trying to squelch possible new pathways:

- John responded negatively to feedback challenging his self-perceived perfection. Old pathways screamed, "No, not right!"

- The information required for the development of new pathways created discomfort.

- In his individual psychotherapy, John experienced engaging with an appropriately supportive mother figure and learned to be more comfortable in the presence of a competent woman. This challenged old pathways that dismissed women, and it required John to build new pathways more respectful of women.

As John's treatment advanced, we added group therapy to the regimen. This forum stimulated family associations and invited old responses. Group members responded to John's contempt for women, as had his sister and friends. He expected women to put aside their needs in the interest of his needs. He tried to manipulate them. For example, if a women started speaking about her issues and John had something he wanted to discuss, with a winning smile on his face he would claim, "What I have to talk about will only take a minute. Let me go first and then you won't be rushed." Initially women would accede to his logic, usually feeling appreciative of his thoughtfulness. Inevitably, though, John's concerns would occupy most of the group's time, and in spite of the woman's attempts to cut him off, little time would remain for her.

Group therapy provided an outstanding forum for women to confront his dismissiveness, for men to support him in the struggles of change, and for me, as his therapist, to provide him with appropriate parenting—setting limits that were supportive and useful. Participation in group therapy provided John with the stimulus necessary to influence the modification of his neurological pathways. This, coupled with John's dogged determination to change, positively affected his relations with women both in the group and, later, outside it.

Reflections on John's experience of the family system and his role as his father's favorite child steered his psychotherapy. Prior to John's beginning treatment, Alex died, causing profound discomfort for John, since he had to function without his father's uncontested praise. Yet, his father's death permitted John the freedom to question Alex's views of the world. With his dad taking up less space in the family, Joan's presence increased. Healing occurred in John's relationship with his mother prior to her death.

It is unlikely that John as an infant set out to replace his mother in his father's heart. As Anna Freud said, every child most wants parents to be intimates with each other, providing the security required for a strong, healthy identity. From his conception, when his parents' DNA shaped his personality, through his childhood, when the family system reinforced his emerging personality, John developed as the quintessential favorite child of his father. In therapy, we challenged his belief system so that his relationships with women became respectful and fulfilling, while he maintained the skills central to an outstanding career.

John's therapy continued throughout the writing of this book. By this time, many (though not all) of his goals were accomplished:

- John's view of himself became more realistic. He grew less self-absorbed and less troubled when not experiencing adoration.

- John's relationship with his mother matured and he grew to respect her. With the death of his father, his mother's personality grew fuller and richer. John's heart opened to her.

- John's relationship with Carole continued to grow. After her participation in John's therapy, she committed herself to her own. John and Carole became, and have remained, trusted intimates.

- John's professional relationships with women improved, with many actively pursuing assignment to cases in which he was the lead attorney.

- At the time when this was written, John had not yet married but had had long and increasingly healthier relationships with women. When a relationship ended, he acknowledged how he had contributed to both the tension and the problems of the relationship.

- John is using his growing self-awareness to explore and develop strategies that will provide greater satisfaction in future relationships.

John began his therapy to support his quest for a marriage partner. In his therapy, he grew to understand how Alex unconsciously used him, rigidly and forcefully, to meet profound needs stemming from Alex's mother's abandonment when Alex and his father emigrated from Hungary. John appreciated how his own attitudes and relations with women were governed by his father's experiences and values. John grasped how his delusions of grandeur and self-importance adversely affected his relationships with people. While not married, John has now experienced committed relationships with women who have been healthy potential partners. He experiences contentment with his life and is at peace.

FATHERS AND FAVORITE SONS

John's story is not unique. Favorite sons, like John, identify with fathers they perceive as powerful. As these sons work to maintain their cherished status, they develop the skills and confidence that foster professional success.

Fathers' favorite sons often grow up not respecting women, which makes their quest for rich, mature, adult love difficult. If they marry, commonly these men replicate their fathers' journeys and marry weak women, attach themselves to their favorite male child, and look to their favorite son to fill their needs for intimacy and stimulation that are unmet by their wives.

According to John and Carole, this cycle was evident in the marriage of their sister Betty. Betty, meek like her mother, married an imposing man like her father. Betty's husband, himself the favorite son of a strong father and weak mother, dominated Betty while looking to his favorite son to meet his needs for closeness that were unmet by Betty.

While the status of father's favorite son is empowering and often professionally gratifying, it can also cause profound unhappiness and loneliness. Through psychotherapy or other healing work, a father's favorite son can challenge a belief system that has been passed down from previous generations. As illustrated by John's story, emancipation takes time and persistence, and the payoff can be enormous.

CHAPTER EIGHT
FATHER'S FAVORITE DAUGHTER

Every Christmas morning I'd tear open the gift in front of the whole family, including my mother. I'd been eyeing it for days. Wrapped in beautiful paper with lots of ribbon, it was the only gift not wrapped in the reused, partially torn paper my mother used. When opening my present, I'd squeal with delight. It was always just what I wanted. The gift—from my father's mistress.

—Teri's reflection

I loved Sundays—just Dad and me. It wasn't until I turned ten that it seemed strange. I remember the day vividly: we'd gone to the zoo, Lincoln Park, and then to Tonnelli's. As I slurped spaghetti, I realized that the restaurant was packed with families celebrating Mother's Day while my mother stayed home with my younger brother. As on other Sundays, Dad called Mom, asking her to join us for dinner. As always, she turned him down flat. But [that] Mother's Day, I remember feeling unusually awkward—alone with my dad in a restaurant surrounded by families celebrating mothers while my mother chose to be home without us.

—Beth's reflections

Teri and Beth lived dramatically different lives, one an esteemed artist pushing boundaries to the extreme and the other an eminent physician adhering rigidly to rules. Teri struggled with addictions, overeating until she was thirty, and then turning to alcohol. Having heard of my interest in favoritism within families, Teri contacted me. She wanted to talk with me about her experiences. She spoke freely with me over several meetings, as if trying to get the courage to commit to the therapeutic experience necessary for healing. She wanted to control her addictions, to have healthy intimate relationships, to no longer live with the pain caused by depression and anxiety. Aware of her reluctance to heal, Teri lived with chronic discomfort and self-contempt. She could not overcome her inability to commit to a program directed at healing. She remained resistant to participating in AA, psychotherapy, or church groups for children from dysfunctional families.

Beth, a client of mine, was committed to her psychotherapy. She arrived on time for all her appointments, often making complicated arrangements for coverage at work or home that required extra effort from many people. Beth wanted better relationships with her husband and children. She thought her relationship with her husband too business-like, aware of the fact that she avoided time alone with him. When they were together, she resisted relaxed and free-flowing conversations, instead wanting to chatter nonstop about their son and daughter. Concerned about her preference for doing things *for* her children rather than playing games or riding bikes *with* them, she worried that her parenting skills were inadequate. She felt envious of the laughter and spontaneity permeating her husband's relationship with their children. She knew the issues to be hers. She did not like herself in those moments.

Common to both Teri and Beth was the importance of their fathers in their lives. Each lived lives sculpted by the role of father's favorite daughter. This role empowered Teri to escape her mother's claws and function outside the family with more success and pleasure than her siblings. It conveyed to Beth the confidence necessary to complete the rigors of medical training, begin her practice, and secure a reputation as an eminent physician.

Teri and Beth both grew up knowing little about the dance of intimacy with anyone other than their fathers. Like John in chapter 7, their knowledge of intimacy developed from abnormal closeness with their fathers, together with their mothers' absence. As explored in chapter 7, the fear of stealing one parent from the other is a child's nightmare. Believing that this feat has been accomplished is a child's delusion. Children want the unquestioned love of both parents. Teri and Beth, though growing up in families with dramatically different dynamics, were both scarred by their position as the father's favorite daughter.

TERI: SURVIVING A DYSFUNCTIONAL FAMILY

Teri was the youngest of three children. When she was born, Katherine, the oldest, enjoyed the independence that came with adolescence. Cecilia, the second child, was born with severe developmental delays. According to family legend, Cecilia replaced Katherine, the oldest, as their mother's favorite child. Their mother, totally immersed in caring for her child with disabilities, thrived on the accolades she received for her devoted caretaking. When Teri was born, according to family friends, it was Katherine who cared for her, changing her diapers and giving her bottles. Her mother remained consumed with Cecilia and her father was seldom home.

Teri told me she sometimes pondered her conception. "It's a family joke," she said. "No one knows how it happened. Katherine insists it was Immaculate Conception! Apparently, after Cecilia was born, Mother paid no attention to Dad. All I know for sure is that physically I resemble *both* parents, so I do believe that *I am* their child."

Teri had no delusion that her birth was the product of passionate lovemaking between her parents, Ann and Marcus. In looking through family picture albums, Teri found no pictures of her parents together after Cecilia's birth. Teri reported that Katherine, as well as aunts and uncles, agreed that before Cecilia's birth, the atmosphere in the family was more loving and accepting, and after her birth, more restrained and uncomfortable. Katherine did not recall fights between their parents, just Marcus begging Ann to be less consumed with Cecilia.

When Teri reviewed her childhood, her memories lacked loving recollections involving her mother. She found no evidence in family photo albums of her mother holding her or smiling at her. In the pictures, it was always Katherine or Marcus who engaged with her. Her reflections of family life when she was growing up echoed those of her sister and brother—no fights, but icy cold.

Teri credited her mother with sending her to boarding school during high school. "Mother, recognizing that I was bright and artistic, thought I'd thrive in an edgy boarding school. Now I wonder about her real motrivation for sending me—whether she truly had my best interest at heart or if it was her wish to get me out of the house. Whatever, getting out of the house was a gift to me. I loved school and it set me up for life."

While Ann and Marcus lived together, their lives followed divergent paths. Ann consumed herself with Cecilia's needs. After Cecilia died at ten years old, Ann absorbed herself with organizations dedicated to the needs of people with developmental delays. Ann replaced caring for Cecilia with caring for her own older, disabled sister. "Aunt Margie lived in a residential facility, about forty-five minutes from our house. Mother visited her almost every day, to oversee her baths, diet, and exercise," Teri explained.

Marcus immersed himself in work, travel, a mistress, and Teri. These were the antidotes for his loneliness. Teri and Marcus found companionship and comfort in one another. Marcus told Teri of his delight in holding her as a young child: "My dad told me that when he walked into the room, I ran to him. I hugged him and kissed him. I didn't want him to put me down, and I didn't want to be with anyone else. Dad said he loved my responses. It made him happy. He smiled from ear to ear." Tears flooded Teri's eyes when, as an adult, she talked with me about his joyous responses: "I think of the comfort I felt as he held me," she said. "With him, my pain of feeling so alone disappeared."

The Wrong Threesome: Teri, Her Father, His Lover

Teri recalled meeting Caroline for the first time around the time of Cecilia's death. "I wasn't quite a teenager," Teri told me. "Dad took me to the county fair. On the way to the fair, he told me that we would stop to pick up a friend of his who would join us. He assured me that I'd like her, that she was fun, adventuresome, and had a great laugh. When Caroline got into the car, I was awed. I had never been with someone who wore nail polish!"

That outing was the beginning of a long threesome. Teri's memories of trips to the beach or overseas were of trips with Marcus and Caroline. She remembers summers when she and Caroline accompanied Marcus on business trips to Munich, Vienna, London, or Madrid. While Marcus worked, Teri and Caroline toured and shopped.

If Teri needed to discuss specific issues with an adult woman, she turned to Caroline. She remembered shopping for prom and graduation dresses with Caroline, not her mother. Teri held Caroline, not Ann, to be a loving, interested female guide. The depth of their relationship is reflected in the exuberance portrayed in the anecdote that opened this chapter, describing Christmas morning.

"Dad's having a mistress was just a fact of life in the family. I don't have the foggiest idea if Mom felt furious that he had a lover or relieved because it took pressure off her. I sometimes think Mom just didn't like men. When men were in the house, she always seemed uncomfortable, her foot never stopped tapping. I never sensed there was another man, that she had a lover. As for her feelings about me, sometimes I imagine she sent me to boarding school to get me away from Dad and Caroline, sort of a punishment."

Teri described her sister, like her mother, as appearing indifferent to Caroline's presence in Marcus's life and in hers. Teri admitted to me, "Even now, years later, I don't know how Katherine feels about our family experiences, about Caroline's blatant presence. We don't talk about it. It's one of *those* subjects, off limits."

Christmas morning highlighted the tension Teri experienced with her sister. She described the morning ritual: "As I opened this magnificent gift, Katherine pretended not to care. In her silence, I sensed her criticism. I'd squeal with delight, louder and louder, wanting her attention and wanting her to be happy for me. The more I clamored, the more she ignored me. I felt like an outsider."

Teri imagined that her sibling's treatment of her on Christmas morning reflected her jealousy of Teri's position as their father's favorite child. She alone was included in the rich life Marcus shared with Caroline. Teri acknowledged that it may have been easier or safer for Katherine to be angry with her than with their parents for having imposed this charade on the family.

Everyone Is Injured

While relishing favored status in relation to her father, Teri, like John in chapter 7, suffered from maternal neglect and delusions regarding her role. Like infants, previously cited, neither Teri nor John were "bad" children. Their mothers' rejection had little, if anything, to do with them. And while their fathers' affirmation protected their young psyches from deeper harm, neither father could obliterate the injuries incurred from maternal neglect.

All of the members of Teri's family perpetuated the dysfunction. None of them acknowledged their discomfort evoked by the arrangement between Ann and Marcus. As a result:

- Respect and open communication between the parents were absent. (This illustrates the destructiveness of inadequate dialogue as described in chapter 6.)

- The mother and father did not look to fulfill each other's needs. Inappropriately, Ann looked to Cecilia and then Margie. Marcus looked to Teri and Caroline. (This family drama parallels that of James's family as described in chapter 6.)

- In accepting Caroline into the Christmas morning celebration, the family agreed to perpetuate a sadomasochistic ritual causing pain for all.

All of the members of Teri's family were injured by their tragic interactions. Premature death, alcoholism, loneliness, and commitment issues plagued different family members.

Marcus

Marcus was killed in his early fifties while racing cars. Prior to his death, he and Caroline had considered marriage. Those reviewing the accident noted that Marcus drove with extreme recklessness. Friends acknowledged that his usual caution had diminished over the months prior to his fatal accident and wondered if this reflected exhaustion from living such a complicated life. After his death, the relationship between Teri and Caroline ended.

Ann

Ann, alone and depressed, drank heavily. She lived with chronic aches and pains, which doctors believed to be stress induced. She could no longer volunteer with associations for people with developmental delays or tend her gardens, one of the few activities that gave her pleasure. Her self-absorption alienated those attempting to have a relationship with her, even her beloved Katherine. Teri, still craving her mother's love, became her principal caretaker and tolerated Ann's indifference toward her, never experiencing her mother's affection.

Katherine

Katherine, as an adult, lived a compromised life. She was lonely and could not establish intimacy. She was married several times, but no relationship proved satisfying. She achieved job security in her role as a dietician in a local hospital.

Teri

Teri's compulsive eating was replaced by compulsive drinking in her thirties. "As a kid I used eating to comfort myself," she told me, "I remember eating so much on Christmas Day, telling myself I didn't want any more food, that I felt sick to my stomach, but still, I couldn't stop. As a teenager, I remember sitting on the porch with my mother. She would drink martinis and I would eat candy bars. We'd match each other, one for one."

Teri lived with guilt regarding Katherine. Teri understood that, as her father's favorite child, she grew up with skills permitting her a higher level of functioning than Katherine. Teri appreciated Katherine's mothering of her as an infant and young child; she struggled with shame because she had left her sister behind to enjoy a more satisfying life with Marcus and Caroline. As an adult reflecting on the past, Teri respected her need to be anesthetized against the pain of her mother's rejection of her.

In spite of her drinking, Teri's career as an artist thrived. Her career as a commercial artist supported her passion as a painter. She acknowledged that, when sober, her thoughts became clearer and her art more expansive. But when she was sober, emotions overwhelmed her and she turned to liquor and food as her elixir. Her distrust of people compromised her career as a fine artist, as she could not trust agents to sell and market her work. Thus, she was left to support herself through commercial art, which took away energy from her creative expression as a painter.

Teri married for the first time at fifty-five. She married a man with whom she had lived for fifteen years. He, having been raised by aunts and uncles, also had issues with intimacy. Neither pressured the other for closeness, yet, according to Teri, their relationship was growing and slowly maturing.

As we talked about her addictions, Teri reconsidered her resistance to OE and AA. During our last conversation, she told me she had gone to AA meetings and spoken to people about sponsoring her. Teri seemed increasingly curious about her relationship to food and alcohol.

During our time together, Teri grew to appreciate that underneath her addictions was an unhappy woman. She pondered her confused feelings for each parent, disliking them while craving them. She missed her father profoundly, grieving for him as much as she did the day he died; she also admitted hating him for drawing her into his double life. She continued to crave her mother's affirmation while at the same time she was angry that Ann overlooked her. Teri hoped that, by joining AA and controlling the symptom of her depression, she could better access the complicated emotions impinging on the quality of her life.

Teri found comfort in our relationship and relief in our honest exchanges. After our conversations, at the time of our goodbye, her goals were first to stop drinking and second to begin sustained therapy. She expressed interest in wanting to begin intensive therapy with me. We agreed that after she stopped drinking, she would contact me. We would meet to explore whether a client/therapist relationship could evolve from the more free-flowing one that we had, or whether it would be in Teri's best interest for me to assist her with a referral.

BETH: A DAUGHTER OVERLOOKED BY HER MOTHER

Beth, in contrast to Teri, had a strong marriage and a satisfying career. She and Martin, married for twenty years, functioned as a team. They shared the responsibilities for raising their children, Tammy and Jonathan, and for managing their home. Each contributed significantly to the family income and participated in financial decisions. Beth began therapy on the recommendation of her internist, who believed her stomach problems were a reflection of stress. Beth's husband emphatically endorsed her physician's recommendation.

"I don't get it," she said during our first session. "I have a great life. I am married to the best man in the world, have two adorable kids who are happy and healthy, and I love my work. I even get to the gym two or three times a week."

Beth represented her life as idyllic. "My parents, they were the best," she commented. "My father, I adored him. He was kind and loving. One of us—Martin, Tammy, Jonathan, or me—would talk to him almost every day. Dad picked up the phone to tell us a joke he thought we'd like, to ask the kids about a soccer game or test they had taken. He'd call me just to tell me that he loved me. Since he died, we miss him enormously."

Beth portrayed her mother, Cheryl, who was alive and healthy, as "terrific." "When my research assistant got sick, I fell behind on notices to participants in the study. I mentioned it to Mom and she got on the next plane to come help. I don't know what I would have done without her."

Beth continued talking about her mother, appreciating her mother's support during her teenage years. "I have great memories of my mother taking me shopping for clothes. While my parents didn't have a lot of extra money, it was always important to Mom that I look nice. My breasts developed when I was ten. Not only was I the first of my friends but my breasts were big, and I felt self-conscious. All I wanted to do was hide my chest. Mom had the patience of a saint as we shopped for outfits. We'd shop and shop until we found clothes we could agree on."

If Beth's life was so good, then why, I wondered, was this woman here? I noted the perfection she described in her life. I wondered if her session with me mirrored her association of shopping with her mother: was she working to conceal something in her therapy that made her feel as uncomfortable now as her breasts did then? Since she was invested in presenting a life that looked good, I knew that it would take time and patience for Beth's story to unfold. As it did, it came to reflect an image dramatically different from that of Beth's initial presentation.

Beth, the older of two children, talked about her childhood as the daughter of a mother with heart disease: "In second grade, I knew that on Tuesdays I couldn't dawdle walking home from the school bus. I had to get home before my mother returned from the doctor. She'd collapse on the sofa in the living room. She didn't have the strength to make it to the bedroom. Sometimes, she'd lie there and breathe so loud I thought she was dying. When my baby brother woke up from his nap crying, I had to decide who to take care of first—Mom or Ben."

Cheryl tired easily. Her diseased heart did not circulate sufficient blood. Diagnosed during her pregnancy with Ben, Cheryl struggled for three years until the odds of surviving mitral valve surgery increased to ten percent. She decided to risk the surgery when doctors told her that without surgery she would be dead in five years, before Beth reached adolescence. It took two years after the surgery for her to fully recover.

During those years, the family activity centered on Cheryl's illness. Beth and her father relied upon each other: he depended on Beth to care for Cheryl during his absence and to help care for Ben. He expected Beth to be "a good girl" and not upset her mother. Beth smiled as she remembered her father's lavish praise for "being so responsible." The reward, accompanying his compliment, was his unrestrained attention.

Beth was lonely. During the week she went to school, and when she came home, she was her mother's and brother's caretaker. They lived in a neighborhood with no children her age. Her "best friend" was Pat, the twenty-four-year-old newlywed who lived next door. Pat was a teacher, and when she got home from work, Beth would go to her house for cookies and milk.

Beth craved the attention of Matt, her dad. Her anticipation of Sunday outings, such as the outing described at the beginning of this chapter, framed her week. During these outings, she had her dad all to herself. On Sundays, she thrived, imagining herself his companion. She had fun and enjoyed temporary relief from the burdensome responsibilities of her week. Her loneliness temporarily abated.

Cheryl lived with complications from heart disease and surgery until Beth turned nine. After Cheryl recovered, the relationship between this mother and daughter faltered. Cheryl did not extend herself to Beth, largely ignoring her except for clothes shopping. In her therapy, Beth reminisced: "We lived far from everything. When my mother was sick, it couldn't be avoided that sometimes I'd go to school without supplies we were supposed to have. After Mom's surgery, when she started driving again, I thought things would be different, that my life would be a little easier. But, it wasn't. She still didn't take me to get what I needed. The time was never right: either my brother was sleeping or she had laundry to do." As an adult, Beth continued to be pained by memories of maternal neglect.

The Threesome: Beth, Her Mother, Her Father

Beth recalled her parents fighting about the experiences that should appropriately be provided for her. She remembers her father wanting her world broadened with exposure to dance, ice-skating, swimming, and tennis lessons. Her mother believed in a more minimal approach: less is better. Cheryl espoused greater self-sufficiency. Beth, in her therapy, put words to long-forgotten memories challenging her mother's Spartan persona. Beth recollected her mother's agreeing that lessons were fine but complaining that she did not want to spend the time or exert the effort to transport her daughter.

Beth remembered clearly a fight between her parents over whether or not she should join the Brownies. Her father insisted she needed more contact with girls her age, but, though her mother agreed, she resented picking up Beth rather than having her come home on the school bus. Beth did join the Brownies and remembers her mother being chronically late when picking her up. Beth recalled the troop leader waiting impatiently, long after all the other girls had left. "When the leader couldn't wait any longer, I remember shaking as I sat on the curb in the dark. I did not know if I was cold or frightened. When Mom got there, I'd burst into tears. She'd call me a crybaby."

As Beth grew older, the issues regarding the threesome consisting of herself, her mother, and her father remained unchanged. Matt and Beth continued to go out, having more grown-up versions of the experiences described at the opening of this chapter. Matt took Beth to the ballet, opera, and theater, performances that Cheryl refused to attend. She thought them "absurd, a waste of money, and not worth the effort to attend." Matt and Beth ensured that each enjoyed birthday celebrations, rituals scorned by Cheryl. Beth and Matt grew closer and closer, confiding in each other and treasuring their relationship. As with John in chapter 7, Beth's perception of her importance to her father was distorted.

Beth talked with me about her associations with clothes and shopping. "I loved to go clothes shopping with my mother. It was the one thing we did together. But, as I think about it now, it makes me uncomfortable. She'd put my dad into the mix. 'Your father will love this or hate that' influenced the outfits she'd want to buy me.

And when we'd get home, she'd pressure me to model the clothes for him. When I was in high school, Dad and Mom fought about what clothes were okay for me to wear. Dad wanted me to wear clothes that concealed my figure. Mom wanted me to wear clothes that, in hindsight, were too suggestive. What a mess!"

Beth explored with me the possibility that her mother's preferences were rooted in sadism, in her mother's desire to make Matt uncomfortable in the presence of his voluptuous daughter. Alternatively, Beth wondered if her mother's interest in her daughter's clothes reflected Cheryl's self-interest, keeping the focus off herself and on her sexual daughter. As for her father's role, Beth wondered if he tried to minimize his sexual feelings for her by preferring her to wear clothing that minimized her figure. Whatever their motivations, as Beth thought about her experiences, she understood that her discomfort related to the fact that her parents had used her, her clothes, and her appearance, as tools that might enable them to provoke each other and protect themselves. Beth did not trust Cheryl or Matt to put her interests first.

Family History Reenacted

In her therapy, Beth journeyed deeper into her psyche. She became aware that the tension between her parents reflected issues far greater than just different strategies for raising her.

Her parents' personality differences were pronounced and not easily reconciled. Beth acknowledged that her mother craved alone time. During Cheryl's illness, the family easily understood her need for rest and minimal activity, but after her full recovery, Cheryl still demonstrated little interest in participating in activities with Beth, Matt, or both. She continued to exclude herself, encouraging father and daughter to spend time together. Beth recalled an evening on which Matt came home from work exuberant. He had just received a raise and wanted to take the family out to dinner. Cheryl refused and insisted that he take Beth out. Were Cheryl's feelings hurt that Matt did not suggest they go out alone, or did Cheryl just not want to be with him?

In contrast, Matt enjoyed people and thrived in relationships.

Long after Cheryl's full recovery, Matt continued to experience the loneliness that he had felt during Cheryl's illness, as she did not readily engage with him. When friends called for an evening of bridge or movies, seldom did she agree willingly. Cheryl would accompany Matt to work-related social events, but always grudgingly.

In his choice of Cheryl as his partner, Matt selected a woman who was the opposite of his mother. His mother pressured him for kisses and hugged him too tightly. Matt's father, described universally by the family as a wimp, never saved Matt from his wife's inappropriate behaviors. Rather, Matt's father listened to the Yankees on the radio and ignored everything else. Cheryl, in contrast, made no physical or emotional demands on Matt. He thought he wanted such a relationship, but Cheryl's coldness proved painful. In selecting Cheryl, he unconsciously selected a person with personality traits resembling those of his father. Matt reenacted his desire to be seen by his father, to be rescued from his mother's overbearing involvement.

Cheryl, in contrast, was the daughter of a quiet man, Papa, who,

Selecting Husbands and Wives

Throughout their lives, women and men work to be loved by both of their parents. In selecting a marriage partner, adults often unconsciously select partners who evoke feelings similar to those evoked by the parents with whom they have the most troubling, unresolved issues. This provides people with yet another opportunity to "get it right" and secure the affirmation they desire from a parental surrogate.

This dynamic is powerfully illustrated when we bring families together to heal, as Carl Whitaker did. (See chapter 6.) As husbands and wives struggle with each other in the presence of parents with whom they have similar difficulties, it is often difficult to track who is struggling with whom. When partners struggle with one another, their struggles naturally migrate from their partner to the relevant parent. In the fury of the moment, patients often exclaim, "You are just like my [hated] father," or "You are just like my mother [who never loved me]." In the moment, a member of the prior generation often erupts with "Yes, that is the same issue I have with your mother [or father]."

As Whitaker observed, the family dance, left untreated, perpetuates itself.

even when he was present, remained invisible. Beth recalled the summer when he came for a long visit. Papa happily ate the homemade borscht made by her mother every Monday and Friday, with a dab of sour cream and two scallions. In the afternoons he bought Beth and her brother ice cream from the white truck of the Good Humor man, chocolate for her brother and toasted almond for her, and at night, he played casino with Beth at the kitchen table. Aside from those experiences, Papa, with his laconic nature, remained a stranger to Beth.

Curious about him, Beth asked her mother to tell stories about Papa. Cheryl, annoyed at the request, said little. She described him as, "a quiet man and a good provider. He was the first in his family to immigrate from Russia and helped family members who followed get jobs and homes," she reported in a monotone. "But my mother, she was the center of attention," Cheryl added quickly and with intensity. Pushing for more information about her grandfather, Beth learned that he had a nice smile. Talks with her aunts and uncles unearthed little else. Among the five sisters and brothers, there were no stories. Papa remained a mystery.

Beth brought Cheryl to a psychotherapy session, wanting more closeness between them to evolve. Cheryl, defensive, maintained that her relationship with her daughter was "fine." She described Beth as "never satisfied, like her father. They both always wanted more from me, not like Ben."

Cheryl was less guarded when talking about her own parents. She stated emphatically that her mother dominated everyone in the family, especially her father. She lamented the fact that she did not know him better. She blamed her mother, characterizing her as overbearing. The desire for a closer relationship with Papa lingered throughout Cheryl's life. In marrying Matt, she married a man less hidden, more forthcoming, and more engaging than her father. Ultimately, this generated feelings of significant discomfort, as she felt ill prepared to engage with a man who wanted interaction. Cheryl felt angry with Matt, just as she felt angry with her mother, experiencing him as overbearing, like her mother. Cheryl admitted she would have been more comfortable if she had married a man more like her father.

Path to Healing

In Cheryl's marriage, she unconsciously acted out her confused feelings about men, a reflection of her troubled relationship with her father. On the one hand, she longed to know her father, to be involved with him. So she married a man who was engaging, a man whom she could know. In marrying him, she probably unconsciously fantasized that he would satisfy her need to have more involvement with her father. On the other hand, she preferred her father's isolation, mirroring his behavior in her marriage. Cheryl's illness allowed her to behave as she was most comfortable, disengaged, so she pressured Matt into an active relationship with Beth. Matt grew to look to Beth for social companionship, and Beth to him. While Matt and Beth continued to turn to Cheryl for companionship, she remained as removed as her father had been from her.

Cheryl's illness forced into play family patterns that accommodated her personality, patterns that became woven into the family fiber. During the earlier years of her illness, she retreated from interactions that were not essential. At about this time, Beth was going through the developmental stage in which children work to resolve their Oedipal struggles. The dynamics and needs of the family required Beth to act as her mother's stand-in, which was a profoundly confusing experience for a child at this developmental stage. Beth grew up gloating, believing that she had, in fact, taken care of her mother and that her mother had contributed little to raising her.

Beth and Matt grew increasingly comfortable with each other, experiencing comfort that was absent from their relationships with Cheryl. Beth saw herself as closer to her father than her mother was. She believed she had won the ultimate competitive struggle, the struggle for her father's heart. Beth grew up feeling powerful.

The stress of her parents' relationship with each other and the requirements flowing from her mother's illness influenced Beth's personality development. Beth's hard wiring, resembling her father's, also impacted her maturation. In her, Matt saw himself. Beth looked like him and interacted with people as he did, warmly and enthusiastically. When participating in Beth's therapy, Cheryl commented that Beth was just like her father: her feelings were easily hurt, as his had been. Both "always had to be with people. They just couldn't amuse themselves," she said critically, comparing them to her son Ben and herself, who could.

Beth healed in the course of her therapy. Her health improved and her relationships with her husband and children became more satisfying:

- Beth developed more compassion for her mother. She appreciated Cheryl's experience of growing up dominated by one parent and overlooked by the other. Beth's anguish at not having felt her mother's love was mitigated as she accepted Cheryl's inadequacies as a function of her anxieties, not as cruelty.

- Beth learned to love her father as a mortal, not an idol. She grew to hold him responsible for some of the difficulties in his marriage, rather than blaming everything on her mother. Beth learned to appreciate her father's discomfort in her presence as her appearance became more sexual; Beth came to understand his need for her to dress conservatively to help him repress his discomfort in the presence of his sexual daughter.

- Beth accepted more fully her role in the family drama. As a player in the infamous triangle, she accepted that her rigid belief that her mother was "bad" and her father was "good" had added to the tension in the home. Accepting her role permitted her to give up the guilt and the shame she carried in believing she had displaced her mother.

- Beth grew to accept her parents as people with strengths and weaknesses. This permitted her to better accept herself with her own strengths and weaknesses.

- Beth's health improved markedly. Her stomach problems ceased as she lived with greater self-acceptance and less tension and anxiety.

- Beth's marriage grew stronger. No longer unconsciously plagued by feelings related to the complexities of her relationship with her mother and father, Beth made room for a more vibrant relationship with her husband. She grew more comfortable with the intimacy of her marriage.

- Beth's relationship with her children became more playful. In exploring her family history, Beth realized that at a young age, she was burdened with adultlike responsibilities. Her therapy permitted her to relax and play with her children.

REWARDS AND SCARS OF FATHER'S FAVORITE DAUGHTER

Teri and Beth are two women who grew up as the apple of their father's eye. As children, both reveled in the position of unquestionably being their father's favorite child. As favorite children, these young women were rescued from greater injury emanating from the destructiveness of their relationships with their mothers. Identifying with their fathers, Teri and Beth emerged from childhood with skills required for professional success, Teri as an artist and Beth as a physician. The confidence and power they gained from their favored relationships with their fathers—similar to the confidence and power gained by John, described in chapter 7—were character traits essential to climbing the professional ladders in their chosen fields.

The repercussions of their mothers' absences were also profound. Teri and Beth grew up without the psychological safety provided by the healthy presence of a mother and a father, which allows daughters to work out their sexual feelings in a safe environment. Without their mothers' support, Teri and Beth struggled with their identities as women:

- They lacked role models to emulate. Neither Teri nor Beth was comfortable with her femininity. Caroline functioned as a surrogate for Teri, but that relationship had its own complexities, and it did not survive Marcus's death. Beth's discomfort with her body was reflected in her confusion regarding clothing, and whether or not it should conceal her sexuality.

- They were confused about their inappropriate attachments to their fathers. As adults, both Teri and Beth transferred their discomfort with their fathers onto their partners. Teri would cohabit but was frightened of committing herself to marriage. Beth felt comfortable in her marriage as long as it functioned as a business arrangement.

- Their career choices may have reflected their unsettled relationships with their mothers. As an artist, Teri described her style as "an abstract representation of how [she] wanted the world to be." Beth speculated that choosing to be a physician reflected her ambivalence toward her mother: as a doctor, she could be close to her mother in taking care of her.

Overall, the quality of Teri's life suffered more than Beth's. Teri was lonely and her career did not flourish in a manner commensurate with her skills. She turned to food and alcohol to soothe herself. Beth, in contrast, was not incapacitated by loneliness and her career thrived. She married a man willing to tolerate her shortcomings as his partner and the mother of their children, and he encouraged her growth. While Teri's addictions became a severe handicap, Beth's foibles did not.

Both women grew up with the advantage of having been their fathers' favorite daughters. Why the dramatic difference in the quality of their lives? First, as an infant, Teri lived with maternal deprivation, and Beth did not. Teri's deprivation impeded the healthy functioning of her brain. As examined in chapter 7, this deficiency probably contributes to children's distrust of others. (See "The Brain: Negotiator between Our Inner and Outer Worlds"). Thus, throughout her life, Teri had difficulty committing to associations that would have fostered her growth. When I met Teri, as an adult, she was continuing to shy away from relationships that could have contributed to her healing. Beth, in contrast, was not rejected during infancy by her mother. Beth matured from a more stable emotional foundation than Teri's.

Second, Teri's mother and father made no obvious attempts to resolve their issues respectfully while Beth's parents did make such attempts. Teri's father rescued her from loneliness and used her to further his agenda. Through her, he brought cruelty into the house, as in the Christmas morning display. He also engaged Teri in two father/mother/daughter triangles, one with his wife and the other with his lover. While Teri won the struggle with her mother, she lost the one with Caroline. Teri was alternately happy and sad with regard to both her victories and her defeats. She appreciated the fact that her father saved her from the ramifications of her mother's profound neglect while feeling rage at his use of her as an instrument of cruelty in the family. Teri lived with confusion that felt like torture at times.

In contrast, Beth grew up in a family where her parents struggled with their differences. While Beth's father looked to her as a companion, he did not use her blatantly to hurt his wife. In fact, he fought to have more time with his wife. This factor—his not using his daughter to further an agenda with his wife—is crucial to appreciating why Beth's adult life was less challenged than Teri's. Matt, Beth's father, worked actively to avoid filling the emotional void he felt in his marriage with the attachment he felt for his daughter.

Beth's parents, with all their shortcomings, provided Beth with an emotional foundation that offered her opportunities for a life that was more satisfying than the life provided by Teri's parents.

FATHERS' FAVORITE DAUGHTERS

The issues posed for Teri and Beth by their relationships with their fathers mirror those common to daughters who have grown up as the father's favorite. Believing themselves to have won the Oedipal struggle, their sense of power in the world is distorted. Discomfort in the father/mother/daughter triangle undermines the depth of their intimate relationships.

CHAPTER NINE
MOTHER'S FAVORITE SON

My father died when I was six. I have three older sisters but being the only male, Mother told me it was my job to protect her and my sisters. She proclaimed me "man of the house." I loved the position. She praised me all the time. Anything I wanted I got. I felt bad that she was critical of my sisters, but not that bad.

—Ed's reflections

Ed, a White House Fellow, accompanied his wife, Marion, to her psychotherapy session. Marion, a respected chief of staff for a senator, described her marriage as "frustrating" and at the breaking point. She complained that Ed drank after she went to bed at night and lied to her about it. She objected to his lying, not his drinking, and was furious that he agreed to all her requests but never came through on them.

"I ask you to pick up my dress at the cleaners. You say 'Sure,' kiss me on the cheek and then come home without my dress," she complained.

"My meeting lasted longer than expected. By the time I got to the cleaners, it was closed," he said.

"You *never* follow through. I can't trust you to do anything you promise," Marion said, gritting her teeth.

Calmly, Ed attempted to elaborate his good intentions.

Marion cut him off, her exasperation intensifying. "You don't get it," she shouted. "I can't live any longer with your deceit."

Struggling to stay calm in the face of her attack, Ed defended his integrity.

"Deceit?! I can't believe you're making such a big deal about the cleaners. Your closet is filled with . . ."

"I wish you would just tell me the truth," Marion exploded, throwing up her hands. "If you can't do something that I ask, tell me. If you think my demands outrageous, tell me. Don't agree and then not follow through."

Ed shifted uncomfortably in his seat and began tapping his foot.

Crying, Marion stammered, "I am so angry with you for letting me down *and* for making me feel so bad about myself . . . like I am a demanding bitch."

The pace of Ed's tapping increased. He grimaced as his eyes fixated on the clock.

Marion pleaded for Ed to be honest. "If you turn me down, I may be furious but at least we have a starting point."

ED'S STORY

Telling the truth may be a simple request for many people, but not for Ed. As his mother's favorite son, Ed finessed the art of telling women what they wanted to hear, convincing himself, and often them, of his exquisite caring. He then proceeded on his preplanned course and ignored his commitment. In my first session with Ed and Marion, the texture of their relationship surfaced immediately as they described their fight of the previous evening:

Marion felt sick and Ed encouraged her to go directly home to get the rest she needed. He committed himself to bringing home their dinner. This was Marion's wish: to be seen, acknowledged, and cared for. But Ed not only arrived home late; he brought no food.

Marion was not swayed by his excuses, his claim of a last minute crisis at work and of his overwhelming concern for her. Her rage at his tardiness and the growling of her empty stomach provoked an expression of unfettered emotion that she had contained for many years. "If you were so worried about me, then why were you so much later than usual?" she demanded.

Ed absorbed the reprimand. "You're right," he replied flatly.

"I don't care about being right. I don't get why, if you were so worried about me, you arrived late and without dinner," Marion continued with intensity.

During the ensuing discussion, Ed alternatively apologized and withdrew. He felt misunderstood. He tried harder and harder to explain himself, to justify his behavior.

He searched for the "perfect" word that would elicit Marion's understanding. The strategy did not work.

Marion became increasingly agitated. She, too, felt misunderstood. She was not interested in discussing the specific transgression of the evening before. The repetitive pattern of their marriage disturbed her: Ed's holding out the carrot of caring but not following through. He always justified his behavior with a spin.

Frightened by the possible demise of his marriage, accentuated by an intensity he had never before witnessed in Marion, Ed followed this initial visit with a consultation to consider individual psychotherapy for himself. After a couple of consultations, he committed to ongoing therapy for himself. This, enhanced by couples psychotherapy and sessions with his mother, accelerated the growth of his self-awareness. Therapy motivated him to prod his mother and older sisters into sharing stories and memories about the past, especially about the father who was unknown to him.

Mother's Favorite Son

Ed was not only his mother's favorite son; he was his mother's favorite child.

After giving birth to two daughters, Ed's mother Sarah desired more than anything to give her husband a son. Finally Ed Jr. was born. Sarah recollected feeling unprecedented joy at his birth, knowing that she had given her husband, "a gift that no one else could. A son. A namesake." "I felt something special with you that I didn't feel with any of the others," Sarah reminisced, "I wanted to call you 'Ed Junior' but your father said 'no.' He wanted you to have your own name. We agreed on 'Ed.'" This resulted in three generations of men who shared names: Edward Senior, Edward, and Ed.

Six years later, Ed's father died of a heart attack while at work. Ed recounted his memories of the funeral. "I was old enough to grasp that something major happened but really didn't get it. Mother was a mess. I had never seen anyone cry so much or so loud. She clutched my hand and wouldn't let it go. People asked her if she was okay and she'd say, 'As long as Ed is at my side. He's the man of the house now.' And as man of the house, at my father's funeral, I was given my first beer."

Ed's mother expected him to fill his father's enormous shoes. He succeeded in making his mother feel important through his successes in the world and his expressions of love for her. Academic excellence led Ed to Amherst, where he graduated with honors, and then to Duke, where he served on the law review. At home he catered to his mother's wishes, sensing and responding to her most subtle attitude changes. "Mom, are you okay?" were words his sisters, and now his wife, associated with Ed.

The relationship between Ed and his mother was mutually beneficial. Sarah's attention and approval fostered Ed's academic and intellectual skills. As Ed excelled, he kept his mother at the center of his world. Sarah—a single parent with no college degree—felt unmitigated pride.

Stemming from her need to believe Ed "perfect," Sarah often overlooked her son's destructive behaviors. At ten, he began drinking beer regularly, but Sarah was oblivious of this. When Ed was in middle school and high school, she ignored the evidence of wild after-school parties held at home while she was at work. In exchange for being the son that Sarah needed him to be, Ed was rewarded—he got his own way, without any consequences. Believing that he walked on water, he grew up expecting no less.

Ed's relationship with his mother hindered her emotional well-being. Ed, the recipient of her idealized memories of her husband, remained the focus of her life. Sarah's attachment to memories and illusions of her deceased husband was so intense that she psychologically stagnated from the time of his death. Her fantasies of what would be pleasing to Edward steered her choices. Sarah's lack of interest in developing healthy relationships with other adult men only served to leave her lonelier.

Sarah's parenting skills faltered. All three of her children suffered. Sarah's preoccupation with Ed gave him a false impression of his importance. She neglected her two daughters. As adults, one of Ed's sisters lamented to him, "When Dad died, it was awful, but I didn't realize then that I had lost both parents. Mom was never the same." She continued: "When you were born, we all loved having a baby brother. But after Dad died, it was too much. You were too important. I often wonder if you were *always* that important to Mom and it was Dad's influence that diluted your importance; or if after Dad died, Mom elevated you. Male attention is very important to Mom."

Ed's relationship with both men and women suffered. His mother was so important that he believed his relationship with men to be inconsequential. Lacking athletic abilities, he did not benefit from the camaraderie of being on a team or having the guidance of a coach. Rather, he associated the idea of men with his humiliation at being the last chosen for a team in physical education class. In contrast, his success in chess, an individual and intellectual sport, comforted him and reinforced his ease in limited male interactions.

His relationships with women were difficult. Ed grew up believing that if he told women what they wanted to hear, he would be adored whether or not he actually followed through on his promises. His sisters, colluding with his mother on Ed's importance in the family, seldom confronted him with his meaningless promises. One of his sisters treated him as his mother did: accepting what he said, never challenging him, adoring him regardless of his behaviors. He, in turn, showered them with empty words of love. His other sister, the rebel of the family, despised him, keeping distant. In her adult life, she continued to refuse contact with him.

Sarah's consistent focus on Ed hindered her daughters' development. In spite of their keen intellects, neither of Ed's sisters attended college. His older sister, who had the clearest and most loving memories of their father, married soon after high school graduation and lived ten miles from their mother. This sister remained totally devoted to her alcoholic husband. His other sister became pregnant during her senior year in high school. The day after her graduation, she moved thousands of miles from home, and since then has had little contact with the family and no contact with Ed.

In Dad's Footsteps

Dead or alive, Ed's father, Edward, affected the lives of his three children and his wife. Edward, in fact, had been his mother's favorite child. According to Sarah, the community snickered at her mother-in-law's indulgence of Edward. Edward and his older brother David were opposites: Edward was social whereas David was a loner. Edward adored his doting mother while David's attachment was to the family's maid. Edward took on challenges while David seemed frightened of the world, hiding or playing it safe. Both sons attended boarding school, where Edward thrived and David became even more isolated. Sarah reported that the family described her husband's brother as "depressed" and "strange."

She recalled her mother-in-law, Caroline, lighting up when Edward walked into the room. Even when Edward was an adult, Caroline talked incessantly about his prep school and college accomplishments—his grades, his position as a class officer, his tennis victories, job offers, and invitations to exclusive gatherings. Edward was the apple of his mother's eye, her favorite child showered with special privileges.

Stories of her visiting him at prep school recalled conversations at home and in the community: Caroline brought cartons of his favorite foods and, if challenged by the headmaster, she reminded him of the buildings on campus named for family members.

Caroline paraded Edward and many of his classmates into popular restaurants, demanding to be seated at tables immediately, regardless of the wait endured by others. Seldom did she miss one of Edward's tennis tournaments, and she always indulged his team after matches with special ice cream flown on dry ice from Boston or cookies from Edward's favorite bakery in New York. If Edward and his friends wanted to go skiing for the weekend, a driver was sent to take them. Sarah noted that "the absence of my father-in-law and brother-in-law in family stories chilled me to the bone."

When reminiscing about Edward, their father, Ed's oldest sister, who was a teenager when their father died, recalled him as easy-going except when anyone mentioned his own father, Edward Senior. "There was an unspoken rule—never, ever mention his name. If anyone slipped, our usually mild-mannered father erupted like a volcano," she recalled.

Sarah speculated, "My husband longed for his father's attention and love. When Edward died, he was an unhappy man. I sometimes think he died of a broken heart. For all his achievements, he never accomplished what he most wanted, his father's love and affections."

According to Sarah, Edward fell in love with her the first time he laid eyes on her. Her smile and sparkling eyes captivated him. To Edward's family this young, sexy receptionist who wore tight skirts, high heels, and "too much makeup" was no match for the handsome, wealthy, Harvard-educated Brahmin. Regardless of their dramatically different backgrounds, they married. They lived close to Edward's parents, in the neighborhood inhabited by his well-connected childhood friends.

After the wedding, Caroline continued to hover over her son, remaining enmeshed in his life. Having heard that Sarah, the young bride, had purchased the ingredients to make stew, "his favorite," for dinner, Caroline rushed to their home with stew, "his favorite preparation," made by the family cook. It was unlikely that any woman would have been good enough for Edward in the eyes of Ed's grandmother, and Sarah, a high school graduate of pedestrian breeding, missed the mark totally.

Ed remembered his mother's recounting the pain she suffered from the daily jabs inflicted by her mother-in-law. Her husband's feverish attempts to reassure her were unsuccessful. Edward explained that Caroline's nasty intrusions were expressions of her pain at having been displaced by his marriage to Sarah. This left his mother to a lonely, empty existence. After ten years of attempting to mitigate the tension between his wife and his mother, Edward gave up. He changed the scenario and left New England—his mother and a secure future—and moved his wife and young daughters to Georgia to establish a new life.

The story, with all its romance, came to an abrupt stop, however.

The courageous husband, who had rescued the love of his life from the claws of his mother, died of a heart attack. Seven years after the move, Ed's mother became a single parent to three daughters and a son. Edward, idealized by his mother in his life, was idealized by his widow in his death. Shocked and alone, Sarah anchored herself with obsessive thoughts about her deceased husband. Without him, she had no partner to challenge her special treatment of Ed. Unknowingly, she cultivated a relationship with Ed that emotionally mirrored and replicated the relationship between her mother-in-law and Edward.

Repeating Family History

The story of Ed and his family, of both past and present generations, once again illustrates Carl Whitaker's philosophy, as explored earlier: without a focused and determined intervention, family history repeats itself.

First, Edward did not resolve the complicated feelings generated by his relationship with his mother. He acted out these feelings by unconsciously selecting a marital partner who evoked issues similar to those stimulated by his mother. In marrying Sarah, he perpetuated his issues.

People commonly select marriage partners who unconsciously help them unravel disquieting issues with the parent who emotionally dominated their lives. Edward's mother loomed large in his life. Her looming presence was integral to his identity. In marrying Sarah, Edward may have been courting his mother's disapproval, hoping to create distance from her. Since that strategy did not work, he moved, leaving his home, work, and friends. While this move could have been prompted by the punishing tension expressed by Sarah, her unhappiness may have been only a pretext for the move: maybe the move was prompted by Edward's desire to cut the cord with his mother once and for all.

Characterizing the move as grounded in Sarah's interests, and not his, permitted Edward to perpetuate his image as a man who unselfishly met the needs of women close to him, while he, at the same time, concealed his self-interest. Lacking psychological intervention, as recommended by Whitaker, to help Edward resolve his issues with his mother, Edward tried to run away from her, in the first place by marrying Sarah and in the second place by moving to Georgia. Denying his personal motivation for moving pushed Edward deeper into his Shadow (as discussed in chapter 1).

Second, Ed grew up with an adoring mother and absent father, as had his father. Though she was contemptuous of her mother-in-law, who looked to her son to fill her emptiness, Sarah replicated Caroline's behavior in looking to Ed to fill her void. Neither woman saw her son for who he was; instead, each saw her son for what she needed him to be. Consequently, both sons grew up estranged from themselves, motivated to meet their mothers' needs in exchange for the status of favorite son. (See chapters 4 and 6.)

Both Edward Sr. and Edward were absent from the lives of their wives as well as the lives of their sons. Though the reasons differed, in one case because of a lack of interest and in the other case because of death, the repercussions were similar: Edward and Ed grew up without the assistance of adult men to help them navigate the complicated terrain of the mother/son relationship. (See chapter 4.)

Sarah's conjecture that her husband Edward died "of a broken heart" may have some veracity to it, but the problem was not necessarily rooted only in his relationship with his father. Edward's broken heart could have resulted from unexpressed rage directed at both his mother and father, his mother for permitting him so little space to live his own life and his father for having left him alone to deal with his mother's inappropriate behavior.

Edward lived his life accepting the family dance. He buried uneasy feelings deep in his Shadow. Living with the continued stress of a mother who was too close and of a father who was too distant may have contributed to Edward's premature and sudden death. The human body is not meant to live under prolonged stress. A return to a state of calm, or homeostasis, is required for the body to heal itself. Without such a reprieve, people are more vulnerable to premature aging and death.

Unlike his father, Ed married a woman unwilling to perpetuate the family dance. Marion was driven to break out of her role, maybe replicating ambitions felt but unattained by Edward. When confronted by Marion, Ed panicked, which reflected his unease in modifying his role in this multigeneration family dance. He was dubious about his ability to play a different role and resorted to his old standby: alcohol. Other than telling Marion what he thought she wanted to hear, he did not know how to behave.

Third, Ed replicated his father's dance with women. In return for behaving in ways that appeared loving, his father expected women to adore him, using skills that he perfected as the favorite son and that were reenacted in his marriage. Ed learned these skills as a young boy observing his father's treatment of his mother. These behaviors were further perfected in his role as his mother's favorite son.

Ed treated Marion, his wife, as he treated his mother. He told her what he thought she wanted to hear. In return, he expected she would adore him as his mother had. When Marion attached behavioral expectations to the praise, Ed faltered—the world known to him was threatened. His behavioral repertoire with women was so limited that he did not know how to act. With hindsight, Ed acknowledged that Marion's ultimatum—change or divorce—made him anxious. He developed sleep problems and his drinking increased.

In summary, the power of the reenactment of this family history is grasped in acknowledging the similarities between Caroline, Edward's mother, and Sarah, Edward's wife. These two women were not genetically related; nor did one grow up influenced by the other. Yet they responded similarly to emotional loneliness, by attaching themselves to their favored sons. Their relationships with their sons focused on serving their own needs, not their sons' best interests.

These women were locked into a competitive struggle, each wanting to prove she loved Edward the most. Both were oblivious to the difference between a mother's love and that of a wife. As much as Sarah hated Caroline's attachment to Edward, she replicated that relationship with her son Ed, perpetuating the family drama.

Ed, throughout his therapy, was curious about his family legacy. He came to appreciate more fully the dynamics with his wife, which helped him begin his journey of psychological healing. Learning to tell her the truth, as she demanded, was challenging. First, Ed had to become more comfortable with what he wanted for himself. This necessitated total abstinence from alcohol. Then, Ed had to learn he would be safe in the world without putting forth the appearance that his primary mission in life was to please his wife. After Ed learned to argue openly with his wife, not in the underhanded style he had mastered with his mother, he learned to trust the power of honesty.

MOTHERS AND SONS

Relationships between mothers and sons stimulate fantasies. Writers from Sophocles (*Oedipus*) through Shakespeare (*Coriolanus*) to Mike Nichols (*The Graduate*) and David Chase (*The Sopranos*) have tantalized viewers with erotic mother/son stories.

"Oedipal," is the Freudian term while "Mama's boy" is its street spin. It is commonly known that Oedipus killed his father and married his mother, and that Freud believed young boys wanted to sleep with their mothers.

The first sexy woman known to a young boy is his mother. As an infant, he is sexually aroused by her presence, and this arousal is as normal as other bodily functions. As children grow older and become more aware, their infantile sexual expressions become suppressed. The mental health of mothers and fathers, as well as the relationship between parents, impacts profoundly on children's feelings about their own sexuality and those for their mother. Children learn that to have sexual feelings is normal and different from enacting those feelings.

A son's worst nightmare is sleeping with his mother. A son's greatest wish is being surrounded by parents who love and trust one another. Boundaries secured by such parents provide the naturally inquisitive child with the safety that is necessary to develop healthy sexual feelings for himself and for the opposite-sex parent. The child learns through observing his parents that sexual feelings are normal, that the love between a husband and wife differs from that between mother and son.

Parents working cooperatively, agreeing and disagreeing, foster the child's healthy psychological growth. As described previously, Edward challenged his wife's desire to call their son "Edward Junior," as he believed that calling him "Ed" would be in their son's best interest.

Absent the presence of an engaged father or father figure, a mother's favorite son can develop an overinflated sense of himself in the world. He can grow up believing that if he can replace his father as his mother's intimate, he can successfully take on any challenge, getting anything he wants. This son feels enormously entitled and develops a false sense of power.

Fathers' presence in families affects the resolution of intimate feelings existing between mothers and sons. This, in turn, impacts the mental health of sons. Edward Senior's emotional absence from his family overshadowed his physical presence. The bond that developed between Caroline and Edward was inappropriate, and proved tragic.

Like his father, Ed grew up without the advantages of having two parents present in his life. But, unlike Edward, Ed benefited from his father's involvement until he was six years old. This engagement may have provided Ed with the emotional foundation required for him to resolve successfully the interpersonal struggles that were hampering his adulthood. Ed did not have to run away from home to salvage his independence, as did his father.

Ed's story, the son of a deceased father and an omnipresent mother, exemplifies the mother/son dynamics that can evolve when fathers are absent from the home. But it is Edward's story that captures the more common mother/father/son scenario—family relationships influenced by fathers who are emotionally detached though physically present. Edward's ploys—using work and time with friends—to distance himself from family involvement are commonplace.

In my practice, I hear many stories like that of Ed's father, Edward, stories of detached fathers. Some fathers distance themselves through working long hours, others through spectator sports, drinking, affairs, or travel. Some marriages reflect the belief that husbands financially support the family and leave child rearing to their wives. Ethnic backgrounds can also promote particular family patterns that minimize fathers' direct contact with their children while magnifying the role of mothers.

For example, Jewish families may reflect the tradition in which oldest sons are most valued. Historically, men studied the Torah, leaving child rearing to the women. Strong attachments between mothers and their oldest sons evolved. While these historical antecedents are long forgotten, the cherished position of the oldest son commonly continues. A client reported the following story:

> My brother, a doctor, arranged to have Mother moved to a nursing home in his community so that he could better follow her care. She broke a hip and required surgery. He decided not to go to the hospital during the operation. He said he was too busy.
>
> I lived a thousand miles away, worked full-time and had an infant. It was unfathomable to me that our mother, suffering from dementia and with heart problems, be alone during the process of surgery. So I went.
>
> I arrived at the hospital about thirty minutes before she was taken in to surgery. "Mother," I said. "This is Cathy. I will be here when you awake from your surgery. I love you."
>
> Mother did not respond. There was no recognition of my presence.
>
> As the nurses rolled her bed from the room, the phone rang. It was my brother. "No, Andy," I said. "They have already taken Mother to surgery." Mother, who was in the hall, sat up and said to the nurses, "Take me back. That is my son on the phone. I want to talk to him."

The relationship between mothers and sons can be so powerful that it can subconsciously ignite erotic feeling between them. A healthy resolution of these unconscious feelings is enabled by the active involvement of a trusted husband and respected father. The presence of this adult male conveys to his son, "I am here. I am the partner to this woman whom you love. You can love her as a mother. I love her as my wife." In a father's presence, the son can experience the security required to resolve his sexual feelings for his mother and mature appropriately.

If fathers are absent, either literally or psychologically, and sons are left to mediate their own complex sexual feelings, they may be uncertain regarding the appropriateness of feelings for their mothers, the objects of their love. If their mothers are lonely and crave male attention, they may invite inappropriate attention from their sons. When mothers behave this way, they may exploit their sons' normal developmental processes, colluding with their fantasies. The stories of Edward and Ed capture this dynamic.

The relationships between mothers and favorite sons are often complicated. Some mothers aspire to make statements to their own fathers through their sons, as we saw with Sara Roosevelt, mother of Franklin. It was important to Sara to have a son who would make her father proud of her, and in fact, she seemed more devoted to her son than to her husband.

Other mothers aspire to have loving associations with their fathers or father figures stimulated by their cherished sons. This was illustrated in James's story, told in chapter 6, and may also have contributed to the relationship between Scooter Libby and his mother. My mother-in-law, always attached to her grandfather, lost her own father when she was a young adolescent. Her parents divorced; her father moved across the country, and apparently, Janis never had contact with him again. At the time of her parents' divorce, Janis, her sister, and her mother moved back to Janis's beloved grandfather's home. When my mother-in-law married my father-in-law, she married a man who was neither warm nor demonstrative, maybe mirroring the distance she felt from her own father. Scooter, as a young adult, physically resembled my mother-in-law's loving grandfather, the one embracing, gentle male figure in her life. Most likely, this strong resemblance further reinforced Scooter's favorite son status. (See chapter 1.)

Mothers' favorite sons grow up feeling powerful, especially if their life experiences support their fantasies of replacing their fathers in their mothers' hearts. These sons expect the world to be as adoring of them as their mothers were, and they struggle to understand why the love of their wives and lovers may not be as encompassing. As mothers' favorite sons navigate the world, they are usually ill prepared for unexpected, often troubling, consequences.

CHAPTER TEN
MOTHER'S FAVORITE DAUGHTER

Look at me. I'm fifty years old, pre-diabetic, overweight, and can't lose an ounce. I've never been married. My claim to fame—my mother depends on me. Growing up, my brothers and sisters were jealous of me. Now, I don't think any of them would trade places with me, and I don't blame them.

—Faith's reflection

Faith's succinct summary typifies the experiences of some favorite daughters of mothers. They begin life in an esteemed position, which transforms into hardship over time. Once the envy of their siblings, these favorite children, as adults, often become the symbol of dread. The burdens of lifelong attachments to their mothers become obvious in adulthood when ill health, addictions, or stressful relationships replace the childhood pleasures that accompanied favored child status. The emotional costs of not having been mothered, but mothering mother instead, become apparent.

DEVELOPMENTAL DELAYS

The developmental milestones of mothers' favorite daughters are often compromised. These children, busy functioning as mothers' caretakers, are robbed of important childhood experiences that are necessary for their psychological and intellectual growth, such as playing with friends and pushing the boundaries of acceptable behavior. They suffer the consequences of inadequate mothering, growing up without being able to trust an adult to take care of their emotional needs.

Inadequate Mothering

Mothers' favorite daughters typically mother their mothers. These daughters deceive themselves with the erroneous belief that they do not require mothering. They grow up believing they mother themselves better than anyone else could. Their arrogance is protected behind a thick veneer, conveying to the world an attitude of "I know best."

Trisha, the daughter of a U.S. senator, explained: "I first realized I was mothering myself at about six or seven. My dad was on the campaign trail and my mother sick. I didn't want to leave her side and she didn't want me to. If she needed anything, I made sure she got it. I felt like the responsible adult in the house, not a kid."

"I just did my thing," Trisha continued, "making my own decisions, taking care of myself. I never asked for much or needed much. There were people in the house to give me meals, get me to school, and drive me wherever I needed to go. I felt like I was my own parent, bringing myself up. I believed I took better care of myself than anyone else could. I felt like hot stuff."

Henrietta echoed Trisha's sentiments: "I never thought I needed anybody. My mother was sick for so many years, and I was the oldest daughter. I did all the cooking and shopping, looked after my brother and sister, and most of all, was at my mother's beck and call. I never imagined anyone looking after me. I didn't want or need anything from anyone. I became a master at providing for myself."

The apparent role reversal between mothers' favorite daughters and their mothers impeded the emotional growth of these young women. Their ability to take the risks necessary for growth was restricted; they were confined to small safe harbors they created for themselves. They grew up without the encouragement of mothers to broaden their horizons and expand their worlds. These women grew up believing they could do it all, knew it all, and needed no one.

In truth, their worlds were limited to what they *could* do. They did not have the security they needed, which emerges from healthy mothering. They did not have the requisite skills, learned from play, to challenge their boundaries, expand their worlds, and push them to tackle new experiences beyond those with which they were comfortable. Their worlds did not expand; rather they remained confined to what these women were comfortable managing.

Mother/Child Attachment

Mothers are familiar with having to weigh their needs against those of their children. This tension begins during pregnancy when mothers ponder giving up old habits, such as smoking or drinking, in the interests of their unborn children.

When the umbilical cord is cut, physical separation is imposed on mother and child. At this moment, a complicated process begins, a process in which two people forge identities that are separate and distinct from one another. This process lasts throughout the child's life, changing with the child's age and developmental issues. Mothers of toddlers struggle with letting their children be independent and go down the slide unattended. Mothers of school-age children have difficulty remembering that the successful completion of homework is their children's responsibility, not theirs. As children grow older, issues regarding their emerging identities become more complicated. Children focus more on friends and fight with their parents about curfews, attire, smoking, drinking, and driving.

The mother/child experience of establishing separate boundaries is complex. Psychologists, physicians, and researchers from varied disciplines devote their careers to exploring this complicated process. In general, there is consensus on important points:

- The process of mother/child separation occurs across species. Ducks push babies from nests, and humans introduce babies to the world outside of the home.

- When separation does not evolve, the well-being of mothers and babies is impeded. Some species of birds are known to kill the weak chick, the one having difficulty leaving the nest. For humans, a criterion for the diagnosis of numerous mental illnesses is an inappropriate attachment between mother and child—the cord seems never to have been severed.

- As separation between children and same-sex parents occurs, the dynamics differ from those between children and opposite-sex parents. This is exemplified in the discussion on the relevance of the Oedipal complex. (See chapter 7.)

- The process of separation between mothers and children is unending, taking place over a lifetime, and often influencing the mother/child relationships of subsequent generations.

For mothers' favorite daughters, the struggles to establish their identity as separate from that of their mothers are uniquely complex. These women are discouraged by their mothers from the natural process of growing and moving out into the world. As fetuses grow too large to survive in their mother's womb and, at birth, are forced into the bigger world of life, children grow too large for the world defined by their mother. To continue growing, children move into the world of friends and schools, establishing lives of their own, removed and separate from their mothers. The attachment between favored daughters and their mothers commonly impedes, but does not necessarily block, this natural movement.

Mothers, like magnets, attract their favorite daughters. Daughters experience the pull as hard, if not impossible, to resist. These daughters feel comfort and security in their attachment to their mothers, unaware of the extent to which their relationships with their mothers have hindered their psychological and intellectual growth. Trisha's and Henrietta's sentiments reflect those of mothers' favorite daughters—misguided confidence in their ability to function unimpeded in the world without having been mothered.

Play

Play is the work of childhood. It is essential to the growth of children. Through play, children develop their minds and bodies, expanding their worlds. They learn to get along with people inside and outside their families. Play, not caring for parents, is the work of childhood. Since some favorite daughters are busy caring for Mom, these daughters are commonly deprived of playtime. This deprivation is starkly noted when observing the spontaneity of children on playgrounds who are not burdened by being their mother's caretakers.

The importance of play for young children is evident when we watch toddlers and their mothers on playgrounds, which are among the first settings outside the home where children explore the world on their own:

Coming onto the playground, young children often hold their mothers' hands; mothers and children let go of one another as they immerse themselves in their own work. Mothers, knowing their children are safe within the confines of the playground, converse with other mothers; children sprint off to explore the world in front of them, which is their day's work. Children play for a while, then reconnect with their mothers, running over to them with a hug or a tug. If the attempt is "long distance," through a wave, eye contact, or a smile, and mothers do not respond, then toddlers generally come to their mothers to physically ensure their reconnection. Once secure, children return to their work of play, the world again safe to explore. On the playground we witness mothers providing their toddlers a safe harbor in which to take the risks necessary to grow.

This scene is replicated at a swimming pool where we witness parents in the water, hovering along the sides while coaxing their toddlers to jump into their arms. At first, children are skeptical: the expanse between where they stand and their parents wait seems enormous. With each jump, parents shout approval and children feel pride in their accomplishment. With successive jumps, parents move back, a tiny bit farther, and children accept encouragement to

Importance of Play

Play facilitates children's growth—mentally, physically, interpersonally, and cognitively.

First, play stimulates brain activity, fostering the establishment of permanent neurological connections. If neural structures are not increased, the potential of the human mind is limited. The brain is a developing organ and requires ongoing stimulation. Play, a form of food for the brain, is vital throughout life.[1]

Limited in their play, favorite daughters can be limited in their exposure to life experiences. As people get older, new neurological connections become harder to establish.

Second, play generally involves physical activity. Joan Packer Isenberg and Nancy Quisenberry, for the Association for Childhood Education International, observe that "as children vigorously and joyfully use their bodies in physical exercise, they simultaneously refine and develop skills that enable them to feel confident, secure, and self-assured."[2]

For young women, acceptance of their emerging bodies, essential to their development, is furthered through shared experiences with friends as they struggle with similar issues. Play, ranging from playing sports to other forms of exercise to shopping for funky clothes, helps young women feel better about themselves. These experiences can be dramatically limited for mothers' favorite daughters.

Third, play teaches people vital interpersonal skills. Through play, people learn to cooperate and compete, to compromise and take charge, and to express feelings acceptably.

When these important social skills develop in the context of a relationship with a mother rather than with contemporaries, favorite daughters learn more about getting along with adults than about getting along with peers, hindering these daughters from developing lives separate from their mothers.

Fourth, play fosters cognitive development. Through play, creative and factual intelligence grows. The organizational skills required for executing tasks develop. Memory is enhanced. The cognitive development of mothers' favorite daughters may be largely limited to learning either at home or in the more structured world of school.

make the jump. As the physical space between parents and children grows, so does children's confidence in themselves. Parents create a secure harbor, inviting their children to take chances and have new experiences.

Mothers' favorite daughters too often develop in a world without the psychological safety and encouragement given to children on the playground or in the swimming pool. Starting as toddlers, these daughters may have gone infrequently to the playground with their mothers, maybe because of mothers' ill health or their self-absorption. If they did go to the playground, these children were probably hovered over by their mothers, who may have feared their daughters' separation from them. Mothers who are insecure with themselves may fear that their physical or emotional limitations preclude their protecting or rescuing their daughters from harm. These daughters learn to stay close to their mothers, discouraged from pursuing their natural inclination to explore the world beyond that of their mothers.

Growing up without the safety or encouragement necessary to explore an expanding world, mothers' favorite daughters function in a small, contained world, one in which they can feel relatively safe. Venturing beyond these secure harbors, which they create for themselves, is uncharacteristic. The skills they develop to tackle life's more complicated problems are limited.

Once they are adults, having grown up with their mother as their best friend, these daughters characteristically find that their social worlds suffer because of their impoverished interpersonal skills. Trisha began psychotherapy out of a yearning for an intimate relationship. She craved a relationship where her partner would take care of her, where she would not have to do the caretaking in order to feel valued. Trisha's inability to permit another person to care for her and her inexperience in filling roles other than that of caretaker made the relationship she craved impossible.

Henrietta, also unable to sustain an intimate relationship because of dynamics similar to Trisha's, began therapy encouraged by her physician. He was concerned with her weight gain, believing it to be a mask for her depression. Henrietta worked as the general manager of a prominent hotel, utilizing the skills she had learned as her mother's caretaker. She found herself resenting everything asked of her by guests and turning to food to cloak her unhappiness.

To mother themselves, Trisha and Henrietta limited their worlds to what was safe and manageable. They shied away from new and potentially broadening experiences. The restricted worlds in which they grew up did not provide them with the exposure and resources they needed to live rich, full adult lives.

Work of Motherhood

From the moment of birth, children begin their journey of developing the physical, mental, social, and psychological tools required for living fulfilling, healthy, and independent lives. The work of motherhood is to teach children these skills and to support them in this process. To do this, mothers must often put aside their own anxieties and psychological needs in order to further their children's healthy development.

To ensure that decisions made are in the best interest of their children's growth, mothers must be capable of mediating their own needs. Mothers who turn to daughters to meet their needs do not foster their daughters' healthy independence. The consequences are profound for daughters whose mothers impede their emotional separation. The healthy growth of their emerging personalities is derailed. As mothers cling to their daughters, their daughters are robbed of the childhood experiences required for healthy maturity.

Mothers who look to their daughters to inappropriately fill their needs do so for differing reasons. Some mothers struggling with illness depend on their daughters, as did Trisha's mother. In large families, some mothers look to their oldest daughters for assistance with other children and household responsibilities, far in excess of what is reasonable. Other mothers, overlooked as children or living in barren marriages, expect daughters to fill their emotional emptiness. Frightened or insecure mothers may look to favored daughters for safety and security.

Mothers see themselves as responsible for nurturing their children. Some mothers, consciously or unconsciously, believe themselves incapable of fulfilling this role and unconsciously project these expectations onto their female children. The children, in turn, unconsciously accept the notion that they can nurture as their mothers cannot. Sometimes this may be true, as when mothers are ill. Regardless of the situation, these reversed roles, enacted over the lifetime of the mother/child relationship, deter these favorite daughters from healthy growth. Often this cycle, of mothers expecting daughters to nurture them, continues to breed emotional distress in subsequent generations.

The following are stories illuminating the journeys of three favorite daughters. Each story represents a different script: favorite daughter as mother's helper, as mother's mother, and as mother's nurse.

Zoe: Mother's Helper

At thirty, Zoe began to create emotional distance between herself and her mother. Zoe began psychotherapy, encouraged by her husband, Tom. He forcefully complained about the tension in their marriage generated by Zoe's mother's dependence on her. Though sensing the legitimacy of his complaint, Zoe could go no further. She could not accept her relationship with her mother as problematic.

Two years into her therapy, Zoe's motivation to struggle with reality increased. She was forced to choose between her six-year-old son and her mother. Having established an alliance with me, Zoe had in place a relationship with a woman whose concern was to meet Zoe's needs. Our relationship provided Zoe with the security and trust required to create emotional distance between her mother and herself.

The transformation was ignited when Tommy, Zoe's six-year-old son, broke several bones when riding a tricycle. He required hospitalization. Zoe's mother, Darlene, asked Zoe to leave Tommy in his father's care so that Zoe would be able to accompany Darlene to a doctor's appointment. Ignoring the five hundred miles between herself and Zoe, Darlene found it unacceptable for her two younger daughters to accompany her instead. Hating doctors, she pressured Zoe to accompany her, believing this favorite daughter was the only one who could "ask the doctor the right questions and understand his ramblings." Insisting that the appointment was made with consideration given to Zoe's schedule and that she had ample notice, Darlene's stubbornness and relentlessness struck Zoe as more child-like than that of her six-year-old, hospitalized child. Zoe did not acquiesce and stood by her decision to stay at her son's bedside.

Unlike prior encounters with her mother, this time, with my support and that of others in her psychotherapy group, Zoe resisted the easy option, that of hiding behind her husband, Tom, and blaming her unavailability on him. A salesman, he often traveled for work so Zoe freely represented him as unable to provide childcare, even

Stress and Illness

The autonomic nervous system (ANS), a regulatory branch of the central nervous system, balances the sympathetic and parasympathetic systems. The sympathetic system alerts our body to danger by activating its fight or flight reactions, responses that are necessary to protect the body. The parasympathetic system calms the body, directing the body to rest. The two systems work in concert, calling the body to action and to rest. When stimulated by stressful events, the body's elevated blood pressure, heart, and breathing rates indicate that the body is in "ready position" and energized to fight for its survival. If the sympathetic system remains dominant over the parasympathetic system for prolonged time periods and the body is deprived of rest, the body's immune system, overworked, becomes depressed, and the person becomes more vulnerable to illness.

Unexpected events, such as a poisonous snake sunning itself on a suburban driveway, arouse the sympathetic system. This system is also activated by experiences that we seek but whose outcome is unpredictable, such as ending or significantly altering an important relationship. As different as the unexpected encounter with the snake or the ending of a relationship may appear, our body's response to both of them is grounded in similar factors.

First, the more novel the experience, the less confident we are of surviving the experience. The body alerts us to this fear and anxiety through a racing heartbeat, cold sweats, and clammy palms. Zoe, accustomed to her familiar role as her mother's favorite daughter, did not know how she would survive not living out that role. Her body first expressed its anxiety through sleepless nights.

Second, the longer our bodies are on alert, the more stressed they become, ultimately resulting in illness. For some people, prolonged stress results in uncontrolled crying or nausea. Eventually, illnesses can result, sometimes in a form as when he could. Her mother's disregard for Tommy's hospitalization, or for the pressure felt by Zoe and Tom, generated feelings of rage. Zoe found Darlene's selfishness and self-absorption unbearable. Driven by anger, Zoe clearly told her mother that she *wanted* to stay with her son. She preferred Tommy to her mother.

During the ensuing year, Zoe struggled with a multitude of health issues. While she already lived with back pain, she now developed chronic stomach problems. Menstrual problems, intense headaches, and chest pains followed in rapid succession. Zoe

severe as a heart attack. Zoe developed chronic stomach problems, intense headaches, and chest pains.

Third, past experiences impact the body's response to stress. Success invites calm, and failure heightens anxiety. The response to a second encounter with a snake on the driveway is affected by the first experience: if the individual involved was bitten the first time, his fear is increased the second time, whereas a first response not resulting in injury may invite greater calm the second time.

Unknown psychological terrain generates high stress levels. Our security is heightened by the belief that we can control the world surrounding us. Knowing what to expect, we benefit from an established response pattern that emerges from experience. Modification of this system, even when desired, leads into foreign terrain and away from the calm of predictability.

Zoe's story shows that sometimes psychologically induced stress is unavoidable. Whether she acceded to her mother's demand or rejected it, Zoe would have been confronted with new experiences, directing her relationship with her mother down an unknown path, and thus generating stress. Her mother's request ignited Zoe's fury. If Zoe had agreed to the request, she would have had to manage rage, first directed at herself for setting aside her own feelings, and second, at her mother for her insistence. Had Zoe not expressed her rage outwardly, her body would have been stressed by the suppression of her feelings; had she expressed the rage, her body would have been stressed by the fear generated by the new experience.

Rejecting her mother's demand, as she did, also created stress: Zoe had never turned down a significant request made by her mother. In doing so, Zoe entered the unknown. Zoe could not anticipate her own reaction nor that of her mother.

rejected simplistic or episodic explanations for her illnesses. She located a physician practicing holistic medicine who collaborated with me. With our joint care, Zoe came to accept the relationship between her illnesses and the anxiety she felt at having set up boundaries with her mother. While she was confident in her decision to select her son over her mother, living with the reality of that decision created profound internal tension for Zoe.

Zoe unequivocally wanted to give up the role of the person her mother depended on, but to do so was complicated, generating a deluge of feelings. Zoe's life had been built around being her mother's caretaker, and, while Zoe knew her feelings were irrational, she feared that without this role her life would lose its meaning. She felt shaken by how quickly her sister grabbed the position and by how readily her mother accepted Zoe's replacement. While her mother seemed to have no difficulty replacing Zoe, Zoe struggled to live with the void created by her mother's absence. The stress of this experience contributed to her many illnesses.

When Zoe was a child, Darlene cared for the children at home while Zoe's father, Peter, financially supported the family. He spent evenings bowling and drinking with friends. Peter's involvement with the children was limited to spanking them when directed to do so by his wife, whom everyone affectionately referred to as "the Family General." Darlene spent her life raising children and going to church. Later in life, after her children left home and her father became ill, her father moved in with Darlene and Peter so that Darlene could care for him. Darlene recollected no warmth or companionship between her mother and father. Her mother's life routinely focused on people other than her father.

Zoe portrayed her parents as having two families. The first began prior to their marriage with a child conceived out of wedlock and three more children born about eighteen months apart. After a gap of five years came the second family of three children. Darlene characterized the first family, a daughter followed by three sons, as difficult, and the second, consisting of three daughters, as a breeze. When the first four children were born, money was scarce, life was challenging, as the family lived initially with Peter's parents and then in a tiny apartment. When the last three children were born, the family lived comfortably in their own home, and "You girls were just easy," her mother would say.

Peter Jr., the oldest boy and second child of the first family, held the position of mother's favorite son. Easy as a baby and then throughout his life, he made few demands on her. Unlike the other children, he seldom fought with siblings, acquiescing to their demands. This brother, sensitive to his mother's needs, sought her approval and brought her pride. Becoming a priest, he fulfilled her dream.

Zoe talked about her sister, Carol, the oldest child in the family:

> Even now, with Mom almost eighty and my sister in her sixties, they cannot be in the same room. They hate each other. Mom reminds Carol that when she was born, they had to live with Dad's parents, whom my mother hated. My grandparents wanted the first grandchild to be a grandson, and they let Mom know it. Mom still complains that as a baby, Carol cried all the time, giving Grandma something else to criticize. And, my sister, wow! She still whines whenever she is around Mom.
>
> Mom became pregnant with Carol before she and dad were married, even though Mom denies it. All my aunts remember Mom seventeen and pregnant, not eighteen as Mom insists. Mom was young and had dreams. But once she became pregnant, that was that. I think she holds Carol responsible for a life she didn't want.
>
> I was the first daughter of the second family. When I was born, it was different. The older ones were off at school. Mom didn't know what to do with herself so she had more kids. Apparently, I was the daughter she dreamt of—docile and easy. "It was love at first sight," Mom loved to tell me. I don't know why Mom had more children after me. She expected me to look after them, and I did. My sisters resented me. They wanted Mom, not me. They hated all the attention Mom gave me. Even as adults, they are jealous. When they tease me, they think they are funny but I feel the nastiness in their humor.

The effort required to maintain the position of favorite daughter increased when Zoe was ten. Her brother, Peter Jr., ten years older, left home for the seminary. With his departure, Mom lost companionship. Darlene looked to Zoe, her favorite daughter, to fill this void.

Zoe diminished her resentment of Mom's increased demands after Peter Jr. left home by telling herself that she was more special than he was. He was only their mother's companion but Zoe looked after the younger children, too. Increasingly, Darlene looked to Zoe as a confidante, as someone to depend on, as someone to help her make decisions. Often Darlene discussed inappropriate subjects, such as her unhappiness in her marriage, with Zoe.

By the time she became a teenager, Zoe saw herself as her mother's mother and grew proud of her ability to mother herself. Believing herself to be an adult, Zoe felt entitled to privileges the other children did not enjoy: fewer household responsibilities, a bigger allowance, and laxer discipline. Her favorite foods were likely to be served for dinner and her favorite cookies, Mallomars and graham crackers, filled the pantry.

In high school, she saw peers having fun that she did not have. Growing to resent her mother's attachment to her, Zoe developed a hidden life. Exploiting her freedom and feeling no accountability to any adult, she drank excessively and was sexually active. Her mother continued to indulge her, giving her large sums of money, not disciplining her or holding her accountable for her behaviors. These rewards paid for the alcohol, her ticket of admission to "fun" groups, and gave her the freedom to take part in the activities of these groups. Reflecting on those years, Zoe acknowledged the precariousness of her life, her decisions rooted in anger and her risky behavior accentuated by the fact that her parents did not hold her accountable.

In college, Zoe struggled with relationships. She lacked the skills, commonly learned through childhood play, to negotiate with her peers. Her belief that people needed her the way her mother had, and her arrogance in believing that she knew best, further alienated Zoe from her classmates. Zoe maintained emotional distance from people, not depending on anyone. Behaviors learned in her role as her mother's favorite daughter made friendships more difficult. Living away from home and without her mother's constant affirmation, Zoe was unhappy in her college years.

Tom, her first boyfriend after college, penetrated her defensiveness. She was important to him, and to Zoe, this felt natural. Yet allowing him to feel important to her felt more challenging. Zoe and Tom worked on their relationship and eventually married.

Humbled by life's emotional complexities, Zoe commented during a psychotherapy session: "I can't imagine how compromised my life would be if I hadn't met Tom. I'd never known a man as gentle and loving to be so interested in me. He patiently waited as I learned slowly to trust him. In doing what Mother wanted him to do, Pete lived his life as mama's boy. I was expected to remain at Mother's side, taking care of her. Without Tom, I would never, ever have had my own life."

After Zoe married and moved away, Darlene began fretting continuously about her health, a manipulation directed at keeping Zoe attached to her and interfering with Zoe's attachment to Tom. Zoe struggled with her allegiance as her mother insisted that Zoe was the only person capable of navigating the world of doctors and making decisions on treatment options. Initially, Darlene succeeded, and Zoe made many trips to oversee the treatment of her mother's illnesses. Now, energized by the need to be with her young, hospitalized child, enraged by her mother's selfishness, and supported by her husband, Zoe passionately told her mother, "No, I am not leaving my child for you." Zoe trusted her decision and felt pride in it.

Nonetheless, having chosen an unknown path, she spent sleepless nights, lost weight, and, as described previously, suffered numerous illnesses. Her body was screaming "anxiety," as she entered an unknown existence. Zoe knew how to care for her mother but not for herself, a skill she now had to develop.

Zoe modified her life by employing diverse tools. Her psychotherapy guided her to explore her relationship with her mother and helped her gather confidence in her ability to live life without the role of mother's favorite daughter. Meditation, yoga, and vigorous exercise offered her body outlets for her tension. Eventually, Zoe observed with relief that her sister had become mother's favorite daughter, and as such, her sister met their mother's demands for attachment. Physically, Zoe healed. Emotionally, she strengthened.

Faith: Mother's Mother

Faith, a brilliant graphic artist, sought treatment on the recommendation of her physician. After two years of trying one weight loss program after another, with her weight yo-yoing up and down, and with a bedside table overflowing with self-help weight loss books, Faith conceded that her issues were more complicated than just disciplining herself. Understanding the risks of carrying a hundred extra pounds on her short frame, Faith shed tears, expressing her fear, during her first psychotherapy session.

Mildred, Faith's mother, grew up in Appalachia. Mildred's father worked in the coal mines, came home for dinner, and retreated to the local tavern. He provided a steady income for his wife and two daughters, Dot, older by seven years, and Mildred. Stories related to Faith by her mother and aunt identified Dot as having been their mother's favorite. Their father demanded meat and potatoes every night for dinner, but providing meat for the entire family exceeded the budget; so Dot ate leftover meat and Mildred ate beans or cereal. Extra pennies from the weekly budget, diligently saved, were accumulated to purchase new clothes for Dot. When they were adults, Mildred talked matter-of-factly, and with no animosity, about her sister's favored status.

Faith stammered when relating her mother's and aunt's laughter as they talked about their mother's pregnancy with Mildred. They joked that if their mother could have aborted Mildred with a coat hanger she would have. "After your Mama born, Ma would not let Pop get close enough to her for even a little smooch," Dot said. "Ma was not happy in the hills. She was meant to be a city girl. When she met Pop, the love of her life had just been killed. Within weeks, Ma and Pop were married."

In therapy, Faith described her anguish in contemplating her grandmother's wish to abort her mother with a coat hanger. Horrified by the lightness with which Dot and Mildred talked about the memory, Faith felt shame that she had joined in their laughter. To her, their response seemed as horrific as the story itself. Faith cried profusely as she related this story during a therapy session. This landmark session motivated her to grapple with her weight as she experienced her fat as representing years of stifled emotions.

Mildred married a man as absent from the family as her own father, and she attached herself to Faith just as strongly as her mother attached herself to Dot. In naming her oldest daughter "Faith," Mildred declared, "I had faith God would give me a daughter who would love me, take care of me, and look after me." And Faith did. In exchange for her daughter's care and adoration, Mildred replicated her mother's treatment of Dot, treating Faith as her mother had treated Dot, with special foods and nice clothes.

Mildred and Faith developed a relationship in which their emotions became entwined. If Faith experienced disappointment, Mildred grieved; when Faith complained of someone's bad treatment, the depth of Mildred's rage exceeded Faith's. If Mildred confronted unhappiness, Faith endured sleepless nights. If her mother worried about Faith's brother, Faith would put aside her work to drive two hours to his home and investigate his well-being.

With her mother as her best friend, Faith's friendships with peers suffered. Faith lacked playtime and the opportunities to learn social, cognitive, and physical skills. When she interacted, infrequently, with other children, Faith complained to her mother about their treatment of her. Mildred's expression of outrage left the child feeling vindicated. Faith learned nothing about getting along with others, and her own behaviors, as inappropriate as they may have been, were reinforced.

Faith's parents divorced when she turned twenty, her mother tired of her husband's affairs and her father tired of his wife's preoccupation with her mother, sister, and Faith. With her father absent, the small buffer that existed between Faith and her mother dissipated. Faith's mother became more demanding and clingy, calling several times a day to seek reassurance over even the simplest decision. Lost, but trying to respect Faith's efforts to focus on school and career, Mildred moved to live near her sister Dot, ninety miles away. Yet, on weekends, Faith surrendered to her mother's pressure to join her for Saturday dinner or Sunday lunch.

The men Faith dated were as demanding as her mother. She bolted from them as soon as the extent of their demands surfaced. Faith wondered if all the men she dated were the same, or if she brought out neediness in the men she dated.

Trying to cultivate a life separate from her mother's, Faith participated in church and community service groups. In these groups, her pattern was the same. Initially, Faith became the person people depended on to get the job done. Within a few months, this was followed by Faith's resentment of people's dependence on her. Finally, Faith fled groups as her resentment (that group members did not value her competence as her mother had) surfaced. Faith, inept in working out uncomfortable feelings generated by interactions with peers, turned to food for comfort. Because she was tightly connected to her mother during her childhood, Faith lacked play experiences that would have taught her basic skills required for getting along with the others.

In her therapy, Faith explored the symbolic meaning of food. She associated food with the joy of being her mother's favorite child. The more alienated Faith felt from her peers, the more reassurance she required, and the more she ate. Faith's world became smaller and smaller—work, her mother, food—until her internist directed her to therapy.

In her psychotherapy sessions, Faith acknowledged that she struggled with numerous issues. First, her relationship to food was complex. As her mother had fed Faith "good" foods in acknowledgment that she was special, food symbolized positive feelings about herself. Additionally, Faith acknowledged that she stuffed herself with food the way she stuffed herself with emotions. Second, she had no knowledge of which emotions were truly hers and which she had absorbed from her mother. Third, she neglected herself out of her longing for a mother to mother her as she had mothered her mother. Fourth, she treated people with curtness, an expression of suppressed anger at her mother's not mothering of her. Fifth, her struggles with men stemmed from unrecognized rage intended for her father because he had left the care of his needy wife to Faith.

Though Faith's father was dead, having recognized the relationship between her issues with men and her unresolved issues with her father, Faith worked in therapy to emotionally reconcile with him. She realized that her mother's preoccupation with her own mother and sister precluded any openness on the part of Mildred to a meaningful relationship with her husband. Faith appreciated her father's loneliness in the marriage, and strove to be more receptive to men and less preoccupied with her relationship with her mother.

Faith also struggled with friendships, not knowing the appropriate emotional boundaries or expectations. Her work in group therapy provided a forum for learning skills that she would have learned by playing as a child.

Therapy provided Faith with an arena in which to explore her Shadow, those parts of herself she was frightened to know, and a forum in which to begin to appreciate her value in life as greater than functioning as her mother's caretaker. Wracked with pain at giving up this role, Faith fought against overeating to fill her void and soothe her anxiety. Her journey was slow but, surprisingly, aided by Mildred.

Mildred wanted her daughter to live a healthier life, be thinner, and enjoy satisfying relationships. She was receptive to Faith's desire that they work to create an appropriate distance between them. Faith wanted her mother to participate in our therapy, and she agreed. Faith presented the idea to me.

I refused, even though I work frequently with parents and adult children. Faith claimed little for herself, but she claimed me as *her* therapist, *her* ally. Through our discussion of my refusal to work jointly with her mother and her, Faith appreciated the clarity of my boundaries, that we had our work to do and her mother had her own work separate from Faith's. Tempted to aid Mildred by finding her a therapist, Faith accepted my encouragement to let her mother find her own therapist. Not believing her mother capable of doing this, Faith dreaded telling her mother my recommendation, that she locate her own therapist and their therapies remain separate. She imagined her mother physically dissolving, exhibiting signs of emotional instability and illness. To her astonishment, Mildred agreed to the recommendation, located a therapist, and promptly began treatment.

Though delighted with her mother's interest in becoming more independent, Faith, to her surprise, experienced anxiety. She cried easily and developed sleep problems, physical signs of stress. She became more reclusive, behavior characteristic of someone seeking protection by fleeing from fear. But, rather than retreat to the comfort of familiarity, Faith pushed into her Shadow to continue her road to recovery.

Though her struggle with weight loss was difficult, Faith worked at expressing feelings rather than stuffing them into herself. As she became more emotionally expansive, her weight fell slowly. More aware of the role she assumed as "the responsible one" with people, Faith became more thoughtful about her relationships with others. She sought more give and take in friendships, allowing others the opportunity to offer her more and accepting their overtures. Over time, Faith's world grew larger and her body smaller as her struggles with weight became more manageable. She and her mother established a more satisfying basis for their relationship.

Abigail: Mother's Nurse

Abigail, a fifty-five-year-old divorced mother of two daughters, enjoyed the prestige, wealth, and job satisfaction commensurate with her position as a vice president of a Fortune 500 company. She began therapy bothered by her choice of men and her limitations in sustaining healthy intimate relationships. She lived a life sculpted by her career—her friendships originated at work, and her vacations originated as business trips.

Abigail recalled that during her first marriage, her husband and daughters, accustomed to Abigail's accepting phone calls during dinner, labeled her callers as "Mr. UG," standing for "uninvited guest." Humanizing the phone call reflected the family's effort to manage their disappointment at having their family dinner interrupted. In their pretence that the interruption came from an uninvited guest, the family felt involved with, not excluded from, Abigail's activity.

Kent, Abigail's husband, divorced her as his resentment of her choices grew. He tired of business calls interfering with family dinners. He witnessed his daughters' elevated tension in the presence of their mother. The girls fought more with each other about trivia and with him about household chores, and they had increased difficulty completing their homework.

Kent grew suspicious of the fact that Abigail habitually chose attendance at "urgent" business meetings rather than their couples psychotherapy sessions. Holding their psychotherapy sessions sacrosanct, he seldom missed therapy even though he, too, lived a pressured professional life. Throughout his professional career, he rotated between practicing law in the private sector and serving as a political appointee in the government. Riddled with pain, Kent recognized that his investment in saving the marriage was one-sided. He ended his marriage to Abigail.

Abigail remarried, to a man who was professionally as accomplished as she was. This marriage lasted less than a year. Abigail pursued individual psychotherapy, motivated by two failed marriages, her estrangement from her daughters, and her concern that the men she slept with were old enough to be her father or young enough to be her son.

Abigail described her mother, Sharon, as "not healthy." During childhood, Sharon survived rheumatic fever but the damage done to her heart plagued her in adulthood. She survived multiple heart surgeries. None of them were effective. With each subsequent surgery, her body healed more slowly and with additional scar tissue that further complicated her health issues. Habitually tired, Sharon napped frequently. Abigail characterized her mother as living a life waiting for surgery or recuperating from it. As Abigail recounts:

> As the oldest of four, I was mother in training. I did most of the cooking and laundry. I loved cooking my mother's favorite dishes. I can still see her smile as I served spaghetti with my homemade sauce. I'd walk to the store, even in the rain, to get her something she craved, a Hershey Bar without nuts or a Tootsie Roll.
>
> I looked after my brothers and sister, making their lunches and checking their clothes as Mother would. In the summer, I put suntan lotion on them before our neighbor took us to the beach, and, when we left the beach, I made sure they'd washed the sand off the toys, just the way Mother wanted it done. I'd do anything so Mother wouldn't worry and anything to make her life easier.

Abigail enjoyed her role as Sharon's best friend and considered Sharon hers. "It made me feel special. When my mother confided in me, I thought I was the most important person in the world. We'd share intimate secrets. She told me her secrets and fears and I'd tell her mine. We'd laugh and joke, telling each other stories until late at night."

Abigail gloated over her ability to confront her father on her mother's behalf. Abigail described her mother as uneasy with conflict, and, as her illness advanced, she lacked the stamina required for even minimal confrontation. Her father, a man who hid his emotions, displayed little compassion for his wife's physical limitations or emotional frustrations. Abigail frequently found her mother crying, overwhelmed with the sadness of her life and the loneliness of her marriage.

The financial stinginess of Abigail's father also created resentment. A man of financial means, he refused to move from their two-story home, which posed problems for Sharon, to a one-story home. He considered that a move would be wasteful. Sharon's stamina permitted her to navigate the steps once a day, coming down in the morning and going up in the evening. Before Abigail left for school, her routine included bringing downstairs those items her mother required for the day. When not at school, Abigail, with occasional help from her siblings, made countless trips up and down the stairs fetching items their mother requested.

Abigail fought for her mother as a mother would for a child who had been wronged. Abigail forcefully and persistently confronted her father about his selfishness, financial and emotional. Their confrontations regularly filled the house.

Wanting Sharon to experience joy, Abigail bought cards and gifts for her father to give her mother. He did, and her mother delighted in believing her husband to be more thoughtful and sentimental than he was. Abigail, wanting only happiness for her mother, gave no thought to the deception the gifts represented. Only Abigail and her father knew he had not selected the purchases, and it served the interests of neither of them to admit the truth.

All the members of the family accepted Abigail as her mother's favorite child. Sharon bragged freely about Abigail in front of the other children, loving to comment about her daughter's beauty and buoyant personality. Sharon permitted Abigail free rein in shopping for clothes and shoes, allowing her to charge without restrictions at the local stores. When Abigail came home with new clothes, she tried them on for her mother. Following Mother's lead, the audience of her sisters and brother, and anyone else in the house, applauded her beauty. To conceal these shopping sprees from her husband, Sharon paid in cash on her occasional outings from the house. Abigail enjoyed being a player in her mother's game of deception, as she did in her father's game.

As a child, Sharon dreamed of a college education, envying her younger sister, who attended a university. Sharon wanted Abigail to have such an education and did not trust her husband to provide it. Over the years, Sharon stashed away money, a little at a time, to ensure her daughter's education. With this money, Abigail achieved her degree.

As an adult, Abigail quickly climbed the corporate ladder. She catered to her superiors as she had catered to her mother. They rewarded her, as her mother had, with special privileges. Her abilities to endear people to one another also served her well: she built circles of friends loyal to her and they, in turn, invested in her career advancement.

Reflecting on her first marriage, Abigail grasped the impact of her mother's bias on her choices. Abigail accepted that her drive to be self-sufficient contributed to her unacceptable behaviors in her marriage:

> Kent really was a wonderful man. I still miss him. When we dated, we agreed we both wanted our marriage to be a true partnership—financial, emotional, parenting. He held up his part of the bargain, but I couldn't. The longer we were married, the more frightened I became of losing my independence. I felt driven to make money, to provide for myself. I became consumed with work.
>
> As for my second marriage to Jonathan, I was swept up by someone who adored me as my mother did. He praised me the way my mother had, something Kent never did. I missed someone making me feel so special and important, especially after all the fighting with Kent. Jonathan seduced me. I knew right away I'd made a mistake in marrying Jonathan. I watched him flirt with other women; he wooed them like he had me. He had affairs. As for me, I was still in love with Kent. My heart wasn't open to Jonathan. Maybe in some way he sensed that.

Abigail explained her struggles with men. "Professionally, I get along with men. I respect them as colleagues and confidants. But as soon as a relationship goes beyond work, all hell breaks loose. I become their caretaker, resent it, and pull away." In her adult relationships with men, Abigail oversaw their relations with others, as she had done for her father. She also took responsibility for their physical and psychological needs, as she had done for her mother.

First, in beginning her psychotherapy, Abigail adamantly refused to consider that her life as an adult was impacted by scars remaining from childhood—from the triangle consisting of her mother, her father, and herself. Eventually Abigail accepted that by involving herself in her father's relationship with her mother, she also took care of herself. Involving herself in this way provided Abigail with the psychological safety derived from believing that her parents fundamentally cared for one another. Through this involvement, she created some distance between her mother and herself, while establishing safe boundaries for her relationship with her father. Abigail grew to appreciate that her adult relationships with men reenacted the relationships of her young adulthood: She tempered her closeness to her partners as she had tempered her relationship with her mother, by fostering their relationships with others.

Second, Abigail learned that by feeding her partner's dependence on her, she could continue to operate in the spectrum best known to her, as a caretaker. Maybe she was not fulfilled or satisfied, but she was not threatened by the requirements of new ways of relating.

Abigail told herself that she was her own best parent and did not require parenting from either her mother or her father. Yet she lived in fear of her mother dying, leaving her father as the only parent. The pressure of this contradiction, more than her body was equipped to handle, expressed itself in severe and chronic stomach cramps.

As her therapy unfolded, Abigail trembled with horror as long-forgotten feelings resurfaced, reminding her of the unease she had felt as a teenager modeling clothes. The attention Sharon deflected from her body, riddled with scars, flowed to Abigail, to her young, attractive body, sexy and inviting. As a teen, Abigail thought the intensity of her mother's eagerness to see her in new clothes was strange, as was Sharon's insistence that everyone in the household should put aside their activities to praise her. In the security of her therapeutic relationship with me, Abigail explored her frightening feelings of having been used by her mother. Abigail came to understand the depth of her mother's vicarious identification with her. She explored her confusion about where her identity stopped and her mother's began. She engaged in this important developmental activity without any support from her mother.

Curious about her unwavering motivation to succeed, Abigail, in therapy, identified her disdain for men and her need to be self-sufficient. She struggled with differentiating her beliefs from those of her mother. Abigail acknowledged the insidious impact of her mother's belittling of her father during moments of mother/daughter intimacy. Abigail began to comprehend the power of her mother's repetitive lecture, emphasizing the importance of careers for women so that women would not be dependent on men.

In her therapy, Abigail gradually turned from expressing despair at the emptiness and pain of her mother's life to understanding that of her own. Abigail realized the deprivation she had suffered, emanating from living a childhood with little mothering or play, and few friends. As a child, feeling adultlike was a "high" for her, but, in retrospect, not having had a childhood rich with childlike experiences was extraordinarily harmful.

Abigail explored the old equation. She had accepted that love equals caretaking. She conveyed love to men the only way she knew, taking care of them. Yet she resented men who accepted her caretaking, wanting to give them as little as she did her father. She was confused: was her caretaking loving or not? She grew frightened of her adult expression of closeness.

Abigail also recognized her resentment at having spent her childhood caring for her mother. She slowly understood its impact on the difficulty she found in establishing boundaries in relationships. Boundaries were either nonexistent, as they had been with her mother, or inappropriately distant, as they had been with Kent and her father.

While I was writing this book, Abigail continued in therapy. She remained skeptical of her ability to sustain healthy intimacy with men. "Maybe, someday," she mused. "For now, what I most care about is my relationship with my children. I mothered the only way

I could and it wasn't very good. When they were young, I was either overinvolved with them or too self-absorbed. Now, I want to do better."

As Abigail continues to work on her relationship with her children, she continues to work on her own Shadow (see chapter 1) and demons. Emerging from this exploration, she will likely be more satisfied with, and trusting of, what she brings to relationships—with her children or possible partners—and what she accepts from relationships.

MOTHERS' FAVORITE DAUGHTERS

Zoe, Faith, and Abigail were three favorite daughters who filled three different roles in the lives of their mothers: Zoe, her mother's helper; Faith, her mother's mother; Abigail, her mother's nurse. These three women, their identities fused with their mothers', lacked the emotional tools necessary to establish for themselves identities separate and distinct from those of their mothers. Their mothers, putting their own needs first, made this normal life progression difficult.

Rewarded for staying attached to their mothers, Zoe, Faith, and Abigail relished freedom that was inappropriate for their ages. As they had not successfully completed the developmental tasks of childhood—play and age-appropriate separation from the mother—these women were unprepared for the challenges of adolescence. Zoe indulged in drinking and sex, Faith indulged in eating and became alienated from peers, and Abigail grew uneasy around men. Again, as adolescents, the women were unsuccessful in completing important developmental milestones appropriate to the teenage years: self-regulation, acceptance of a developing body, and growing comfort with age-appropriate intimate relationships.

As adults, these women struggled with the emotional scars created by the inappropriate attachments between them and their mothers. Zoe and Faith fought the physical repercussions of having lived with prolonged stress, and Abigail suffered in her relationships with her daughters and husband. As adults trying to forge healthy, independent lives, these daughters, once the envy of their siblings, fight against what they learned as children to be true and comforting. This battle is fraught with fear and stress; yet these favorite daughters feel no option but to charge forward. Each wants a richer and more satisfying life.

Here we have explored two interrelated processes: first, the mother and child psychologically separating from each other; and second, the child working to establish an identity separate from the mother's. While this is the work of all children, it is severely impaired by mothers who cling to their daughters, expecting these young women to fill needs that mothers should have filled elsewhere. These mothers, with the responsibilities of caretakers, impose these responsibilities on their daughters. Their daughters, flattered by the expectation, cling to this role until, as adults, they acknowledge their suffering.

Taking on the developmental work of separating from one's mother and forging one's own identity is especially difficult when it has to be begun by an adult who has not achieved earlier developmental milestones. To take on the work of separation as an adult requires a daughter to be courageous and to challenge her lifelong assumption that she requires her mother's preferential treatment for her life to have meaning. Motivated by pain, showing itself physically, interpersonally, or emotionally, these women can effectively modify their lives in the context of a trusting therapeutic relationship.

CHAPTER ELEVEN
THE OVERLOOKED CHILD

> *I mentally left home when I was six years old because my family had so little interest in me. For years I felt bad about this. It wasn't until I finished graduate school and was in a training workshop with Carl Whitaker that my attitude about being the overlooked kid changed. I remember the experience vividly. Whitaker said to me, "How many kids have the opportunity to select their own lives without parental interference? You're probably the envy of everyone in this room."*
>
> —Morris's reflections

I offered a training session on favorite children at a professional meeting. Once the allotted slots in the group were filled, people approached me for admission. Not wanting to show favoritism, I said "no" to everyone. As the session was about to begin, Morris quietly entered the room. He asked, pleasantly but firmly, to join the group. At that moment, I was preoccupied with reviewing, in my mind, my opening statements. I was not thinking about those whom I had already refused or about showing favoritism in the moment. And so I agreed.

Morris's role in the group proved to be important. He gave thoughtful expression to the experience of being the overlooked child in a room otherwise filled with impassioned statements about having been favored or not. At the conclusion of the training session, Morris turned to me and said, "I came in here not knowing what to expect. I leave knowing my time has been well spent, with new and useful ways to think about my experiences in the world. Thank you for this gift."

Toxic Families

Synonyms for "toxic" are poisonous, deadly, lethal, noxious, and contaminated. Imagine growing up in a family that is described with any of these words. In her bestselling book, *Toxic Parents*,[1] Susan Forward, described such parents as putting their own needs ahead of responsible parenting. Children growing up in such an environment commonly feel worthless or bad about themselves. The repercussions of toxic parenting are obvious in homes that tolerate physical or sexual abuse or alcoholism. The psychological and moral scars of children affected by emotional abuse are often not as obvious. But they are there, just the same.

The biographies highlighted in chapters 7–10 are stories of men and women whose parents, putting their needs first, impeded the psychological development of their favored children. Bribed with favorite child status, these children worked to fill their parents' needs and voids, and these children did not develop healthy identities separate and distinct from their parents. These children, not trusting their competency and controlled by feelings of guilt and shame, did not challenge their role in their parents' lives or question the toxic environment in which they grew up. They took on this challenge only when confronted with their own life traumas. Because these stories are those of adults working to improve their lives, the stories ring of hope.

Stories not conveying the same optimism are related in chapters 3–6 and interspersed in other chapters. These are vignettes of favorite children who, even as adults, did not challenge the toxic influences of their childhood homes. They continued to cling to the roles they had known as children, regardless of the negative moral, physical, or interpersonal ramifications. As suggested in chapter 9, the premature death of Edward, Ed's father, may have been related to the toxic influence of his childhood family. James, the favored son discussed in chapter 6, who symbolically represented for his mother the father on whom she was dependent, spewed his parents' toxic influence onto his siblings as he maneuvered them out of their rightful inheritance.

Morris's participation in the group was a gift to me, directing my thoughts to the experiences of overlooked children. Long after the meeting ended, Morris continued to talk with me about his journey as an overlooked child in a toxic family.

Vignettes of three overlooked children are given below. The first is Morris's story, that of a person who reaped the benefits of being overlooked. The second is Beatrice's story, that of an otherwise successful adult whose repressed envy of her sister's favorite child status came close to shattering her life when it surfaced in adulthood. The third is Annemarie's story, told from the viewpoint of a sibling who acknowledged the breadth of her family's toxicity only when injured by her older brother, her mother's favorite child. Annemarie's story complements that of James, her brother, as told in chapter 6.

MORRIS: AN OVERLOOKED CHILD WHO THRIVED

As the training session on favoritism concluded, Morris's goodbye mirrored his participation in the group: it was polite, articulate, steady, and thoughtful. An esteemed psychologist who continued to practice psychotherapy in his late eighties, Morris described himself as a man whose life was driven by the desire to seek the recognition that was not offered by his family. He lived his life conveying to others the acknowledgment and affirmation he sought, treating others as he wished to be treated himself.

Family Dynamics

Morris was the son of immigrant parents. His father's first wife died of tuberculosis, leaving him with three young children. Needing a wife to care for his children, he had a matchmaker pair him with a beautiful woman, about five years younger than he. The second wife was Morris's mother.

Morris describes his mother as physically small with a personality to match. "She was inconsequential, not a real presence in the family," he said. "She was unobtrusive and easily overlooked." As an adult thinking about her, Morris explained to himself that she "must have been overwhelmed by life. She was not prepared to mother the three children my father brought into the marriage. She didn't have the competency to deal with them. She never changed. She was stuck there."

As a mother to her own, biological, children, she was no more effective. Morris recounted that "other than feeding us, dressing us, and doing our laundry, she was not up to the task of mothering. There was no physical or emotional contact. She was not a presence in our lives."

Morris described his father, a shoemaker, as intermittently making adequate money. During one of his better-off times, he moved the family to what Morris described as "the good edge of town. We didn't have the money to be in the middle of the good neighborhood but we were on the edge and didn't live in the bad neighborhood." The move proved to be Morris's salvation. It offered him exposure to a world bigger and more inviting than that of his family. His neighborhood friends were children of doctors and lawyers, people with ambition and motivation. Morris found solace in their company and was energized by their companionship.

Morris remembered his father as an irritable man, often fighting, especially with his wife and sons. "My father was mean to my brothers and me. He screamed at us and humiliated us. I tried to lay low, avoid him, and keep my distance. Overall, I was successful. My younger brother tried to do the same but it was harder for him. He was physically small, like my mother, and our father would scream at him about his eating habits. My brother was probably the target of my father's aggression."

In contrast, Morris described his father as favoring his sisters. "My oldest sister, his daughter from his first marriage, was his favorite child. She was beautiful. Maybe she reminded him of his first wife [for] whom he may have continued to grieve." Morris's most vivid memory of his father's treatment of his own sisters involved the competitiveness between his sisters. Even in her nineties, his second oldest sister continued to exude rage at not having received the preferential treatment from their father that her older sister had received.

Morris: His Own Best Friend

Morris described himself as a child who was shy and unsure of himself. He stayed in the background, not getting into trouble and doing those tasks he needed to do. At school, "I flew beneath the radar screen," he reflected. "I kept my head down, did my work, and didn't do anything to bring attention to myself." His personality reflected the survival skills he had mastered at home.

During our conversations, Morris affirmed his resilience, reflecting the emotional riches he found for himself outside of the family. He was drawn to friends, school, and pick-up games of ball in the neighborhood, which nurtured his growth. "Those experiences taught me how to be noticed and appreciated, unknown to me at home." His social world taught him that being noticed is not always dangerous. The skills he honed as a child while playing with peers and interacting with teachers—interest in others, respect, and politeness—were conveyed by Morris when he entered my training group and contributed to the ease with which I agreed to his joining the group.

When he was a junior in high school, life changed for Morris. Persuaded by a teacher, Mr. Lanier, Morris tried out for cheerleading and made the squad. Morris, even as a man in his eighties, did not know the basis of Mr. Lanier's interest. "I didn't think we had a special relationship. But he saw something in me and encouraged me. His suggestion seemed to come out of nowhere. For me, everything changed after that. My world became richer with friends and opportunities. Suddenly, I was the president of clubs and held positions I believed important. I received recognition for the first time in my life. It was great!"

Having escaped his father's cruelty and his mother's indifference, Morris molded a life for himself that was filled with satisfaction. In his life's work as a clinical psychologist, Morris perfected the art of seeing and responding to others, treatment he had craved for himself. In response to his exquisite caring, patients, supervisees, and colleagues have showered him with accolades. As this book was being written, Morris and his wife celebrated their fifty-eighth wedding anniversary, continuing to share their work as practicing psychotherapists. They enjoy good health, each other, their children, and their grandchildren.

In reflecting upon his life, Morris commented: "I ask myself why I didn't crumble as a child, or why I didn't get into trouble, falling off the deep end? I believe I was born with internal strength, that my hard wiring served me well. I don't really know why I wasn't miserable, trying to get my mother's affection when she couldn't give it, or why I maintained my distance from my father, never taking him on. I have to say, I think it is about instinct. I am glad I had the strength to follow it, even as a young child. I feel fortunate."

Morris grew up hiding from his parents, relieved that he was *not* the favorite child in his toxic family. His mother and father were both so inadequate that to have been favored by either of them would have been disastrous, as it was for his oldest sister, who was favored by his father. The basis for Morris's evaluation of his sister's life is vague, as Morris, usually forthcoming, resisted elaborating. His only statement was that "my sister was so much older than me that I don't really know what went on. I only know everyone sensed my father's treatment of her was different than the rest of us. It was definitely more special and a mess. Being my father's favorite was no gift."

Contrasting with Morris is Beatrice, the younger of two daughters. As an adult, Beatrice continued craving her mother's attention, desperately wanting the experience of being her favorite child. Instead, she continued to feel overlooked. The trauma she continued to experience as an adult only magnified the traumas she had experienced as a child.

BEATRICE: DELAYED IMPACT OF BEING OVERLOOKED

Beatrice began therapy with me, in crisis, a few days after her mother's departure after a visit. Her mother, Rosie, had come from Atlanta to help Beatrice recuperate from a cesarean section and to care for her newborn child, Angela. The visit was disastrous. Rosie paid little attention to her infant granddaughter, expected Beatrice to cook and serve meals, and spent inordinate amounts of time talking on the phone to Beatrice's sister, Melia. Upon Rosie's departure, Beatrice was inconsolable, her crying unending. She began therapy, depressed and only marginally functional. She was frightened that she could not adequately mother her beloved infant. What was quickly revealed was a story of an adult woman desperately wanting to be mothered by a mother who overlooked her.

Family Dynamics

According to Beatrice, Rosie, as a young bride, was beautiful and full of the hope that she would flourish as a recognized artist. As a high school student, she was among the first minority women awarded scholarships to study art and tutored by great instructors. Walter, her groom, was dashing and well positioned to provide for his future family. Beatrice brought her parents' wedding picture to show me. Captured in a gilded frame was an image of a young couple, glamorous, vibrant, and worldly. This representation of her mother and father, the only picture Beatrice had of the two of them alone, she proudly displayed on the piano in her living room.

Ten months after the wedding, Melia was born. Surrounded by an involved extended family who helped care for her infant daughter, Rosie was able to continue painting. Her work continued to mature and her reputation flourished. Critics considered her a young artist with great potential. Three years into the marriage, Rosie's world faltered. Her mother, her best friend and trusted partner in caring for Melia, died suddenly. Rosie was pregnant with a second child. Walter worked two jobs to support the family and was seldom home.

Beatrice's memories of her childhood were filled with images of watching from the sidelines as her mother and sister played and laughed. Beatrice recalled them chasing each other on the lawn outside their apartment and playing hopscotch.

Beatrice's one vivid memory of being included with her sister by her mother related to art. "I remember my mother setting up an art table for Melia and me in the middle of the living room or, in the summer when the apartment was too hot, on the street. The table was covered with brushes and paints that were the most beautiful colors. Even now, as an adult, I can feel my mother's exuberance as she would instruct and encourage us. I loved being included and loved painting. I cherish those memories," said Beatrice with tears streaming down her cheeks.

More commonly, Beatrice looked outside the family for affirmation. "We lived in a garden apartment complex filled with kids and nonstop activity," she recalled. "I don't remember spending much time at home. My most vivid memories are of time spent at Lynn's and Charlene's. Their mothers, Aunt Tina and Aunt Wilma, were more like mothers to me than my own mother. They still are."

This childhood pattern—her mother's involvement in Melia's growth while she left Beatrice to fend for herself—held firm throughout Beatrice's life. Left on her own, Beatrice described herself as quiet and circumspect, seldom getting into trouble, and always doing her best. She was liked and counseled by teachers and her friends' parents, such as "Aunt" Tina and "Aunt" Wilma. After graduating from college, Beatrice left Atlanta and moved to Washington to take a job on the Hill. Her stature grew, and she was selected for competitive jobs. Ultimately, she received prestigious political appointments. She married a prominent attorney, and together, they built a secure, loving relationship.

Melia, in contrast, stayed in Atlanta, living close to her mother. She had two children, fathered by different husbands. Ultimately, Melia moved to Washington, DC, with her third husband, a man many years younger than she was. Though she lived in close proximity to Beatrice, the sisters saw little of one another. Beatrice lamented, "Melia only stops by when she needs my husband or me to do a favor for her, or if she needs to borrow money. Other than that, we seldom see her."

Acceptance of Broken Dreams

With the birth of her first and only child, Angela, Beatrice imagined a relationship with her mother previously unknown to her. She remembered her mother as loving to Melia and to Melia's two children, both of whom were of college age when Beatrice's daughter was born. With no competition, Beatrice expected her mother to embrace Angela as she had embraced her nieces. That was not how the scenario played out.

Rosie, during her brief visit, was as indifferent toward Angela as she had been toward Beatrice. At the conclusion of her mother's visit, Beatrice was devastated. While she had been acclimated to life without maternal caring, she had hoped that Angela's birth would invite engaging and loving experiences with her mother that she had never had herself. Forced to confront the truth, she saw that she continued to be overlooked and that her daughter was an overlooked granddaughter as she had been an overlooked daughter. Beatrice was flooded with sadness. She cried endlessly, had difficulty leaving her home, and struggled to care for her beloved newborn daughter. Overwhelmed by her emotions and encouraged by her physician, Beatrice began psychotherapy.

Beatrice's therapy bore fruit as she searched for personal truth. She could not recollect feelings of envy at the relationship between her mother and sister. She remembered her delight in having the freedom to spend time with friends at their homes. Yet, Beatrice acknowledged, her reaction to her mother's emotional indifference around Angela's birth was extreme. Without the presence of her childhood friends to assuage her feelings of rejection, Beatrice was confronted with feelings of turmoil that were generated by her mother's distance. In mothering Angela, Beatrice recognized her agony at not having been emotionally mothered herself.

Beatrice's strong response to her mother's behavior after the birth of Angela reflected Beatrice's long-buried grief for the years of maternal neglect. In an effort to better understand the intensity of her own feelings, and motivated by her therapy, Beatrice pursued her curiosity about her mother's history. She spoke more openly with her mother than she had ever done before.

Beatrice was aware that she had grown up in a home with walls covered by Rosie's exquisite art but had never seen her mother paint seriously, only dabble. Beatrice wondered if her mother had stopped painting seriously when she was born, an image connecting with her mother's coldness. Rosie repudiated this connection and discussed with Beatrice the complexity of factors derailing her from painting.

Rosie acknowledged, first, that when her mother died, she felt she could not function without her support, not even to paint. Even though she was married, Rosie accepted that she was dependent on her mother, not her husband. Second, Rosie described herself as being consumed with mothering Melia. She believed she had to, to make up for her mother's absence. She believed she wanted to, pouring herself into something her mother had done. Third, Rosie portrayed herself as too tired to paint, fatigued by the physical activity of mothering her toddler while being pregnant. With hindsight, Rosie thought that after Beatrice's birth she was too overwhelmed with life to resume her art: her marriage was weak and her life too demanding, and the pain of her mother's absence was too great.

Rosie's story was consistent with Beatrice's thoughts and impressions about her mother's life. Beatrice considered her father a loving but weak man, imagining him as not up to partnering with her mother. Beatrice never felt rejected by her mother but sensed that when she was born her mother was inept at modifying her routine so as to include her in the relationship that had been established with Melia.

Feeling compassion for her mother in her limitations, Beatrice appreciated her own competency in navigating the world without much input from her mother. When she compared her life to her sister's, Beatrice more fully valued the life she had. She appreciated that her sister was as dependent on Rosie as Rosie had been on her mother. Slowly, and over time, Beatrice grew to treasure her adeptness at mothering herself.

Morris and Beatrice, two overlooked children, both found their way without parental encouragement or support. Both were born with emotional strength and resilience, hard wired with the attributes required for self-sufficiency at an early age. While growing up, neither Morris nor Beatrice fought for favorite child status: Morris's father was too dangerous and his mother too weak; Beatrice found a world outside the family that was rich and joyful, meeting her needs.

The third story, Annemarie's, is that of a woman remaining ensconced in her toxic family. As noted, Annemarie's story complements that of her brother, James, told in chapter 6.

ANNEMARIE: OVERLOOKED AND SUFFERING

Growing up as an overlooked child, Annemarie suffered emotional injury inflicted by her mother's insular relationship with her brother as well as by her father's indifference. Annemarie, a client of mine, described herself to me as feeling like Don Quixote in her search for acknowledgment in the world. "In my quest to be seen and known, I felt like I was tilting at windmills. As soon as someone began to appreciate me, I found fault and built a case about why the person wasn't to be trusted. I left that relationship and moved on. The pattern repeated itself countless times. Finally, I accepted the problem had to be mine, not with everyone else."

Annemarie's ability to learn to value her role as an overlooked child grew from years of psychotherapy with many different therapists prior to me.

> It now makes sense to me that I had to establish an ally outside of the family. When I first began therapy, I thought I was crazy. My brothers and sister, who were also overlooked in the family and were my childhood buddies, were falling apart. One sister and brother drank too much, and my other brother continued to ruin his marriages by having affairs. I was concerned, and, when I tried to talk to them or other family members, everyone said the problem was me. They said I was too uptight. I just needed more fun.
>
> During all of this, I decided I wanted to start graduate school and made an appointment to see Mrs. Scott, my beloved high school teacher, to talk over my plans. When I walked into her office, immediately I felt the respite I had felt there so many times as an adolescent. I started crying. I cried and cried. We never made it to lunch or talked about graduate school. We talked about how unsure I was of myself, of how crazy I was feeling. Within a week, I started therapy for the first time.

Annemarie described the beginning of her therapy as difficult. "All I did was cry or fight with my therapist. If she affirmed my sadness or anger, or challenged my statement of my family as 'loving,' I'd scream at her, 'You don't understand,' and proceed to represent my family as I wanted it to be, not as it was."

Breaking away from one's family and achieving an independent identity is challenging work for children. First, children have to confront their parents' "truths," previously maintained as unquestionable. Second, when experiencing the discomfort of altering old roles and relationships, people are inclined to retreat to these precious old and comforting roles. Third, people refuse to consider feelings that could make them question their view of their family as loving. They are more apt to believe something is wrong with them than with their families, and to accept the kind of treatment from family members that they would find unacceptable from strangers. These psy-

Shame and Guilt

Shame reflects feelings of who we are, and guilt reflects feelings of what we have done. If something is amiss, shame evokes feelings of "I *am* the mistake," while guilt evokes feelings of "I *did* something wrong." Shame, the more powerful of the two, reflects an inner self-evaluation, often suppressed and not easily overcome. Guilt reflects awareness of mistakes from which people can learn. The experience of guilt can result in shame. In *Facing Shame: Families in Recovery*, Merle Possum and Marilyn Mason write that "while guilt is a painful feeling of regret and responsibility for one's actions, shame is a painful feeling about oneself as a person."[2]

Guilt and shame are tools parents utilize to mold the behaviors of children, guilt to teach about right and wrong, and shame to forcefully reinforce parental attitudes. In healthy families, children make mistakes, feel guilt, learn, and move on. In toxic families, children make mistakes, feel shame, and become stuck. Over time, they become anxious or depressed.

For example, when children make mistakes, as in breaking a glass of water because they are jumping around the kitchen when holding it, they probably feel guilty. After children accept responsibility for having broken the glass, they can evaluate, by themselves or with their parents, what happened, and learn from their mistake. The lesson is internalized while the incident is forgotten. In toxic families, where children believe they are bad because they create tension, they are burdened with shame. These children feel self-recrimination for having broken a glass. Shame grows.

Parents in toxic families reinforce the belief that their children are wrong for wanting for themselves something different from what the parent wants for them. Shame is used as a mechanism to pressure children into maintaining the status quo. As the magnitude of these children's shame grows, it becomes increasingly difficult for them to forge the separation from their family that is necessary for healthy psychological functioning.

chological currents impede the natural progression of children and adults to the establishment of a life and identity separate from their families. These currents are stronger in inhibiting healthy development in children brought up in toxic families, where shame and guilt are used to control behaviors. Children brought up in unhealthy families are poisoned with shame and guilt.

Annemarie explained the power of shame in influencing her behavior. "I got caught up in appearances," she said. "Everywhere I went, I was identified as James's sister. That gave me status and acceptance. Girls who wanted to date my brother became my friends, thinking that would get them closer to James. I knew it wouldn't and felt ashamed about participating in the charade. But if I told them the truth, that my brother paid no attention to me or my friends, I feared I wouldn't have any friends at all. I truly believed that I had nothing to offer." Annemarie carried into the world her feeling, learned at home, of not being valuable.

Not feeling worthwhile, Annemarie felt inadequate to challenge her position in the family, and she reenacted these behaviors in the world. As an overlooked child, she behaved outside the family as if she were inconsequential. This belief governed her adult behaviors. Only in the presence of her trusted former teacher did Annemarie accept the challenge of confronting her deep Shadow:

> I was sinking deeper and deeper into depression. After my breakdown in Mrs. Scott's office, I knew I could no longer pretend everything was okay. My unhappy feelings became too powerful. Therapy became my lifeline.
>
> I felt such shame with my unhappiness. Everyone in the family was supposed to be happy, accepting our roles in this Ozzie and Harriet–like family. For the longest time I hid my therapy from my friends and family. I couldn't bear the responsibility of being the one denting the family facade.

Slowly, Annemarie began to appreciate the freedom that came with her invisibility in the family. She remembered finally telling her mother about her therapy. Her mother dismissed it as a "waste of money" but otherwise expressed no interest. Annemarie recounted to me that she left her parents' home, got in her car, and screamed at the top of her lungs, "I don't care. It is my life. Thank you Mrs. Scott for having given me permission to live my own life." Annemarie celebrated her growth as she appreciated her refusal to surrender to the potential shame of wasting money on therapy.

Having forged a life separate from her family's, Annemarie was angry, but not devastated, when James's exploitation of his role as mother's favorite surfaced. She understood his adult behaviors as an outgrowth of his prized role in the family. Appropriately, the main thrust of Annemarie's anger was directed at her parents, her mother for having the relationship that she had with James, and her father for his acquiescence in it.

Annemarie believed James's life to be tragic, describing him as robotlike: "He has so little of his own personality or sense of himself. Even in his fifties, he says, thinks, and behaves as our mother directed. I fear for him and his future as he navigates with a minimal moral compass. Would I rather be him, our mother's favorite child, or free to be me and live my own life? Seeing and appreciating myself is far richer with more potential than still working to be seen and appreciated by my mother," Annemarie concluded, with tears streaming down her cheeks.

OVERLOOKED CHILDREN

Morris, Beatrice, and Annemarie are three adults who grew up as overlooked children. Their psychological reactions to this role varied. Morris appreciated the freedom derived from having been overlooked. Beatrice buried her pain until her high level of functioning, as an adult, was threatened. Annemarie repressed her awareness of being overlooked and remained fused with the family until challenged by the emptiness of her adult life.

The quality of life experienced by Morris, Beatrice, and Annemarie is consistent with their responses to being overlooked children. Morris has a successful marriage and a prolific career. He is well liked, respected, and embraced by extended personal and professional communities. Beatrice, too, has a satisfying marriage and a fulfilling relationship with her daughter. She continues to thrive as a teacher while nurturing her own skills as a painter. Unlike Morris and Beatrice, Annemarie regrets never having sustained intimate closeness. She continues her therapy, striving to further develop the character changes necessary for such a relationship.

In conclusion, it should be said that growing up overlooked in a toxic family can vary in its effects. As Morris reflected, internal wiring matters but so does the pull of the family. Morris and Beatrice, as children, were freer to disengage from their families and establish lives more removed from them. They protected themselves from injuries to their mental health. In contrast, Annemarie remained more tightly entwined with the dynamics of her toxic family into her adulthood. Consequently, the process of healing herself has been more difficult. Awareness and acceptance of the role of the overlooked child are critical in directing such children to more satisfying lives.

CHAPTER TWELVE
CONCLUSION

Being favored is not all bad. Although [I'm] quite prejudiced, I think I prefer it to being unfavored. If one must live with distortion, it might as well be one that does not cause immediate pain. Either way, the struggle is how to introduce the real world into your assessment and experience of yourself.

—Zachary's reflections

Growing up as the favored child in a family means growing up believing that one is better than one's siblings. If this belief is transitory, it may be true for the moment and facilitate the child's building of his self-worth and confidence. If this belief is rigid, reflecting an absolute family truth, it is probably false and contributes to the child's growing up with a distorted and overinflated sense of self. How his parents reinforce, or counter, his distorted self-perception will profoundly influence the character of the child.

Zachary, a friend of mine who is quoted above, retired from his successful career as a psychologist to begin a second career as a sailor. In our lengthy discussions about favoritism in families, he acknowledged that, when he was growing up, his mother favored him over his brother. Frightened to change the status quo and lose his position in the family, he continued to work as a psychologist long after realizing that his career did not permit him the life he wanted. "It was connected to living the kind of life my mother needed me to live," he commented. "My life was not about me."

With growing awareness that he did not derive the satisfaction from his life that rationally he knew he should, Zachary became more conscious of the depth of the muted pain residing within his Shadow. After he decided to retire as a psychologist and to begin his career as a sailor, sailing to distant parts of the world with his wife on their forty-two-foot boat, the veil of depression with which he had lived most of his life lifted. He experienced the quality of intimacy with his wife that both of them had desired.

Drawing from his own experiences, Zachary wrote to me: "I think the favorite child frequently must wait until his image of himself is not reflected back to him by the broader world before he is ready to take on the challenge of seeing himself more honestly. Often this is quite a shock. The unfavored child has a leg up. In his unhappiness—in his pain—he may have greater motivation to see himself more realistically in the world, to reject what parents have heaped on [him]."[1]

Like Zachary, favored children are usually less inclined than overlooked or unfavored children to undertake the challenge of self-discovery, because the rewards of favoritism can be so gratifying and seductive. Additionally, these children are often oblivious to their negative impact on others. But, ultimately, favorite children may be motivated to overcome their resistance to self-exploration when they feel constricted in the way they live their lives, or when they are faced with threatened or damaged relationships, or legal improprieties.

People are vulnerable to accepting their parents' viewpoints on them. Whether parents hold children to be "the best" or "the worst," children internalize these beliefs, which become a primary element of their self-evaluation. Favorite children are likely to have overinflated views of themselves, unfavored children to have diminished views, and overlooked children to have uncertain views. Because of the negative emotions attached to feeling "lesser," unfavored children may be more motivated to challenge their self-perception than are their favored counterparts. Though motivated by different experiences, favored, overlooked, and unfavored children commonly struggle with an identical issue—that of perceiving themselves realistically.

As described throughout this book, the favorite child complex impacts the life experiences and personalities of all members of the family—past, present, and future. It is a process that is conscious and unconscious, constructive and destructive, rational and irrational, healthy and unhealthy. Everyone across generations has a role in the favorite child complex and is affected by the experience. The potential rewards of favoritism are enormous—confidence and empowerment—and the risks substantial—self-absorption, self-deception, and corrupted morals.

OUR PARENTS' CHILDREN

Parents' views of their children are reflected in the children's feelings about themselves. These perceptions are an amalgam of family, social, cultural, and genetic histories; parental personalities and needs; the relationship between the adults in the household; and children's temperaments, needs, attributes, physical appearance, sex, and other assorted personality traits. While parents are often unaware of the attitudes they convey to children, siblings commonly adopt their parents' attitude toward specific family members.

Selecting the Favorite

From the beginning, children intuitively know whether or not they are favored. In some families, *all children* begin life knowing how special they are to their mothers, having absorbed this important nonverbal communication as fetuses or newborns. If this pattern continues, children, throughout their lives, rotate in and out of the role as the favorite child, sharing the position with siblings. Ideally, fathers join in, and every twosome within the family experiences a favored relationship.

In other families, *a given child* may be designated as "the" favorite of one or both parents and holds that position, essentially unchallenged, throughout life. The dynamics within each given family influence the impact of favoritism within that family, on the designated favorite, and on other family members.

In Fluid Families

Many opportunities for healthy growth for all family members can be found when two trusting adults establish the framework in which the family functions. In the relationship that each parent has with each child, parents are likely to experience, at different times, each child as a favorite, and all children are likely to have the experience of favoring each parent. These favored relationships may be dictated by the ages of the children or the parents, common interests, similar or complementary temperaments, or other shifting variables.

One father, commenting on the topic of favoritism, stated simply, "I love both my kids and would do anything in the world for either of them, but I do have a favorite, Quinn. He is just more fun, and naturally, I'd rather be with him. Evan is more fun for my wife, and he is her favorite. Essentially, my wife and I each adore both our boys and we enjoy spending time with both of them."

Favoritism shifting from child to child gives all of the children the opportunity to be temporarily overlooked and to be able to function without close parental scrutiny. At these times, children may feel less pressured to perform and freer to try out new activities. Children are less concerned about "getting it right" or protecting themselves from parental judgment. What is important is that no one is stuck in a given role, and all family members have opportunities to reap the benefits of being favored or of being overlooked.

Parents in families where favoritism shifts around often claim that they have no favorites and all their children are treated the same. This is impossible to accomplish. First, people's feelings, reactions, and behaviors fluctuate, and in given moments, they are more attracted to some people than to others. Second, because all children, by genetic definition and personality, are different, no two children can truly be treated the same.

Parents voice their intention of treating all children "fairly." Fairness is in the eye of the beholder and requires objectivity that may be impossible to maintain. When parents are giving Christmas presents, is fairness defined by giving children the same number of gifts or by spending equal amounts of money on them? Do both parents define fairness the same way? Do all children in the family agree? If not, whose definition of fairness is correct?

In fluid families, parents usually do not look to their children to fill their needs. These parents are more likely to fill some of their own needs and look to their partners to fill other needs. Focusing less on themselves in making parenting decisions, these parents are more likely to be steered by what they believe to be their children's best interests, not their own. For example, does a mother's objection to her child skateboarding reflect her nervousness about the activity or genuine concern that her child may break an arm two days before an important swim meet? In the first possibility, the mother wants the child to take care of her nervousness by not skateboarding. In the second possibility, the mother determines the risk is too great for her child.

Trust in the relationship between adults in the household is accentuated by the tenor of their communication. With open discussion between themselves, parents model honest dialogue and lay the groundwork for healthy communication in the family. This permits one parent to confront the other when observing inappropriate displays of favoritism and, if necessary, help the partner to modify the undermining behaviors.

For example, if one parent is overinvested in one child's academic achievement, the other parent may assume the role of monitor, supervising homework or communicating with teachers. Ideally, both parents, in conjunction with the child, work out this role change through open communication. When one parent has removed herself from a role in which she was inappropriately invested, she can reflect on and learn from her misguided projection. Then the issues of achievement can reside, more appropriately, within the child. Moreover, both parents can rotate, spending more time in helping the child's siblings to excel in school as well.

This framework teaches children respectful communication and gives them permission to express themselves honestly within the family. In the example of Christmas gifts cited earlier, voicing envy of their sibling's gifts is healthy for the children doing this and for all relationships within the family—between the child and the parents as well as between the child and his siblings. For the child, submerging disappointment or resentment in his dark Shadow can breed shame and, ultimately, alienation and anger. Families functioning as healthy units reduce the risk that transient displays of favoritism will evolve into favoritism that is rigid and fixed.

In Rigid Families

The needs of one parent are more likely to govern the functioning of families that have rigid dynamics. Commonly, this parent looks to one child, designated as the favorite, to satisfy the significant, usually unconscious, requirements of the parent. The obsessive bolstering of this favored child can exacerbate problems in the parents' marriage, heightening tension between a husband and wife who do not function successfully as partners. Instead of parents attempting to meet each other's healthy needs, the trust between them falters, their communication becomes more perfunctory.

An exclusively favored child is vulnerable to growing up with a personality fused with that of the significant parent. Thus, the child's developmental milestones are unreached, which hinders the emergence of the child's identity and the child's ability to psychologically separate from the parent. When the child remains connected to the parent, feelings of being powerful and entitled take hold in the child. When the child becomes an adult, this sense of self enables the person to tackle difficult challenges but leaves him vulnerable to making self-serving decisions without considering the needs of others. Often, in adulthood, symptoms of mental illness emerge, such as alcoholism, promiscuity, or even sociopathic traits.

GENDER-BASED ADVANTAGES AND DISADVANTAGES OF FAVORITISM

As we have seen, children growing up as *the* favorite generally mature with confidence and power, permitting them to become adults driven to get what they want. Growing up as the favorite taught them the skills necessary to take on difficult challenges—determination, confidence, and entitlement. More specifically, the gender of the dominant parent will influence the favorite children's characteristics.

Children favored by mothers are inclined to be preoccupied with trying to make people important to them feel good, and these children are inclined to seek father substitutes. Children favored by their fathers generally seek achievement outside of relationships, and these children are inclined to seek mother substitutes.

- *Daughters as favorite children of mothers:* These daughters typically mother their mothers. In doing so, these daughters are robbed of their childhoods, erroneously believing themselves to be competent adults. Not having established a firm psychological foundation when growing up, these daughters, as adults, are often vulnerable to having their fragile egos corroded in relationships that replace those they had with their mothers. As their mothers merged identities with them, these daughters are susceptible to merging their identities with people they mother—husbands, children, or lovers.

- *Sons as favorite children of mothers:* These sons typically fill voids in their mothers created by husbands who are absent, emotionally or literally. Sometimes husbands feel relegated to a lesser position by their wives' attachment to their over-adoring fathers. Commonly, these wives train their favorite sons to replace these older, adored men, and then look to them to do this. Growing out of the erroneous belief that they have replaced their fathers, or are substitutes for their grandfathers, mothers' favorite sons are vulnerable to growing up egocentric.

  To protect themselves from the uneasy feelings generated by the Oedipal complex, often these sons unconsciously seek, in their lives outside their families, strong men as mentors and protectors. These relationships can foster their professional achievements. As adults who expect to be adored as their mothers adored them, mothers' favorite sons commonly struggle with intimacy.

- *Daughters as favorite children of fathers:* These daughters typically fill voids that their fathers experience in their marriages, in a function similar to that of mothers' favorite sons. Like their male counterparts, these daughters often grow up with an uneasy feeling; they may unconsciously believe they have replaced their same-sex parent as the partner of their opposite-sex parent.

  Not having been the recipients of maternal affection, fathers' favorite daughters are particularly liable not to trust the caring of others, which makes intimate relationships difficult. Due to their attachment to their fathers, these women commonly focus energies on their careers and are successful in their professional pursuits.

- *Sons as favorite children of fathers:* These sons typically fill voids their fathers experience in their marriages. In some cases this stems from their choice of marrying emotionally distant women who replicate the husbands' emotionally absent mothers. Growing from this position, fathers' favorite sons develop an overinflated sense of their importance in the world. This aspect of their personality is similar to that of mothers' favorite sons and fathers' favorite daughters. Typically high achievers, they are more skilled at achieving outside the home than in close interpersonal relationships.

  These favored sons, like fathers' favorite daughters, were not usually the recipients of maternal affection. Having grown up suffering from maternal deprivation, they find it difficult to form an intimate relationship.

Ultimately, all these favorite children tend to struggle with intimate relationships. The misalliance with the favoring parent contaminates these men and women, reducing their ability to function successfully in healthy relationships, which demand a generous give and take. While mothers' favorite sons and fathers' favorite sons and daughters all tend to excel professionally, their sense of entitlement leaves them vulnerable to moral corruption.

HEALING

The ultimate destructiveness of growing up as the favorite child is the potential alienation from himself or herself that the child experiences. Unaware that they are detached from crucial aspects of their personalities, favorite children can become cognizant of their estrangement from themselves when blindsided by divorce, accusations of addiction, struggles with children, or legal challenges. More subtle signs that something is wrong can include nagging depression, marital tension, or physical ailments. These children benefited from believing the distorted and inflated views about them held by their powerful parent. Why would they want to challenge these beliefs? Because, within these favored children, the Shadows of their own personalities loom large, often suppressing even tentative attempts at honest self-exploration. Favorite children have developed powerful defenses against seeing themselves as they are. Favorite children who tackle the challenge—to work at seeing themselves more honestly—emerge as more effective and trustworthy people.

The Process of Healing

This process is demanding for favored children, requiring them to chisel away at their self-deception and begin to sculpt a more honest self-appraisal. Undertaking this journey requires a willingness to confront and modify the interactions with the primary parent that have been so advantageous.

Recognition

The solution to any problem begins with recognition. As Zachary reflected at the beginning of this chapter, recognizing the corrosiveness of favored child status is often impeded by the seeming benefits of the status. This was true for him. He had learned to accommodate to keep his status, even though the results of his accommodation later manifested themselves in depression. The wake-up call was louder for Dean, a father's favorite son who had a mental breakdown. This story, as told in chapter 4, highlights Dean's investment in denying his own truth for years so as not to disappoint his father.

Language

Putting words to sinister aspects of the favorite child status begins the process of defining, with greater honesty, the problem to be solved. Zoe, her mother's favorite daughter (chapter 10), who opted to care for her son Tommy rather than her mother, was forced by her overwhelming tension to employ language as a means of accurately perceiving her mother's demand: why would she abandon her young son who was hospitalized to take her mother to a routine doctor's visit?

When she applied this clear and simple language to her quandary, the answer resonated: there was no good reason except that Zoe had always put her mother first and acted as her mother's caretaker. The clarification afforded by language permitted Zoe to realize she had a choice: she could behave as she always had, and go with her mother, or she could behave differently and not go. Based on her prior experience, Zoe surmised that, if she did the former, she would feel anxious and guilty over leaving her son. Additionally, Zoe envisioned herself as conveying resentment to her mother through antagonistic comments.

By verbalizing her alternatives in concise language, Zoe realized she had never rejected a request that was important to her mother. If she had elected to do so, she would not have been able to imagine the outcome. In this particular situation, she could only anticipate feeling repulsion at herself for being a mother who would choose to abandon her youngster. Zoe would furthermore be furious with herself for then treating her mother contemptuously and blaming her for Zoe's own decision.

Repercussions

The healing of favorite children gains momentum when they accept that there are varied and often unpredictable ramifications of changing their relationship with their favoring parents. When these adult children are no longer willing to pay the psychological costs of remaining disconnected from their personal truths, they become motivated to take on change. In my extensive work with favorite children, they have consistently told me that their decision to behave differently, in relation to their powerful parent, did not reflect courage. They felt they had no choice.

Zoe believed she had no choice. The impact on her life of deciding to stay with her son was profound. It took her years to learn to live successfully with the repercussions. First, Zoe was replaced as her mother's favorite child, and second, she was beset with many illnesses.

When Zoe chose her son over her mother, Darlene pressured her to change her mind, begging her to maintain the status quo. Darlene shamed Zoe, calling her thoughtless and selfish. Zoe felt devastated by the shame heaped upon her. Observing the futility of Darlerne's efforts to persuade Zoe, Monica, Zoe's sister, navigated herself to the position of favorite child.

When growing up, Monica's resentment festered in her Shadow. She wanted the relationship with her mother that Zoe had. Now, with the demise of the relationship between Zoe and Darlene apparent, Monica leapt into action. She took advantage of the fact that she lived only a few miles from her mother, not five hundred miles away, like Zoe.

Monica's ploy worked. She was at her mother's beck and call. Monica scapegoated Zoe, portraying her as selfish and egotistical. Monica spun Zoe's decision to stay with Tommy as evidence of indifference and lack of caring. Monica joined her mother in demonizing her sister, characterizing Zoe as evil in having violated the religious commandment to honor one's parents. Darlene began praying for Zoe's soul, which Darlene believed was destined for hell. With amazing speed, Zoe was relegated from favorite child to unfavored. Monica obtained the relationship with her mother that she had always wanted—that of favorite child.

The family upheaval upset Zoe. Though consciously understanding her mother's irrationality, Zoe could not accept it. She grieved for the loss of her mother, to whom she had given so much without question. Zoe also grieved for the loss of her sister, for whom Zoe had always advocated. During the ensuing months, Zoe struggled with a myriad of illnesses. Her body expressed the pain resisted by her psyche.

Creating a Separate Identity

Creating an identity separate from the powerful parent equips the favorite child, who is trying to break away, with the tools necessary to begin the process of embracing herself. Zoe had to grow to perceive herself as successful, powerful, lovable, and loving, even when it was not connected to her mother.

Zoe grew up believing her self-worth was connected to being the person her mother needed her to be: the perfect helper. Zoe was her confidante, companion, and decision maker. Zoe filled the void created in her mother's life by the absence of men who were important to her: her father, husband, and son. Zoe mothered her younger sisters, because her mother expected her to. By adolescence, Zoe perceived herself as essential to her mother's ability to function. Darlene's projections onto Zoe were integral to her identity.

The biggest challenge for Zoe was confronting her irrational belief that her survival depended on fulfilling her mother's wishes. In the deepest recesses of her psyche, Zoe did not believe she could survive if she functioned differently. If she was not caring for her mother, she was no one. Teasing out who she was—what *she* thought, believed, and felt—was stressful. Zoe successfully tackled this challenge in her therapy, supported by the ancillary interventions of yoga and meditation, and, without question, by her husband's unwavering support.

Communication

Embracing one's self is the psychological work of a lifetime. When we are feeling most vulnerable, our deep conscious and unconscious roots in our past challenge this objective. It is false to believe this mission is ever easy or completed. Communicating with trusted loved ones—family, friends, or therapeutic agents—helps to ensure the journey is continued.

Zoe, having grown up in a family where the honest expression of feelings was discouraged, had to learn to communicate openly, freely, and honestly. First, to nurture the improvement of her health, Zoe struggled in her individual therapy to develop more functional communication skills. She learned to trust that her ideas had merit and that, when expressing them, she would be safe.

Second, Zoe added a psychotherapy group to her treatment regimen. A group resembles a family where all members affect the dynamics and no one can control for all eventual reactions. In the group, Zoe learned that, when people did not like what she said, or if she did not like what others said, the feelings churned up could be worked out. Through respectful communication, people could grow closer. Most important, speaking her own truth allowed Zoe to make more reliable connections to her own self.

Third, Zoe worked at being the same person in the world that she was in her individual and group therapy. She worked on communication skills with her husband and closest friends, building up a network of people with whom she could freely and easily expose her true self. This network provided support to Zoe when, in moments of vulnerability, she needed help to fight off demons from her past that reared their ugly heads.

Healing within the Family

Families can heal from rifts, such as those that occurred in Zoe's family, but at the time when this book was written, the rift with Zoe and her family had not healed. Neither Monica nor Darlene assumed any responsibility for their treatment of Zoe. When Zoe spent time with them, their cruelty and dishonesty induced severe stomach problems or back pain in her. Though she consciously understood her mother's irrationality, Zoe's body demonstrated her inner struggle.

While struggling to establish an identity distinct from her mother's, Zoe felt the need to maintain regular contact with her mother. At the time this book was written, Zoe had weekly phone conversations with her mother and could tolerate being in her presence only at family gatherings. Her goal was to feel confident enough about herself that, in her mother's presence, Zoe would neither become physically ill nor allow her mother to impinge on her boundaries.

As Zoe slowly learned that she could function without being her mother's favorite daughter, she grew to feel better about herself. She let go of the desperate hope that the hostility emanating from her mother or sister would diminish. Zoe accepted that neither Monica nor Darlene were likely to honestly examine their roles in the family tension. Zoe acknowledged that her increasing mental health was fundamental to any possible reconciliation with her mother. Zoe continued to harbor rage at Monica. Zoe believed her best interests were served by more fully appreciating Monica's malice and potential danger to her.

Dean's family experience is different from Zoe's. As described earlier in this chapter and more fully in chapter 4, Dean's therapist reported to me that all the members of Dean's family worked to understand their contribution to his breakdown. His family was invested in his healing and well-being. As the family worked to free Dean from the pressures of being his father's favorite son, the family grew stronger and healthier, a development I often witness in families I counsel. Common to these families is a culture fostering mutual respect: all of the members, especially the adults, assume responsibility for trying to meet their own needs, rather than looking to others to meet these needs. Family members do not insist on rigidly holding onto their truths and perceptions. They are open to grappling with different observations offered to them by others, and they are equally accepting of feedback from children or spouses.

Other Forms of Healing

Healing takes place in the atmosphere provided by trusting, honest, and constructive relationships. Not all healing needs to take place in the context of psychotherapy. Healing can occur when a person works with clergy or support groups, or commits to calming experiences such as meditation. But sticking with the process for the years required for healing is unlikely unless one is in a committed, ongoing therapeutic relationship. The challenges of healing the scars of favoritism are substantial, and the favorite child needs an objective ally to ensure a safe environment for self-exploration and an honest journey.

POLITICIANS: VULNERABLE TO THE BURDENS OF FAVORITISM

Favorite children, especially favorite daughters and sons of fathers and favorite sons of mothers, grow up with the personality traits of confidence and empowerment that are essential for leadership. Throughout *The Favorite Child,* we have seen countless examples of these children's vulnerability to the development of compromised morals, which affect not only them but their families and society as well. Many of these stories are those of elected and appointed public officials whose identities have been concealed to ensure the anonymity guaranteed to all clients engaging in a therapeutic relationship. From these stories, three conclusions can be drawn.

First, the determination and sense of entitlement characteristic of favorite children, which drive them to tackle the challenges that others would reject, are often skills essential to succeed in Washington and other seats of power. For example, passing important legislation is a challenge that would be insurmountable to many. To succeed in this requires the tenacity both to write a bill that reflects a keen knowledge of the content and the ability to forge alliances with often conflicting interest groups. Favorite children have the personality skills that are necessary for this undertaking.

Second, favorite children grow up as the center of their parents' attention, attention these children have learned to invite in activities and relationships outside their homes. Politics is a natural arena for this reenactment. The mere process of being elected or appointed requires politicians to solicit attention and approval. Having won an election or received an appointment, the politicians' skills in getting what they want are reinforced.

Winning an election reinforces their belief, which they learned while growing up as the favorite, that they are preferred to all others. Unfortunately, these officials can easily distort this reality. Often they come to believe they are preferred over others for endeavors far broader than those for which they were elected. For example, winning an election does not make one a better golfer; although it may make one a preferred golf partner because of the status associated with playing with an elected official. Appreciating this distinction helps to protect the politician from potentially destructive grandiosity.

Third, favorite children grow up permitted, and often encouraged, to misuse their power in their families. This fosters personalities highly vulnerable to the moral corruption witnessed in the world of professional politics.

Having been elected to public service, young politicians come to the city, usually claiming to bring integrity and accountability to government. The longer they are in Washington, the greater their tolerance may become for behaviors they previously deemed questionable. Their professional behaviors come to mirror those enacted in their families—in a cycle in which power and importance dilute accountability.

As illustrated in this book, my brother-in-law, Scooter Libby, appears to be a possible example of at least some of this. Through much of his life, thoughts of public service intrigued him. He returned from working one summer as a college student on the Yakama Indian Reservation in the state of Washington and was disturbed by the contrast between the barrenness of the tribal lands and the lushness of the lands surrounding them. Scooter was eager to attack the injustice. His keen intellect and strong work ethic combined to make him uniquely qualified to do so. For him, college, graduate school, and summer jobs were paths intended to further enable him to achieve his dreams. Ultimately, his future contributions were thwarted by his inability to successfully spin his truth—to the jury that convicted him after finding problems in his previous statements—as he had seemingly learned to do as the favorite child in his family.

TO CONCLUDE

The Favorite Child contrasts the experiences of growing up in families where favoritism rotates among all children and between parents, and in families where favoritism is fixed between one parent and child. Children growing up in families where favoritism is fluid are less likely to experience the acute burdens of favoritism than those growing up in families where favoritism is fixed.

Favorite children are generally powerful and confident. Those who are scrupulous are more likely to have grown up in families where parents, or parent substitutes, met their own needs and did not expect their children to fill the voids in their lives. The importance of open expression of feeling and honest communication within these families was valued.

Favoritism is normal in families. Being the favorite child has benefits for the child as well as for society. The burdens accompanying favoritism are also substantial but can be mitigated by respectful relationships among the adults who are in a position to influence the growth of the child. In taking on this challenge, the challenge of bringing up children with the confidence and power inherent in being favored while also holding these children accountable for their behaviors, parents contribute positively to the characters of their children—our future leaders in all spheres of society.

SUGGESTED READINGS

Angelos, Bonnie. *First Mothers: The Women Who Shaped the Presidents.* New York: Harper, 2001, reprinted 2006.

Black, Conrad. *Franklin Delano Roosevelt: Champion of Freedom.* New York: Public Affairs, 2003.

Bowlby, John. *Attachment and Loss.* Vol. 1, *Attachment.* New York: Basic Books, 1969.

Burns, James MacGregor. *Roosevelt: The Lion and the Fox, 1882–1940.* New York: Harcourt Brace, 1956.

Cozolino, John. *The Neuroscience of Psychotherapy: Building and Rebuilding the Human Brain.* New York: W. W. Norton, 2002.

———. *The Neuroscience of Human Relationships: Attachment and the Developing Social Brain.* New York: W. W. Norton, 2006.

Forward, Susan. *Toxic Parents: Overcoming Their Hurtful Legacy and Reclaiming Your Life.* New York: Bantam Books, 1989.

Frank, Justin A. *Bush on the Couch: Inside the Mind of the President.* New York: Regan Books, 2004.

Hollis, James. *Why Good People Do Bad Things: Understanding Our Darker Selves.* New York: Gotham Books, 2007.

Manchester, William. *American Caesar: Douglas MacArthur, 1880–1964.* New York: Little, Brown, 1978.

Minutaglio, Bill. *First Son: George W. Bush and the Bush Family Dynasty.* New York: Times Books, 1999.

Napier, Augustus Y., with Carl A. Whitaker. *The Family Crucible.* New York: Harper & Row, 1978.

Phillips, Kevin. *American Dynasty: Aristocracy, Fortune, and the Politics of Deceit in the House of Bush*. New York: Viking, 2004.

Radcliffe, Donnie. *Simply Barbara Bush: A Portrait of America's Candid First Lady*. New York: Warner Books, 1989.

Siegel, Daniel J. *The Developing Mind: Toward a Neurobiology of Interpersonal Experience*. New York: Guilford Press, 1999.

Smith, David Livingston. *Why We Lie: The Evolutionary Roots of Deception and the Unconscious Mind*. New York: St. Martin's Press, 2004.

Smith, Jean Edward. *FDR*. New York: Random House, 2007.

Stout, Martha. *The Sociopath Next Door: The Ruthless versus the Rest of Us*. New York: Broadway Books, 2005.

Teitelbaum, Stanley. 2005. *Sports Heroes, Fallen Idols*. Lincoln: University of Nebraska Press, 2005.

Whitaker, Carl A., and William M. Bumberry. *Dancing with the Family: A Symbolic-Experiential Approach*. New York: Brunner/Mazel, 1988.

NOTES

CHAPTER 1: EVERY FAMILY HAS ITS STORY

1. *The Shadow*, radio show, copyright Conde Nast Publications.

2. James Hollis, *Why Good People Do Bad Things: Understanding Our Darker Selves* (New York: Gotham Books, 2007), p. 9.

3. Ibid., p. xiii.

4. Ibid., p. xii.

5. Ibid.

6. U.S. Department of Justice, "Government Exhibit 1, 05Cr.394 (ID) for Grand Jury No. 03-3," March 5, 2004, http://www.usdoj.gov/.

7. Ibid., p. 5.

8. Emma Schwartz, "Sizing Up the Libby Defense Strategy," *Legal Times*, March 12, 2007, p. 8.

9. Ibid.

10. Richard Willing, "Jurors Wonder Why Others Weren't Also on Trial," March 6, 2007, http://usatoday.com/washington/2007-03-06-libby-jury_N.htm; see also Larry King, *Larry King Live*, CNN, March 6, 2007, http://transcripts.cnn.com/TRANSCRIPTS/0703/06/lkl.01.html.

CHAPTER 2: FAVORITISM: KNOWN TO ALL

1. Chip Taylor, "The Baby," quoted with permission from Train Wreck Records.

2. John Bowlby, *Attachment and Loss*, vol. 1, *Attachment* (New York: Basic Books, 1969).

3. Ibid.

4. Nadia Bruschweiler Stern, "Early Emotional Care for Mothers and Infants," *Pediatrics*, 1998, http://pediatrics.org/cgi/content/full/102/5/SE1/1278.

5. Bonnie Angelos, *First Mothers: The Women Who Shaped the Presidents* (New York: Harper, 2006).

6. Ibid., p. 1.

7. Robert Anda and V. J. Felitti, "Adverse Childhood Experiences," http://www.cdc.gov/nccdphp/ACE; Robert Anda and V. J. Felitti, "The Adverse Childhood Experiences (ACE) Study," http://acestudy.org.

8. Robert Anda, "The Many Faces of Fear: Attachment, Trauma and Neuroscience Perspectives" (American Academy of Psychotherapists Institute and Conference, 2007, San Diego, California).

9. John Cozolino, *The Neuroscience of Human Relationships: Attachment and the Developing Social Brain* (New York: W. W. Norton, 2006); John Cozolino, *The Neuroscience of Psychotherapy: Building and Rebuilding the Human Brain* (New York: W. W. Norton, 2002).

10. Cozolino, *The Neuroscience of Psychotherapy*, pp. 173–74.

11. Tiffany M. Field, Robert Woodson, Reena Greenberg, and Deborah Cohen, "Discrimination and Imitation of Facial Expressions by Neonates," *Science* 218, no. 4568, October 8, 1982, 179–81, quoted by Cozolino, *The Neuroscience of Psychotherapy*, p. 174.

12. Bill Minutaglio, *First Son: George W. Bush and the Bush Family Dynasty* (New York: Times Books, 1999), pp. 45–48.

13. Angelos, *First Mothers*, pp. 362–402.

14. Ibid., p. 5; Angelos, *First Mothers*, pp. 415–19.

15. Angelos, *First Mothers*, pp. 413–19.

16. Ibid.

CHAPTER 3: THE FAVORITE CHILD COMPLEX

1. Martha Stout, *The Sociopath Next Door: The Ruthless versus the Rest of Us* (New York: Broadway Books, 2005), p. 105.

CHAPTER 4: WHO'S THE FAVORITE AND WHO ISN'T

1. Robert Anda, "The Many Faces of Fear: Attachment, Trauma and Neuroscience Perspectives" (American Academy of Psychotherapists Institute and Conference, 2007, San Diego, California).

2. David Livingston Smith, *Why We Lie: the Evolutionary Roots of Deception and the Unconscious Mind* (New York: St. Martin's Press, 2004).

3. *Tell Me You Love Me*, HBO, 2007.

4. Joan Edward Smith, *FDR* (New York: Random House, 2007).

5. Bonnie Angelos, *First Mothers: The Women Who Shaped the Presidents* (New York: Harper, 2006), p. 1.

6. Ibid., p. 2.

7. Ibid.

8. William Manchester, *American Caesar: Douglas MacArthur, 1880–1964* (New York: Little, Brown, 1978).

CHAPTER 5: THEY'RE ALL MY FAVORITES

1. Confidential e-mail correspondence, December 8–12, 2008.

2. Laura Bennett, "The Dirty Little Secret of Motherhood," *Daily Beast*, December 9, 2008, http://www.thedailybeast.com/blogs-and-stores/2008/12/09/the-dirty-little-secret-of-motherhood/.

3. Confidential e-mail correspondence, December 2008–January 2009.

4. Ibid.

5. Ibid.

6. Bennett, "The Dirty Little Secret."

7. Ibid.

8. Sarah Pierce, "Understanding Genetics: Human Health and the Genome," in *Understanding Genetics*, Stanford School of Medicine, http://www.thetech.org/genetics/ask.php?id=142.

CHAPTER 6: REWARDS AND RISKS OF BEING THE FAVORITE

1. Carl A. Whitaker, lecture at Berkshire Summer Institute on Family Therapy, 1984.

2. Carl A. Whitaker and William M. Bumberry, *Dancing with the Family: A Symbiotic-Experiential Approach* (New York: Brunner/Mazel, 1988).

3. "Property–Global Variation and Convergence," http://science.jrank.org/pages/10875/prperty-global-variation-convergence.html.

4. Stanley William Rothstein, *Class, Culture, and Race in American Schools: A Handbook* (Westport, CT: Greenwood Press, 1995), p. 148.

5. William J. Starosta and Guo-Ming Chen, eds., *Ferment in the Intercultural Field: Axiology/Value/Praxis* (Thousand Oaks, CA: Sage, 2003), p. 133.

6. Theodore Bestor and Helen Hardacre, "Contemporary Japan: Culture and Society," http://afe.easia.columbia.edu/at_japan_soc_/.

CHAPTER 7: FATHER'S FAVORITE SON

1. "Oedipus and the Riddle of the Sphinx," http://www.essortment.com/all/oedipusandth_rzul.htm; "The Birth of the Oedipus Legend," http://www.answers.com/topic/oedipus.

2. John Cozolino, *The Neuroscience of Psychotherapy: Building and Rebuilding the Human Brain* (New York: W. W. Norton, 2002).

3. Ibid.

4. David Livingston Smith, *Why We Lie: The Evolutionary Roots of Deception and the Unconscious Mind* (New York: St. Martin's Press, 2004).

5. Carl A. Whitaker, lecture at Berkshire Summer Institute on Family Therapy, 1984.

6. Ibid.

CHAPTER 10: MOTHER'S FAVORITE DAUGHTER

1. Bruce Perry, Lea Hogan, and Sarah Martin, "Curiosity, Pleasure and Play: A Neurodevelopmental Perspective," Child Trauma Academy, http://www.childtrauma.org/ctamaterials/Curiosity.asp.

2. Joan Packer Isenberg and Nancy Quisenberry, "Play: Essential for All Children—A Position Paper of the Association for Childhood Education International," http://www.acei.org/playpaper.htm, p. 4.

CHAPTER 11: THE OVERLOOKED CHILD

1. Susan Forward, *Toxic Parents: Overcoming Their Hurtful Legacy and Reclaiming Your Life* (New York: Bantam Books, 1989).
2. Merle A. Fossum and Marilyn J. Masson, *Facing Shame: Families in Recovery* (New York: W. W. Norton, 1986), p. 5.

CHAPTER 12: CONCLUSION

1. Confidential e-mail correspondence, April 10, 2009.

INDEX